AF477851

Mistral! There is something of Olympian Zeus about the way it roars and rages down from Mont Ventoux, always unexpectedly and always at full force, rolling boulders and dust ahead of it and whistling down the river-valleys like a herd of mad bulls. In the dusty plain of the Crau the trees are all hooked into weird shapes, twisted and bent by its force. It is upon you at a moment's notice, cramming the words back into your throat, sending the dust-devils spinning and whirling like so many dervishes among the vineyards. But it belongs faithfully to the landscape, and matches it as the dragon matches the fairy-tale . . .

—Lawrence Durrell, *The Lawrence Durrell Travel Reader*

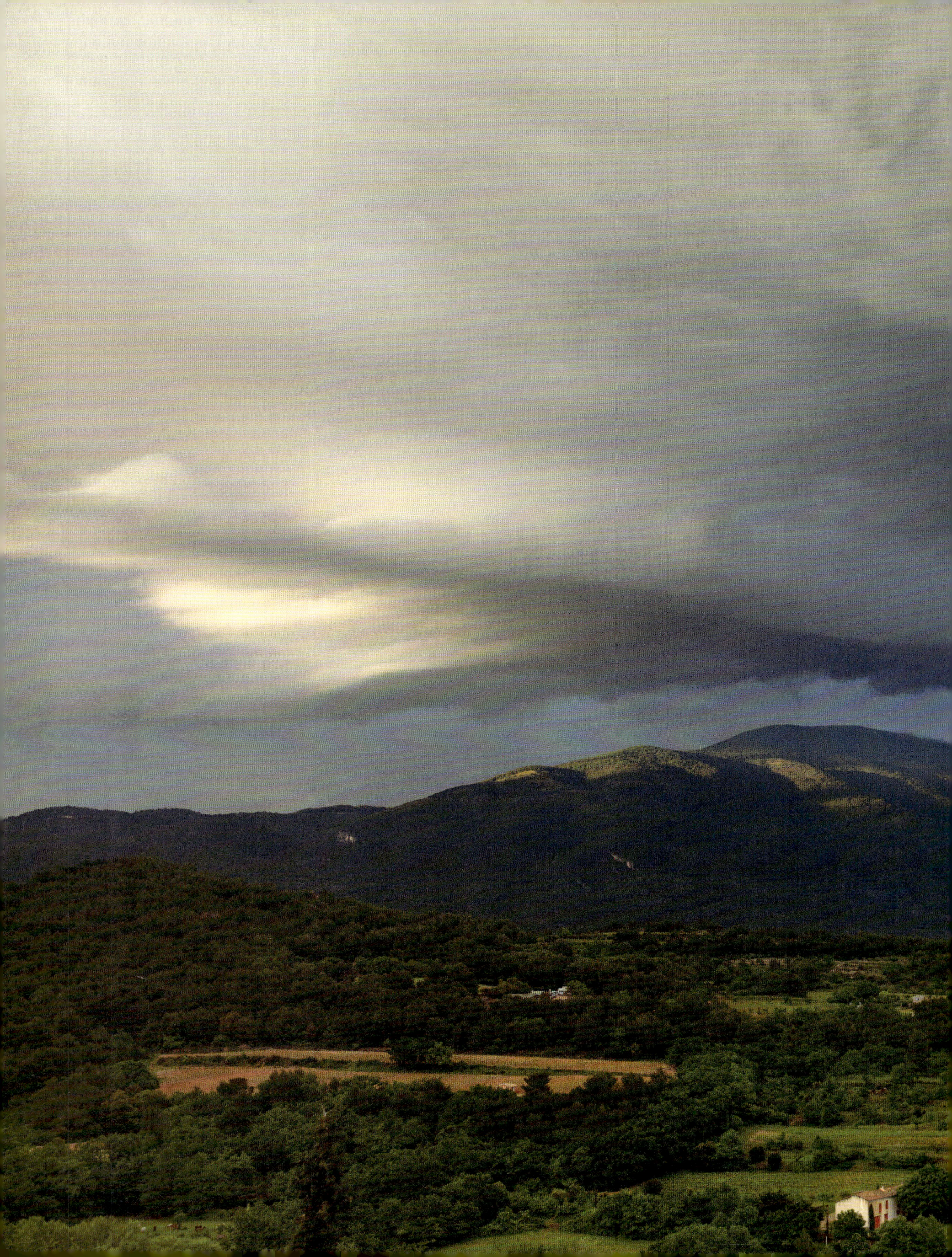

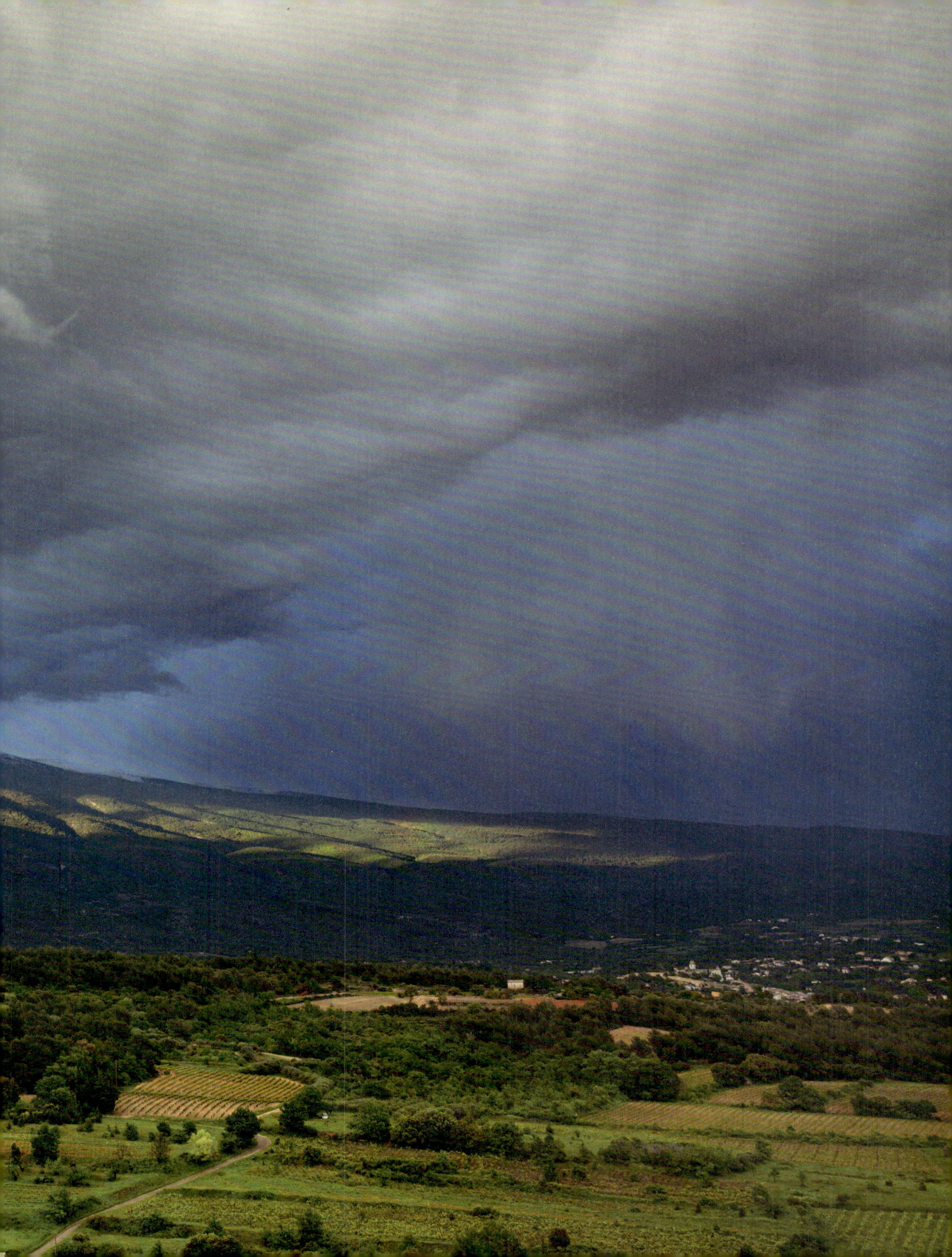

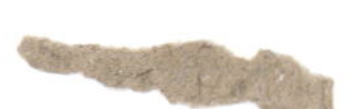

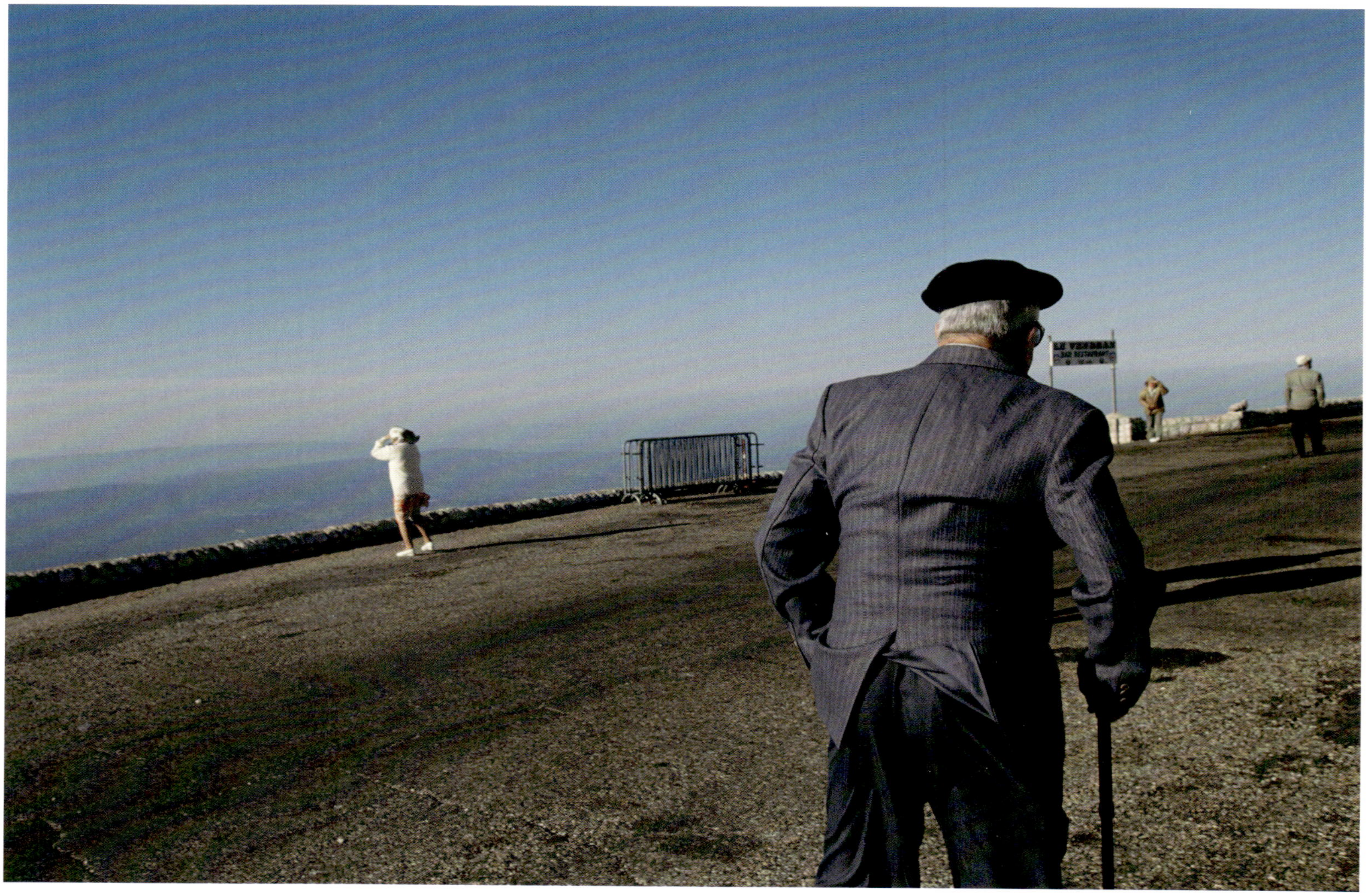

MISTRAL

The Legendary Wind of Provence

RACHEL COBB

Introduction by Bill Buford

DAMIANI

INTRODUCTION

Bill Buford

I know Rachel Cobb as a friend, as a mother of a son the same age as my twin boys, as a fellow journalist, as a fearless photographer, and, for five years, when I was living in Lyon with my family, as a fellow expatriate in France, who, on being visited, had a curious practice of disappearing, often in the early morning.

"Did you feel the temperature drop last night?" she would ask when she returned later in the afternoon. "Did you hear the banging? Were you woken by the slamming door?" She was animated. The animation was in her eyes and voice. She then whispered, "It's the mistral."

I've come to believe that she whispered because she was afraid of scaring it away.

Cobb aspired to do what everyone knows can't be done: she was trying to catch the wind.
Only fools try to catch the wind. And in photographs? If you can't see it, how can you take a picture of it?

She knows (or, maybe I should say, I hope she knows) that, on those cold, brutal days, when she would stalk the wind, in the same way that local Provençal hunters might stalk a wild boar, hoping to come upon it before it got away, hoping to take it by surprise, she wasn't actually photographing the wind as such, but its effects. She was looking for images so aerodynamically impacted that we, like onlookers sheltered nearby, could feel the invisible force, just as her subjects felt it. She wanted us to shiver and sink our heads into our necks and hold ourselves in our own arms.

The mission put her at odds with socially accepted practices. Once, on the stark, bald Mont Ventoux, she found herself waiting, camera ready, for a man to lose his hat. It was cold—the mistral is almost always cold—and the man's hat seemed to be shifting slightly, as though in the tentative moments before liftoff. A hat leaving the head of a man who then reaches out to grab it as it eludes his fingers en route to some celestial high-altitude destination? That is a wind picture. I wasn't there. (No one accompanies Cobb on her stalks.) But I could imagine her, forehead pressed against her viewfinder, adjusting the focus, ready, muttering quietly like Lear: "Blow, winds. Blow." In the event, the man adjusted his headpiece, pulling it down lower. Cobb returned to her houseguests, frustrated.

The mistral ruined weddings. It is uncanny how often a mistral ruins a wedding. Cobb attended many. She loved them. An outdoor wedding during a mistral? With no place to hide? Perfect for the photographer of discomfort. If she can't catch the wind, at least she'll get a loving couple's most important day in its howling, unforeseen ruin.

Like all hunters, Cobb was unlucky. There was a truffle festival in Carpentras. Cobb was unable to attend because her son was ill. It wasn't an issue, her missing the festival, except that, just when it was meant to begin, a wind arrived. A big one. There are many kinds of mistrals, but the mighty ones, the ones that break and destroy and seem like supernatural forces in their wreckingness, are rare.

"Oh, Rachel, how lucky you weren't there," a neighbor reported. Truffles thrown in the air, everyone trying to grab them, tables upturned, the folding chairs airborne. Cobb thought: No, I wasn't lucky at all.

To prevent another double calamity—a mighty mistral and an unwell child—Cobb bought two-way walkie-talkies.

Wind is most often represented in words. With words, you can describe the man's losing his hat even if it never actually leaves his head. With words, you can make wind into more than wind. Friedrich Nietzsche, the philosopher of Dionysian disorder, loved the mistral. Percy Bysshe Shelley thought of wind as a pagan god and wrote an ode to it—a West Wind, he alleges, but in its powerful fury it sounds more like the mistral's cousin, the Tramontane. (Like the Tramontane, the mistral is a northerly wind. But does the direction matter? It seems to come from nothing that can be represented by a compass point; it seems to come from the earth's meanness.)

One of the best evocations of wind is in Joan Didion's account of the Santa Ana, which is, of course, really a story of Los Angeles. The Santa Ana, along with the mistral (or a foehn in Austria, or the Solano in Spain, or the aforementioned Tramontane), is also among the earth's nasty, persistent winds. It arrives with no warning, except a feeling that the air pressure might have dropped (what Didion describes as an ambient uneasiness, "some unnatural stillness, some tension"), and then acts like it will never go away. Didion cites a 1957 Santa Ana that blew for fourteen days.

I spent twelve years of my childhood downwind from the Santa Ana, in a home that was on the then almost rural edge of northern Los Angeles (aka the San Fernando Valley). I can attest to Didion's essential point that, when the Santa Ana is blowing, bad shit happens. My memory includes tumbleweeds that appeared to be larger than houses (I had to dodge them walking home from school; they scratched your arms and face if you got caught in one); and long trunks of eucalyptus trees (Australian imports planted as windbreaks to protect lemon groves) that bent with the force of each gust, their branches scraping against the roof and seeming always about to snap and break (and sometimes did); and fires. The fires were whipped up by the wind. They jumped directions because of the wind. They were controlled by the wind. During one fire, my last, when I was fifteen, the air gray and thick with soot, I stood on the roof of our home, watering it with a garden hose, fearing flying hot embers, fearing that, at any second, I would have to rush down a ladder that had been propped up against a drainpipe and evacuate, when a eucalyptus tree just north of us exploded in a tower of its hot oils. Instantly and inexplicably, the wind changed and blew the fire down a canyon and away from our home.

A Santa Ana is bad. But it was also like living on a rocky beach in bad weather. You could forget about it. It put you to sleep. It never stopped until it stopped for good. A mistral is different. It stops. It starts again. It goes away entirely. It is back, worse than ever. It has no rhythm. It makes you have to think about it.

Lyon is where two rivers come together, the Saône and the Rhône, and their convergence, which occurs just south of the city, is the start of the long Rhône Valley. The valley is the mistral's corridor, its geological wind tunnel.

We lived on the Saône. Sometimes, at night, at the change of the seasons, especially between winter and spring, I was woken by the sound of small winds. I felt I could identify where each one happened. One seemed to be high above the river. One was directly across from us, a couple hundred feet away, in the old Renaissance habitation known as Vieux Lyon. Then nothing. Then three at once. These small winds were aurally so specific that they occurred in my mind like a shape, like a spring that had become stretched out and wiggled nervously in the turbulent air outside. Was this the beginning of a mistral? Who is to know? It is another feature of wind: you can't follow where it goes next. It may have been nothing more than a local wind's eddying in the crevices of old buildings. But it seemed to express a mountain source, some Alpine ravine, air rushing down it like a waterfall, and conveyed hence by a river. It seemed to express our particular perch on this highly particularized patch of earth.

I like all of Cobb's pictures mainly because they make me feel the wind. My favorites seem to imitate its force, its blurry, primary-colored disorder. I can't think of a higher piece of praise than that, after studying them, they make me want to rub my eyes. I feel grit on my skin.

I also like that they are pictures. Cobb described an experiment she conducted with video. A video seemed wrong, and she knew it. It is not the right way for catching the wind, even though technically it seems to depict its effects more comprehensively. She was back on Mont Ventoux. There was a man with a hat. She brought him into focus. She waited and on impulse pressed the record button. The hat flew off. Its flight was depicted as a video. She missed what she wanted: the photograph. The still image. This book's uniqueness, for me, is in the achievement of its still images: still images of a subject in accelerated motion. It seems more like memory. It seems more like the way our brain understands disorder. I don't have videos in my head. I have cognitive pictures. And now I have these.

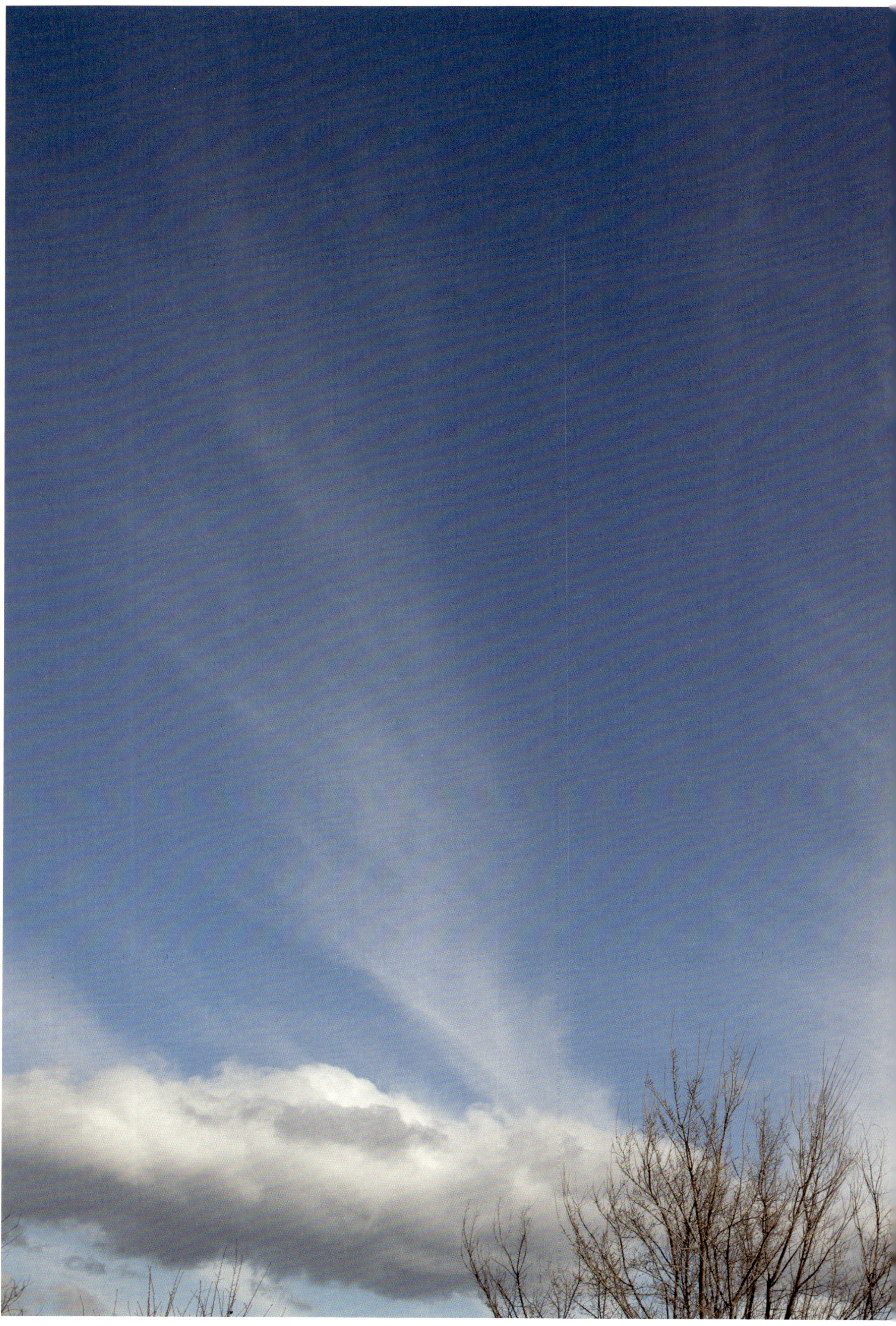

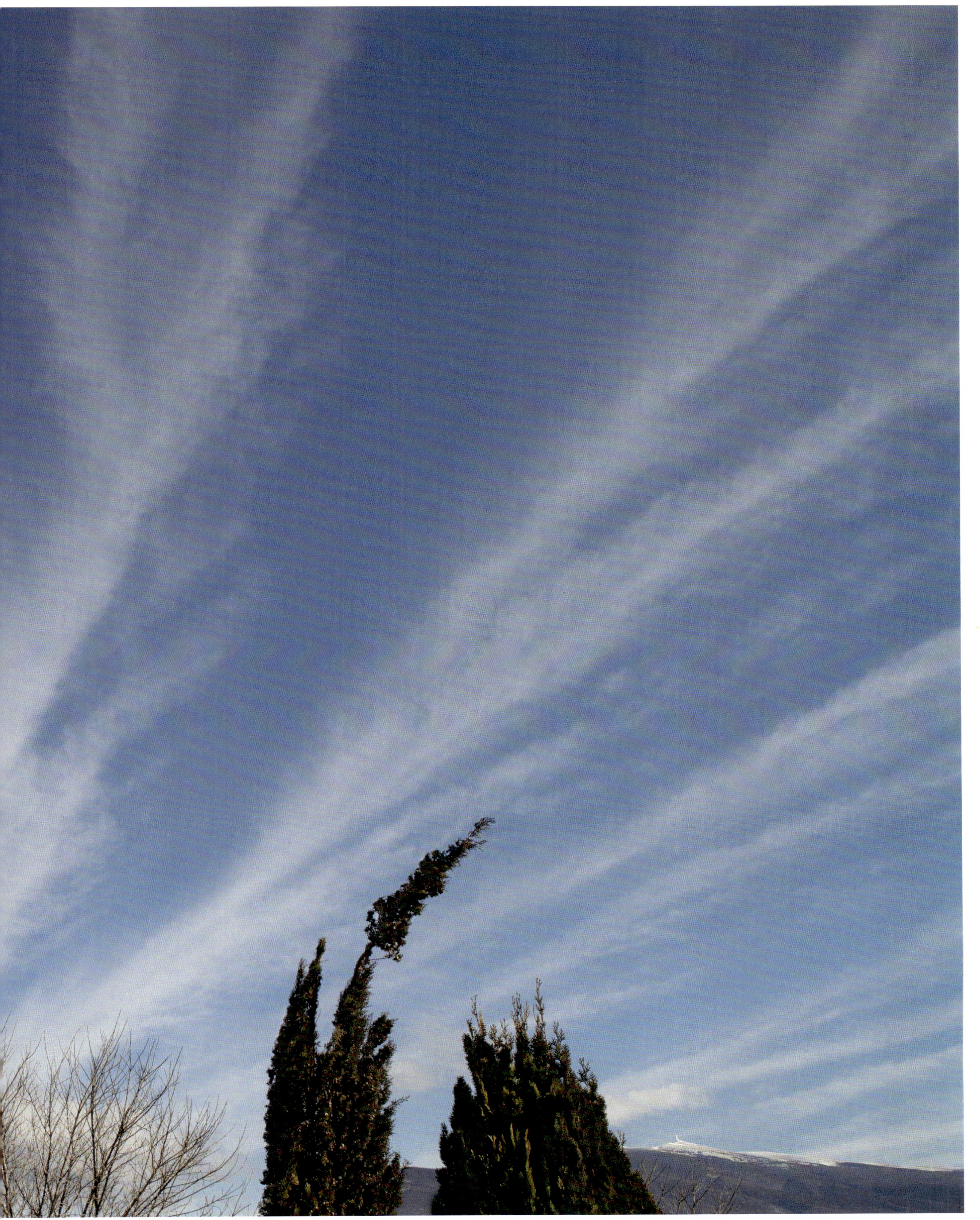

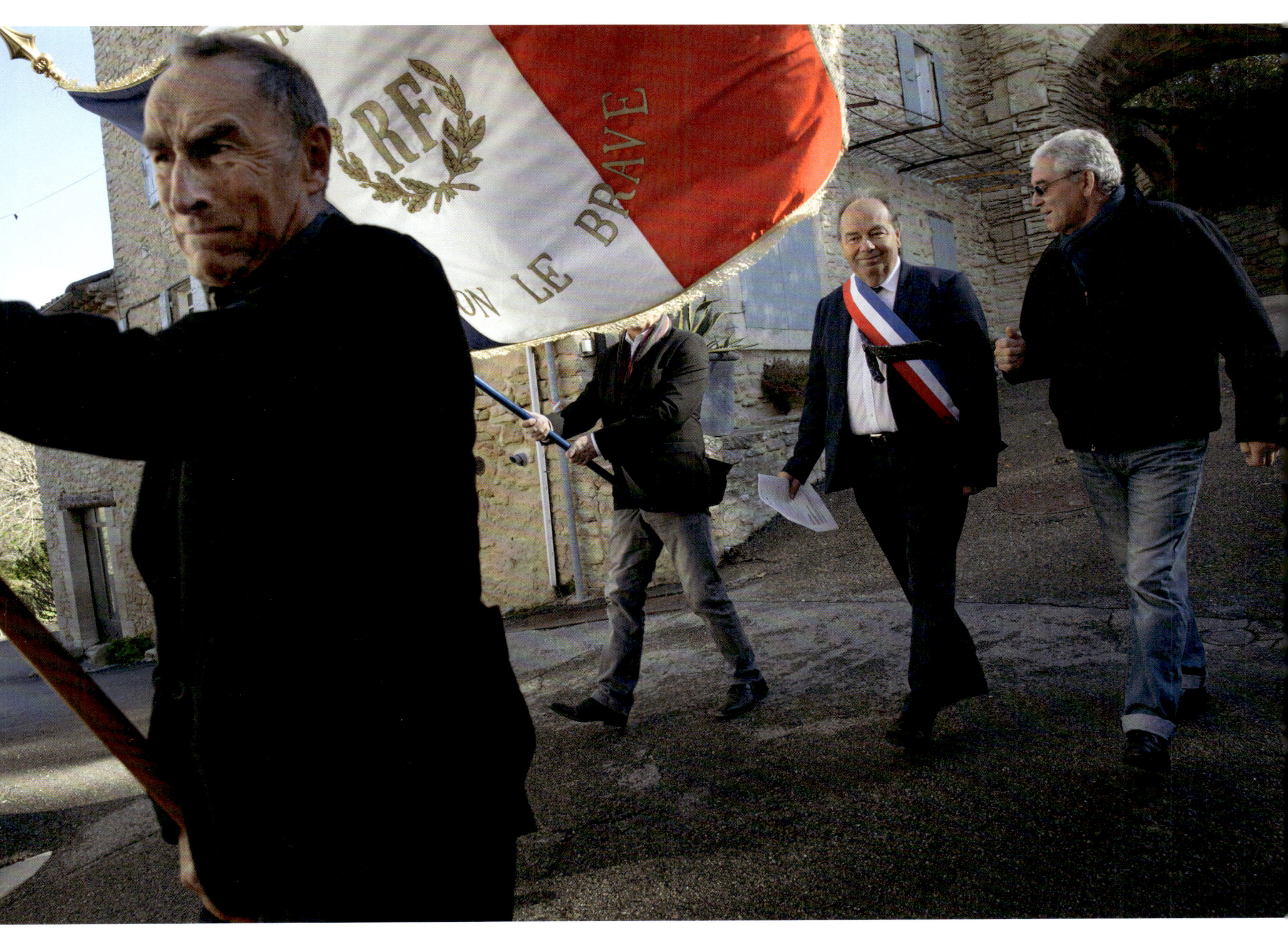
RF
ON LE BRAVE

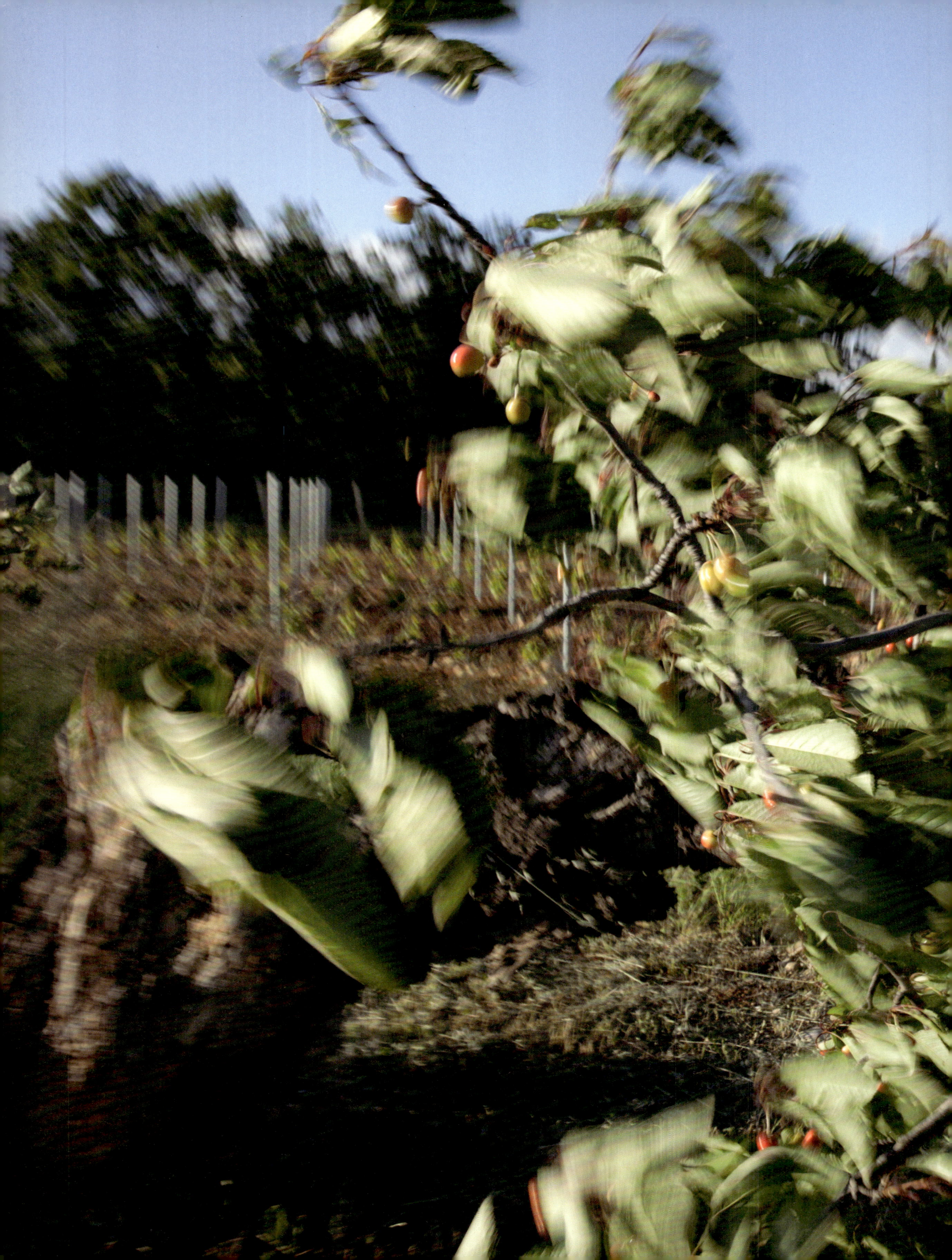

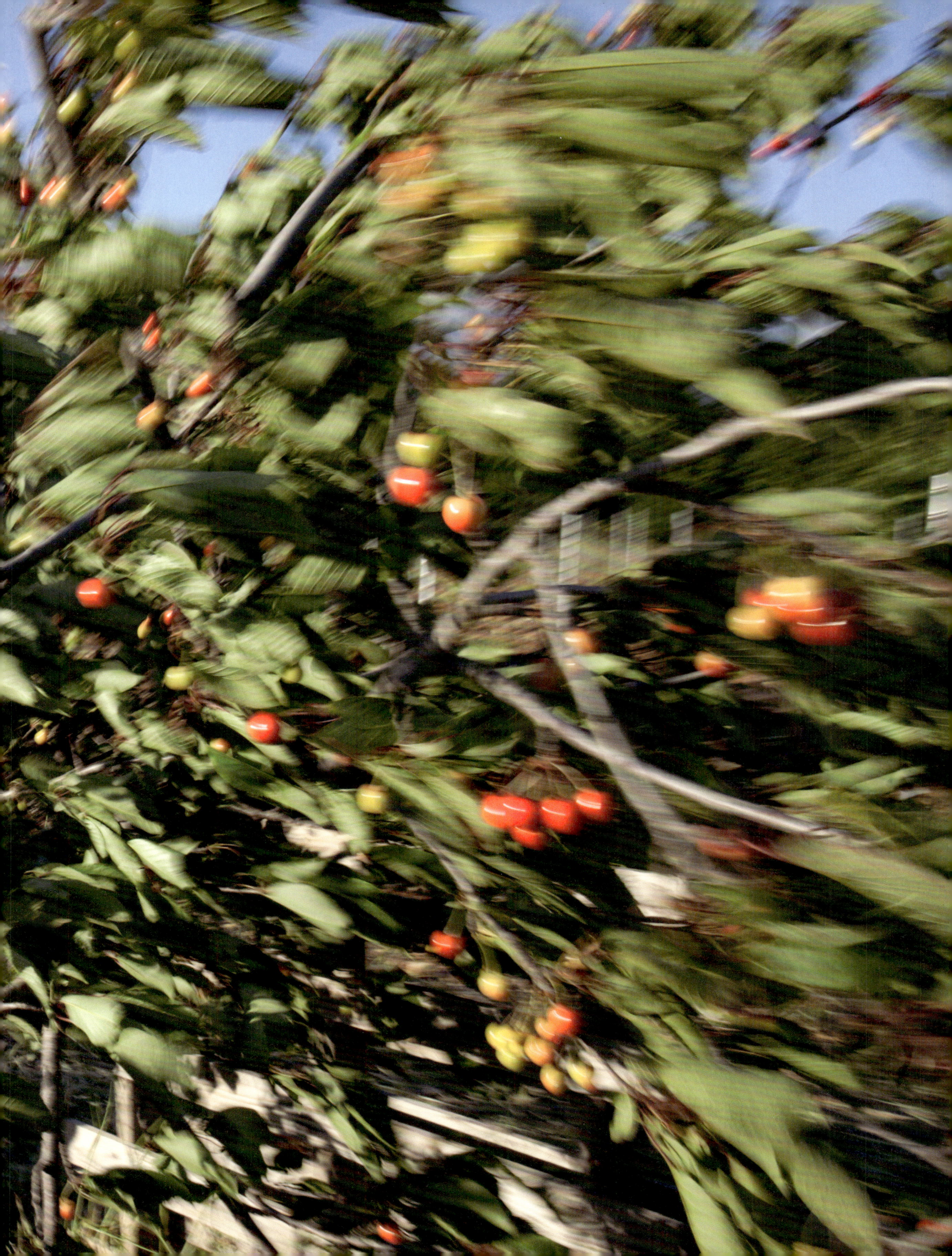

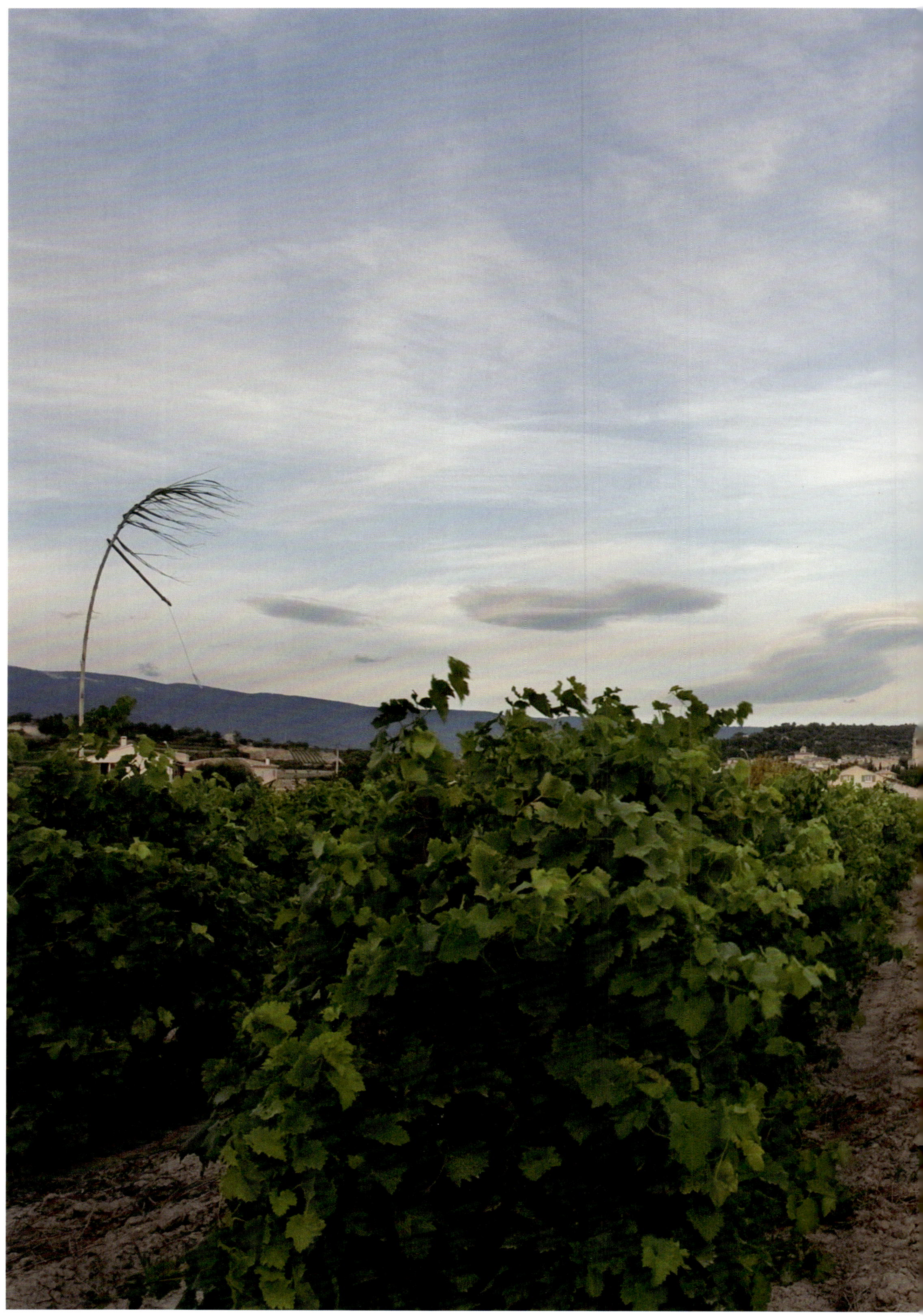

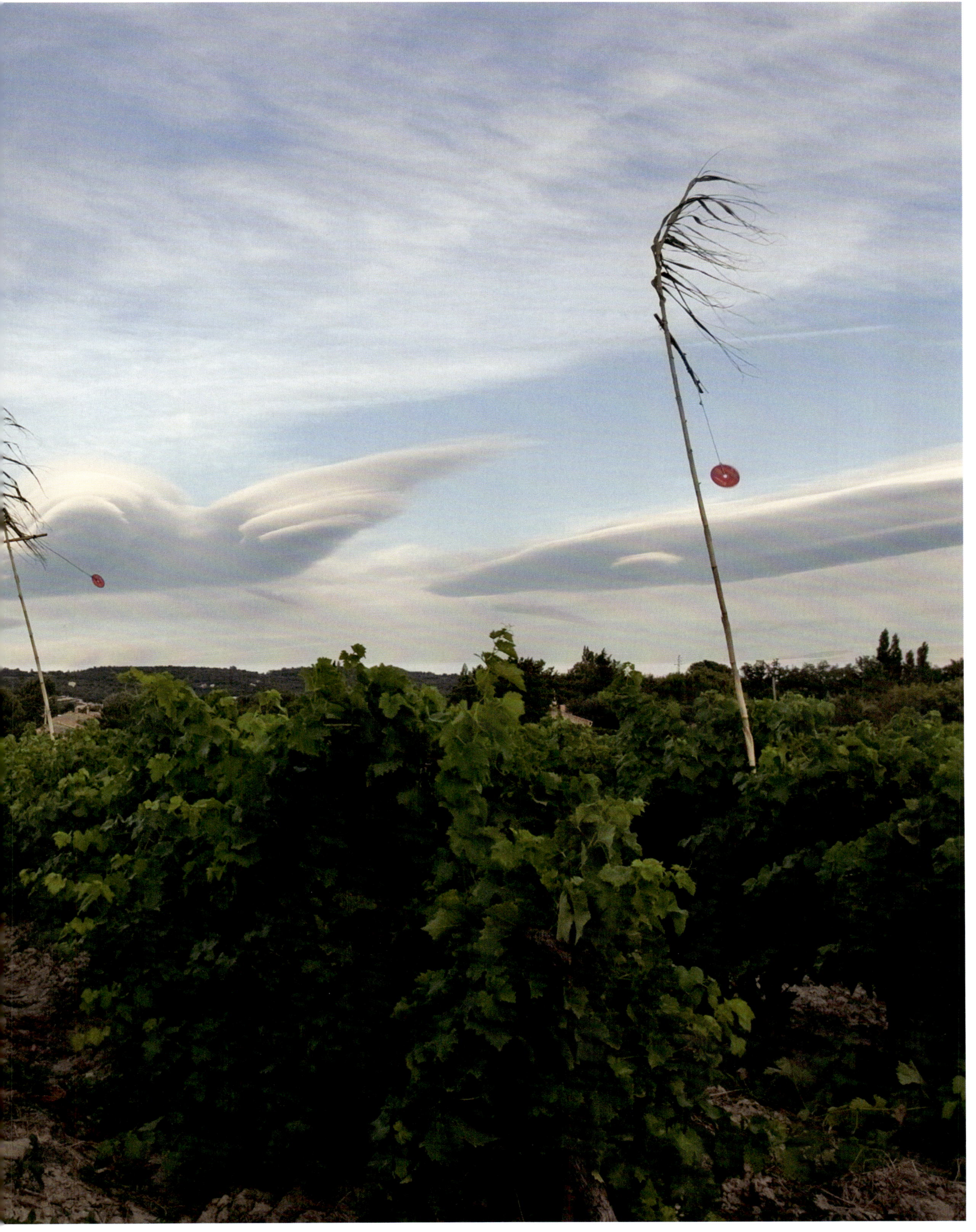

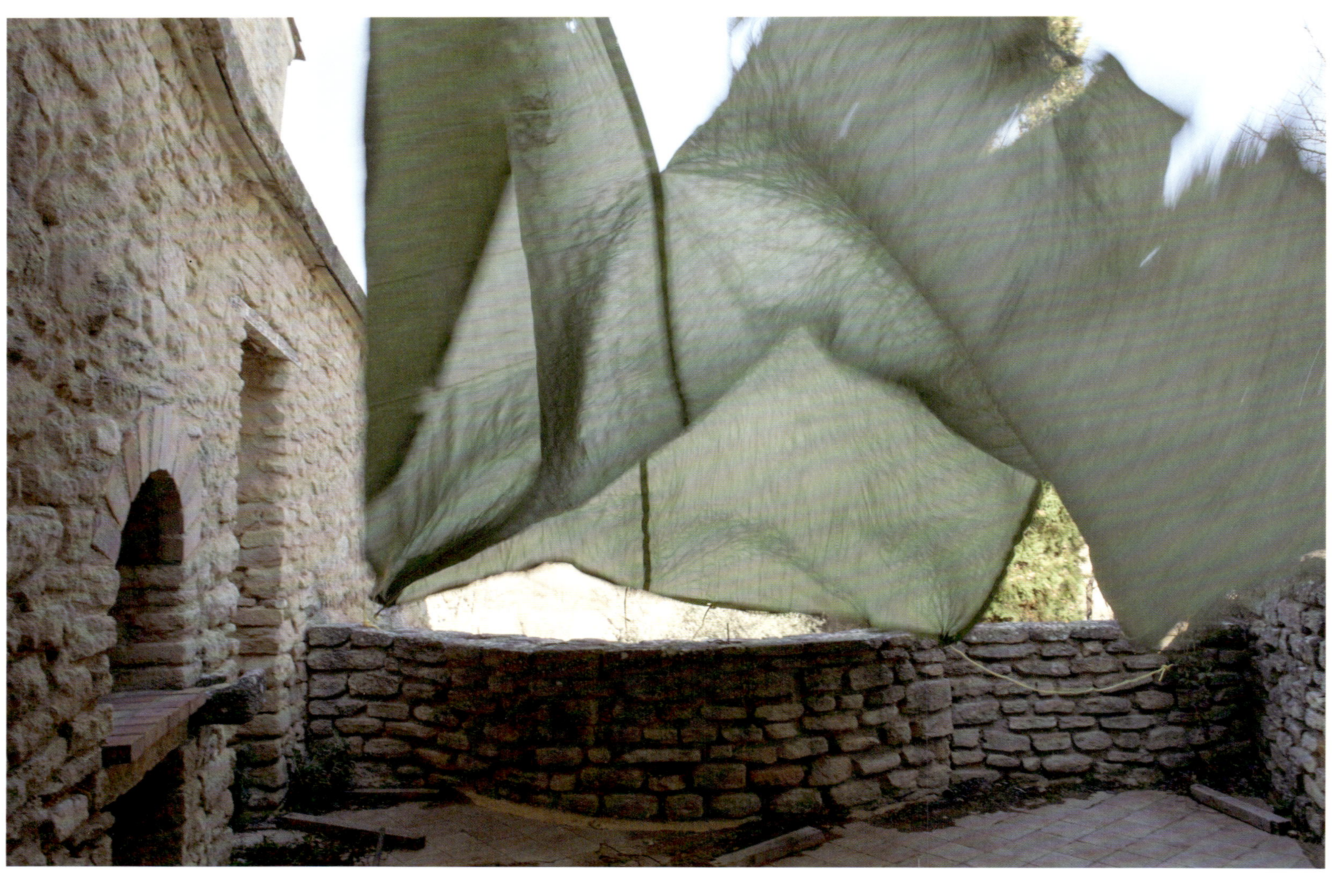

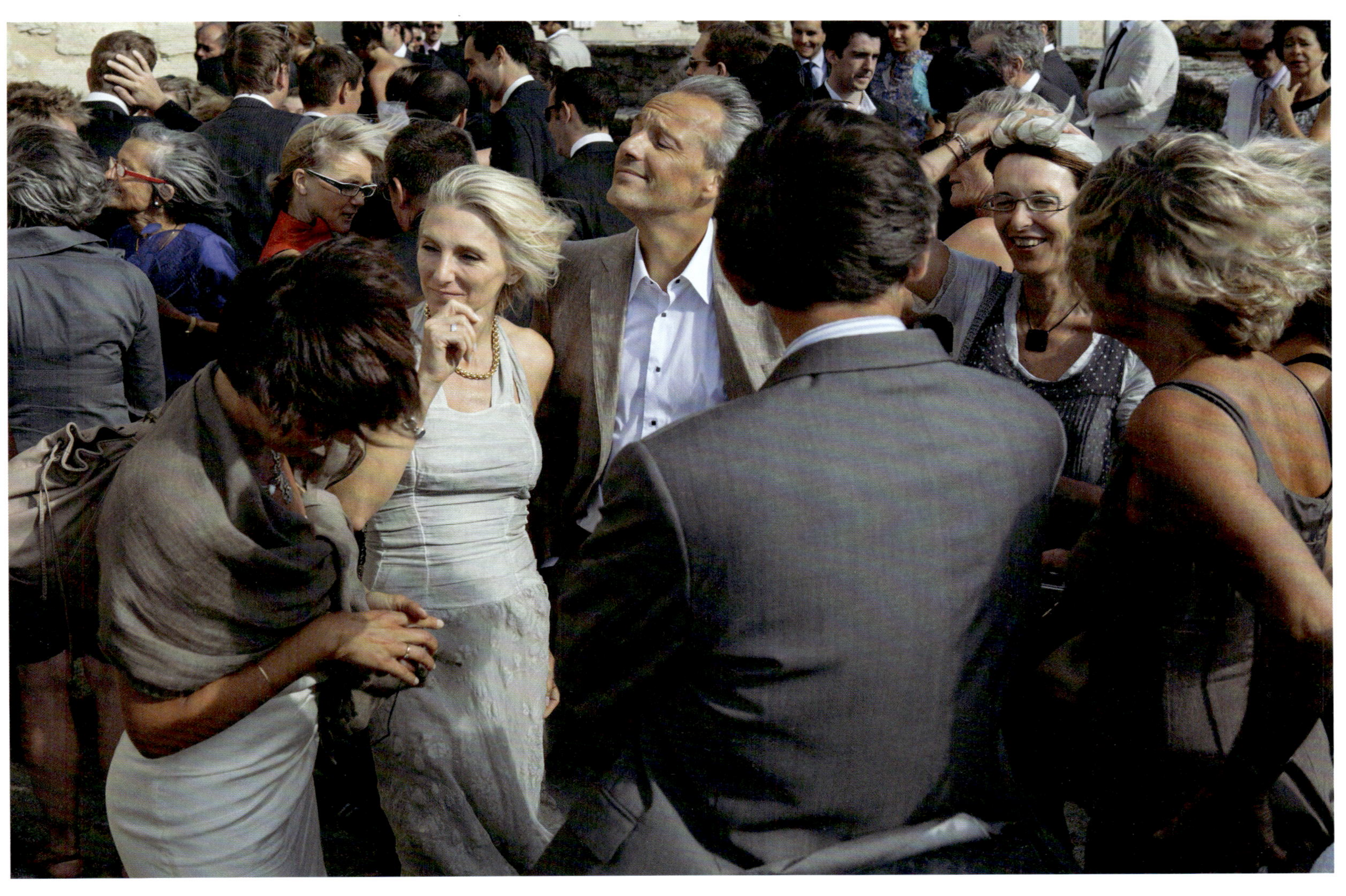

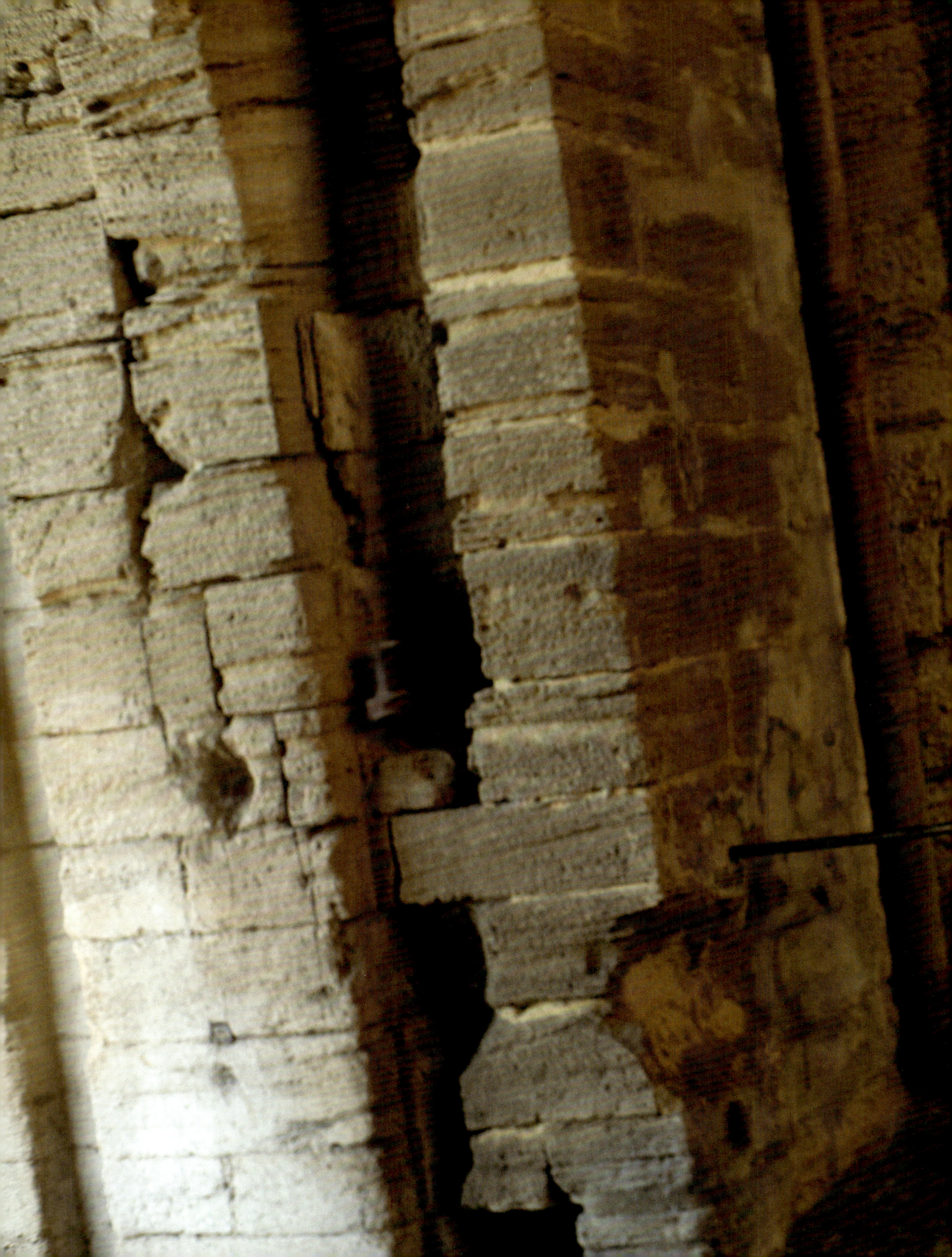

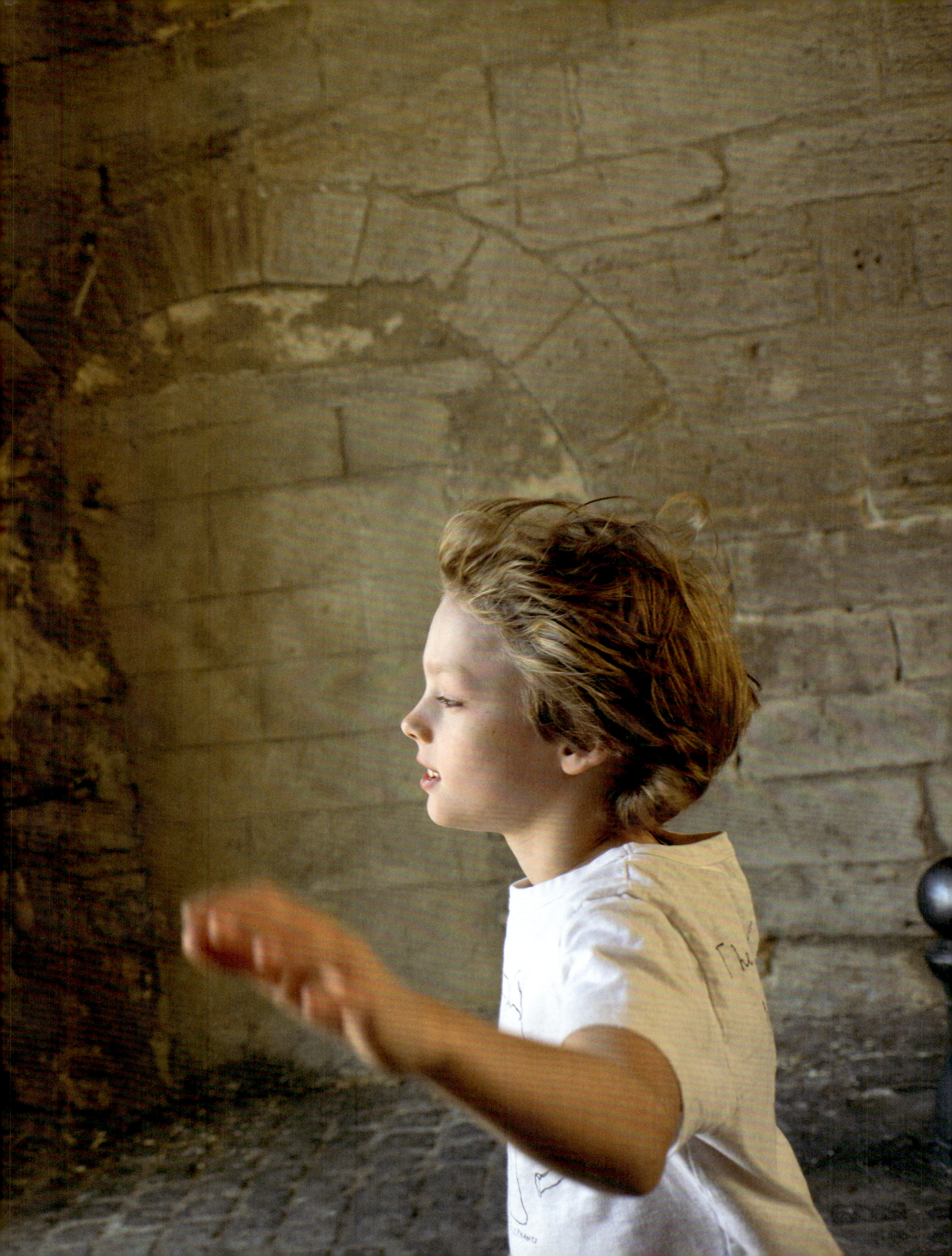

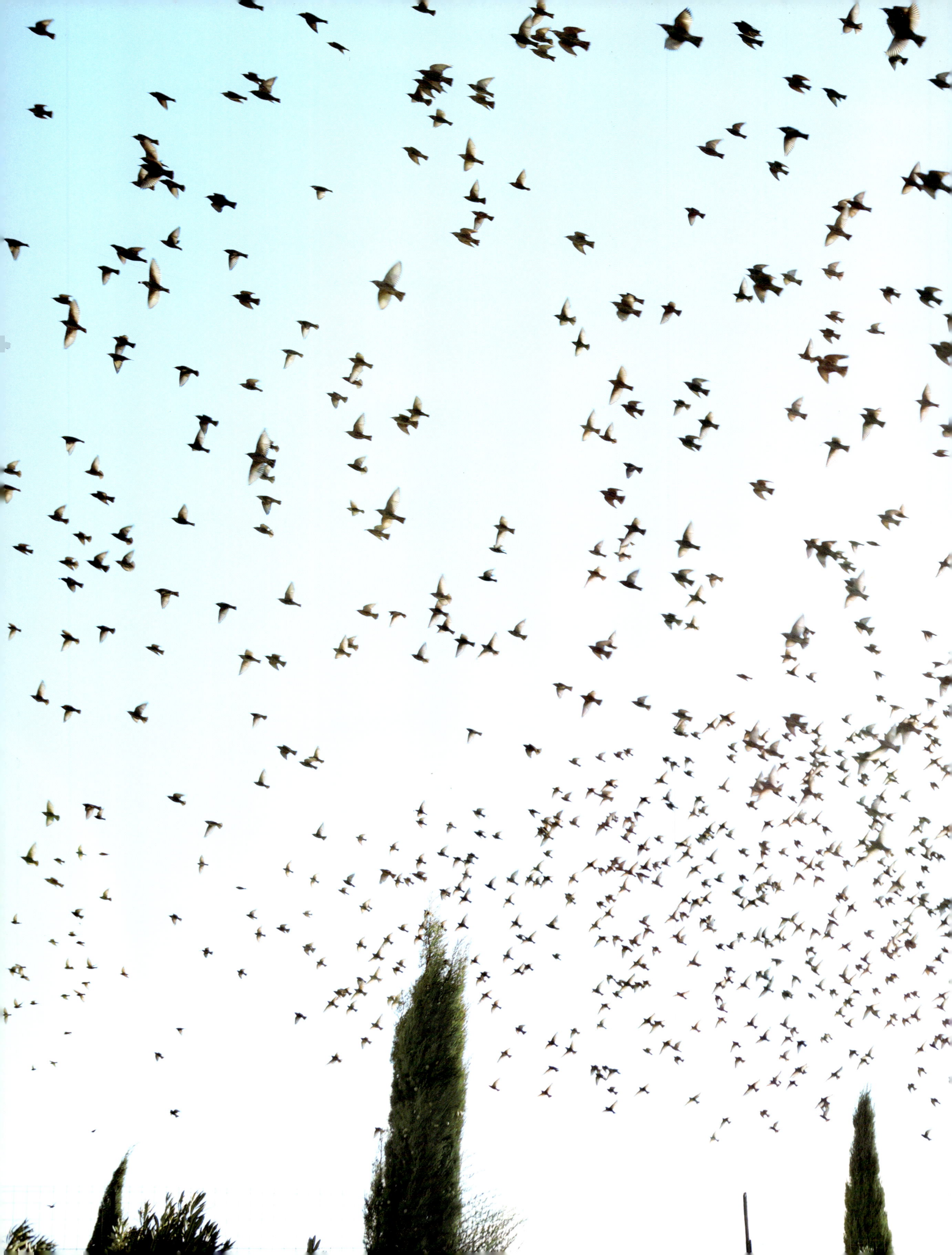

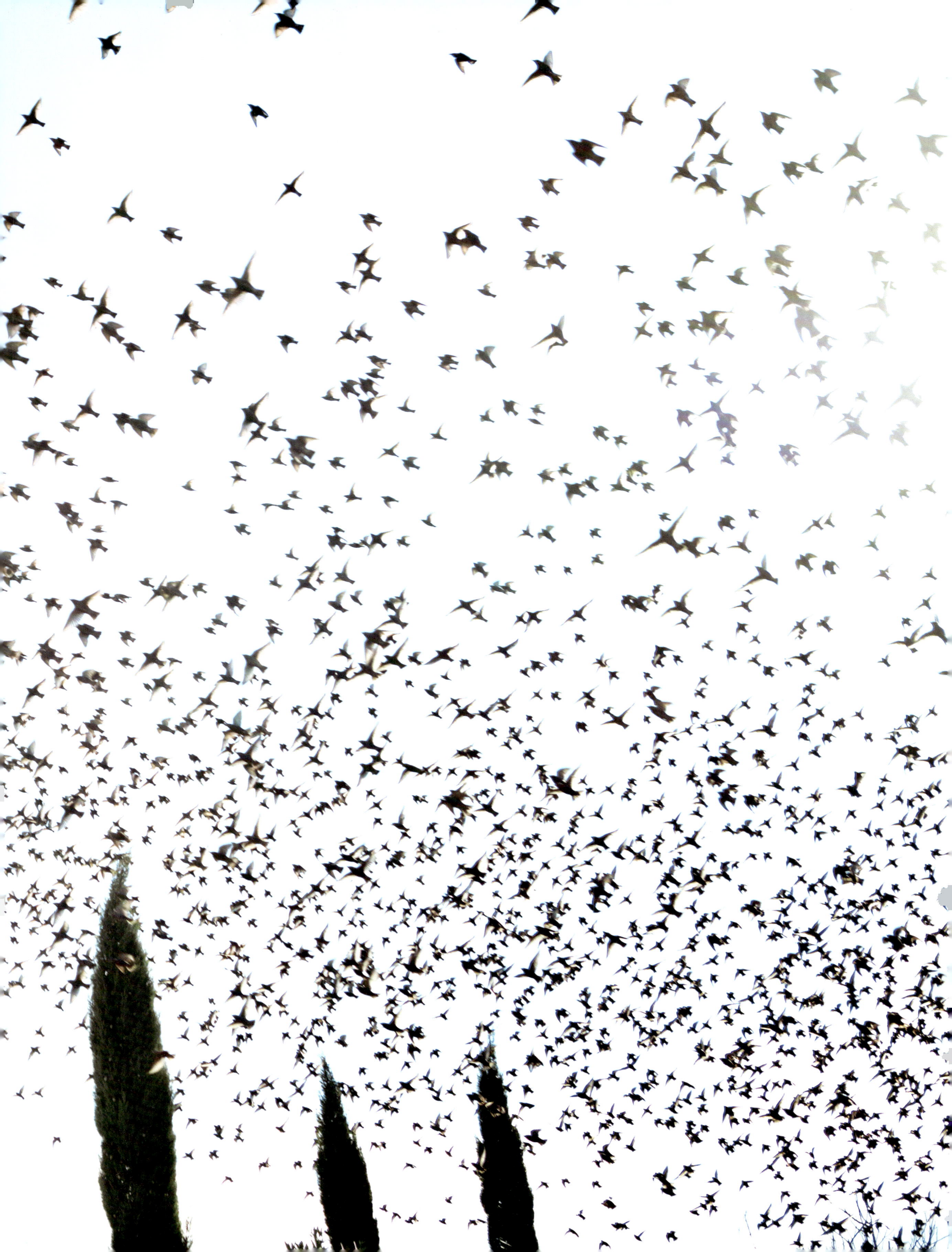

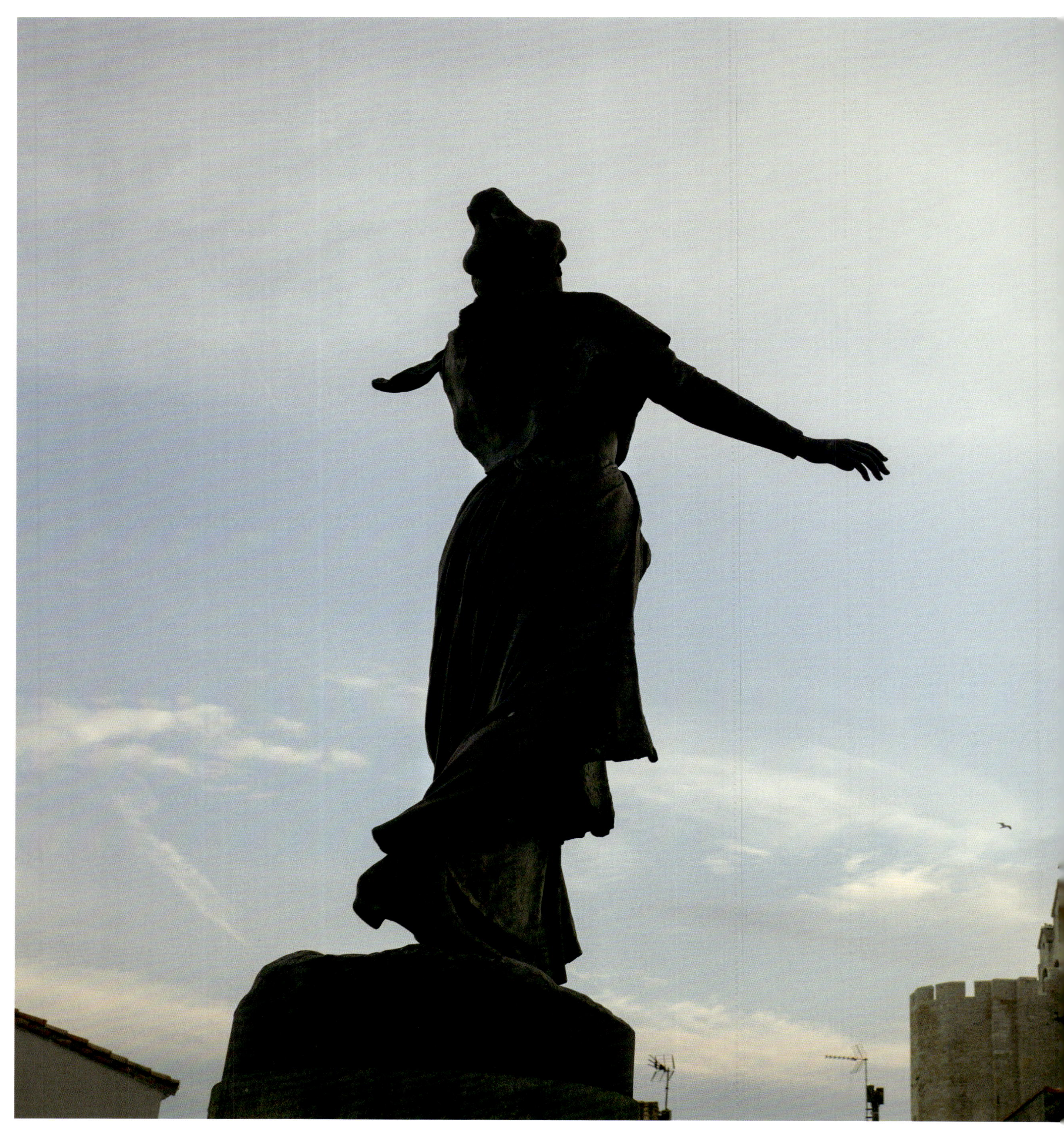

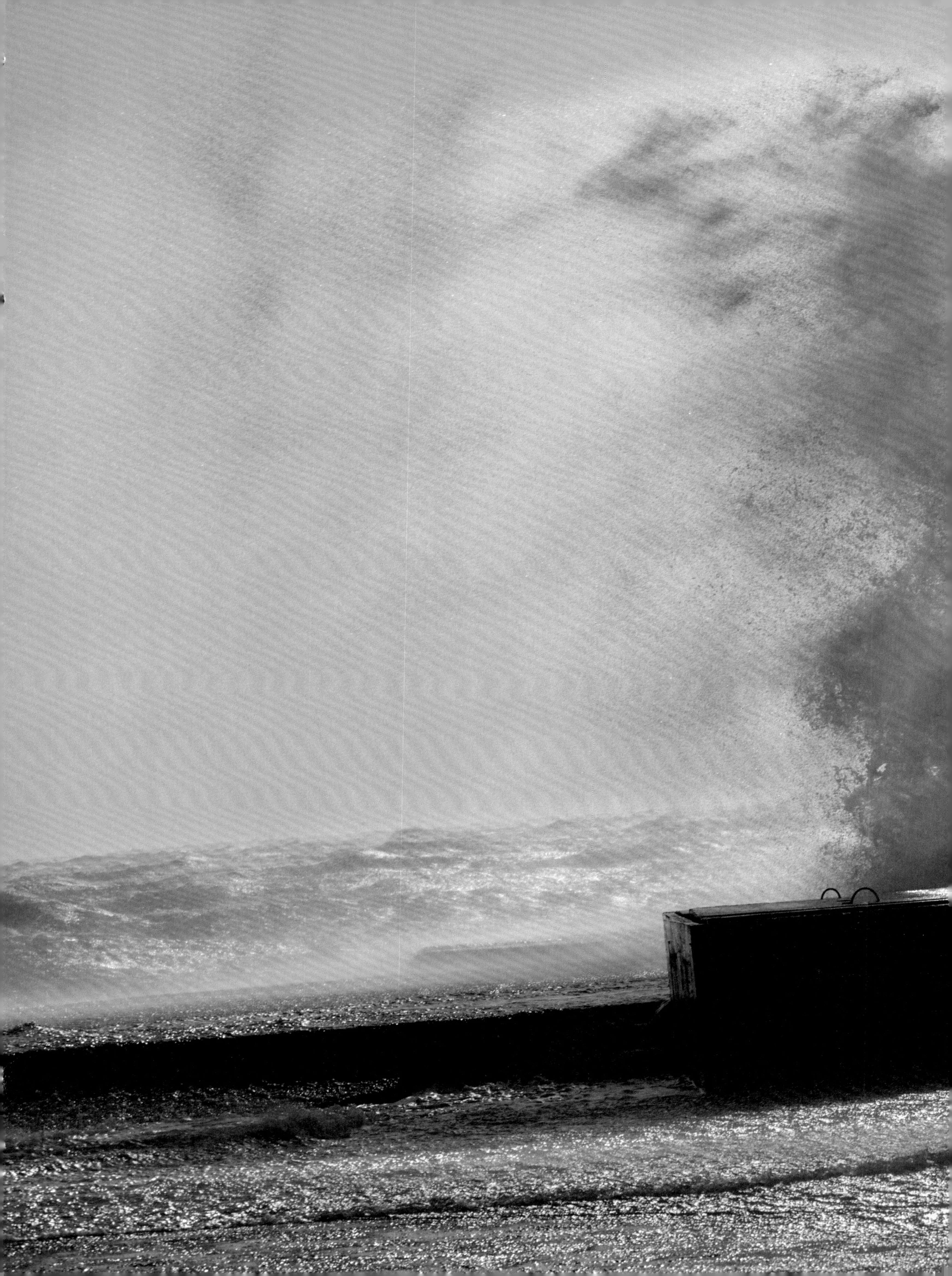

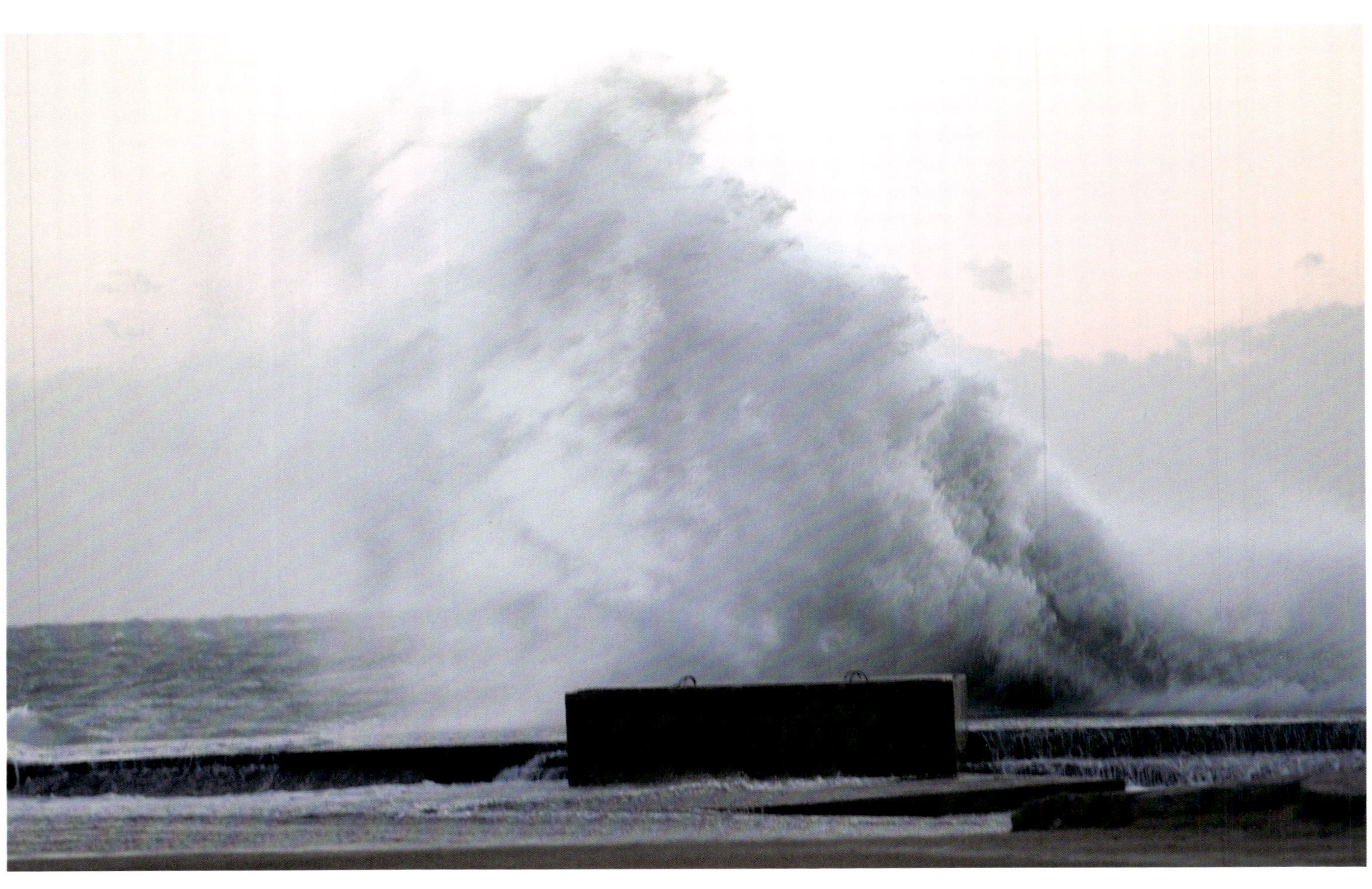

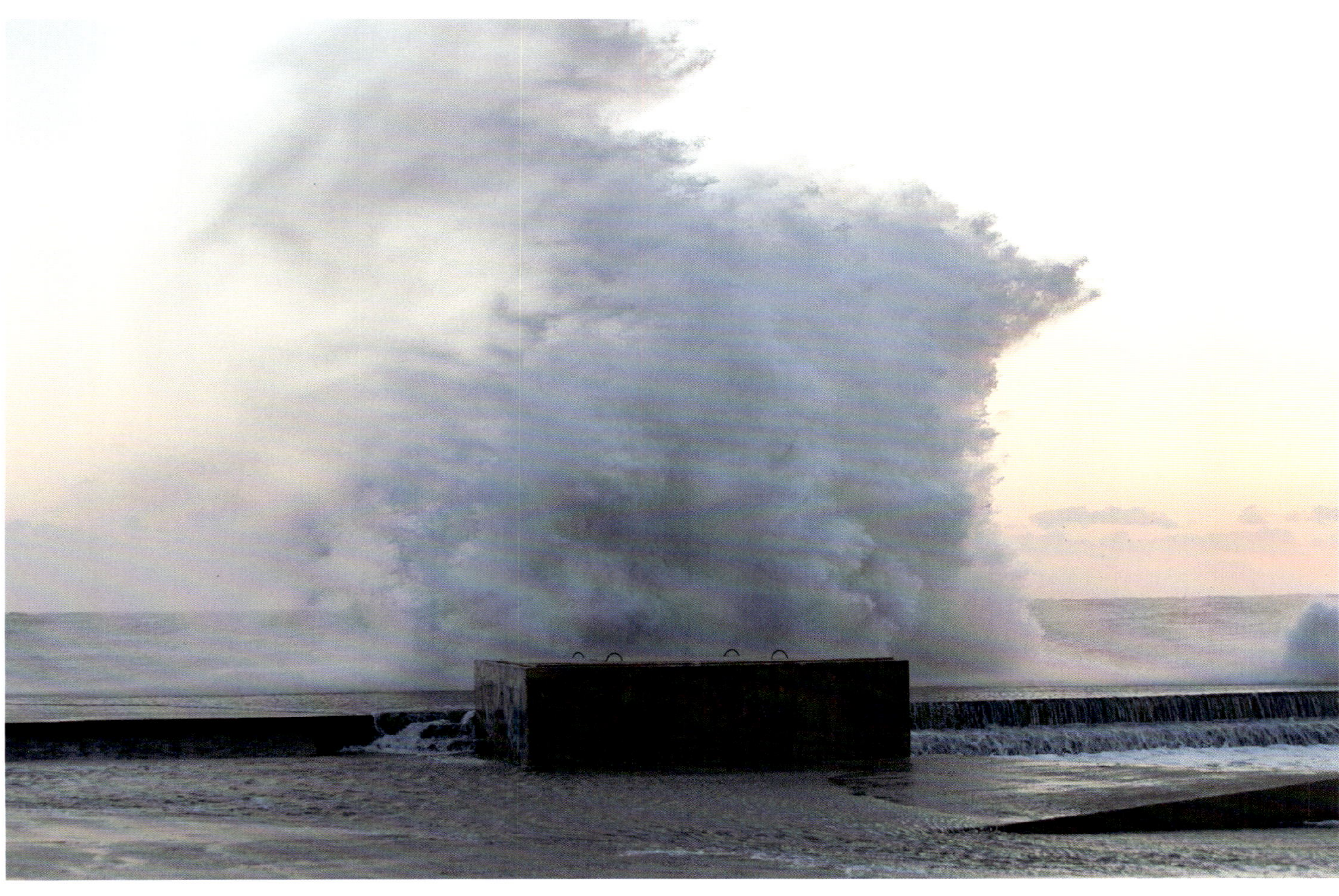

Let us sing to the glory of our fathers
Who throughout history
Have made their way in the world,
And who always, the books tell us,
Have remained free
Like the sea and the mistral.

Chantons la gloire de nos pères
Qui dans l'histoire
Ont fait leur trou,
Et qui toujours, nous disent les livres,
Sont restés libres
Comme la mer et le mistral.

De nòsti paire canten la glòri
Que dins l'istòri
An fa soun trau,
E que de-longo, nous dien li libre,
Soun resta libre
Coume la mar e lou mistrau.

—Frédéric Mistral, *Les îles dor*

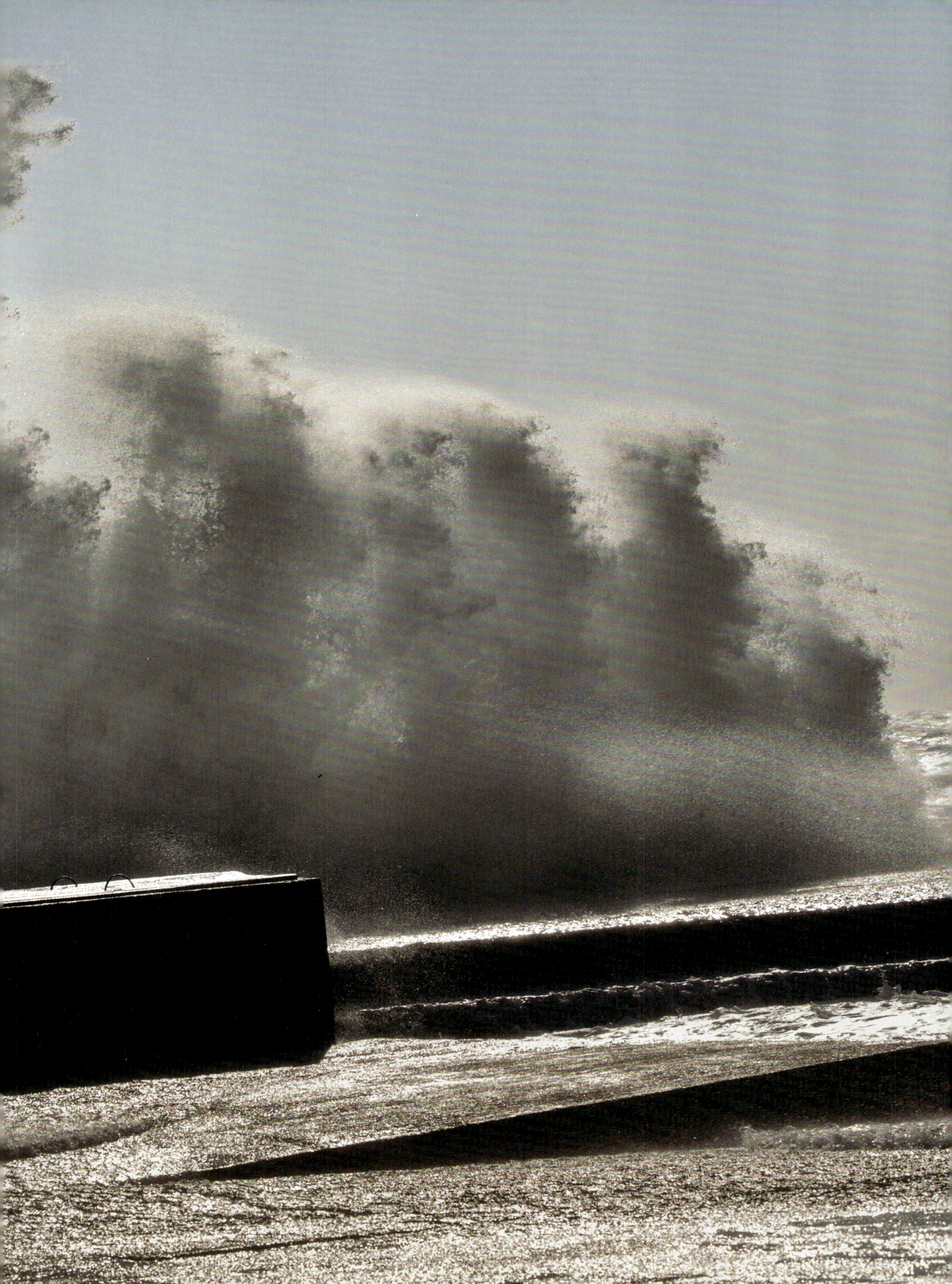

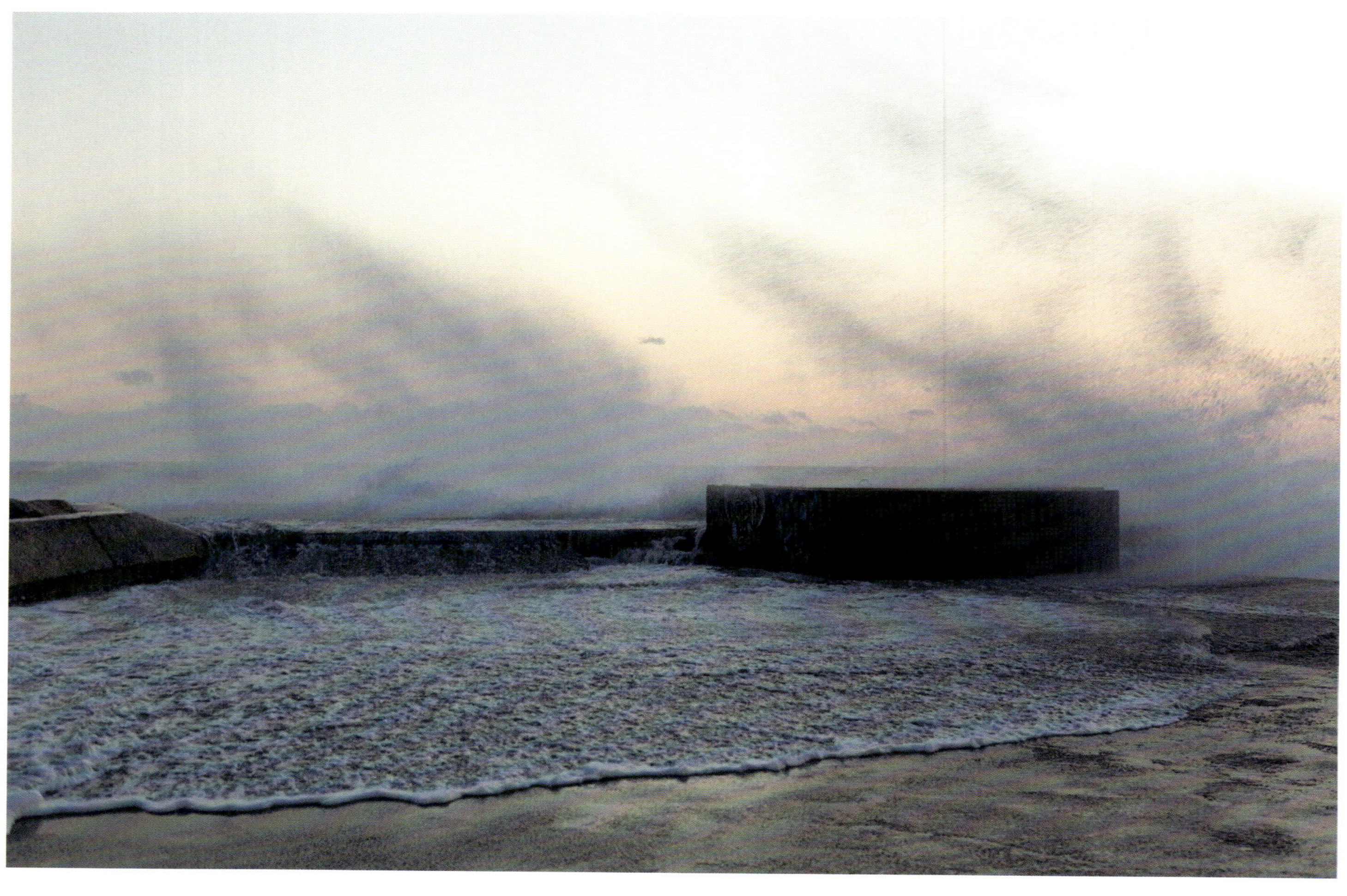

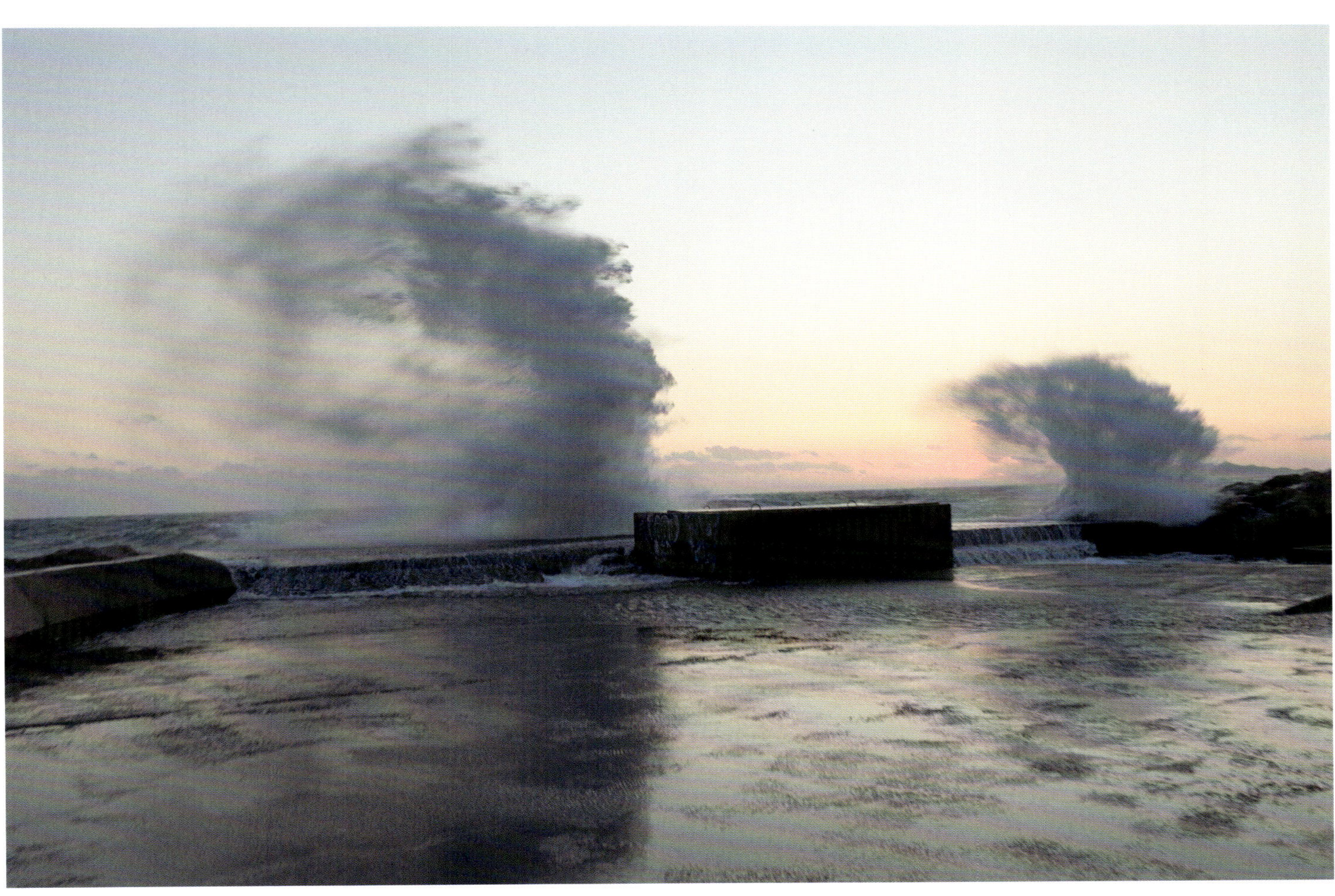

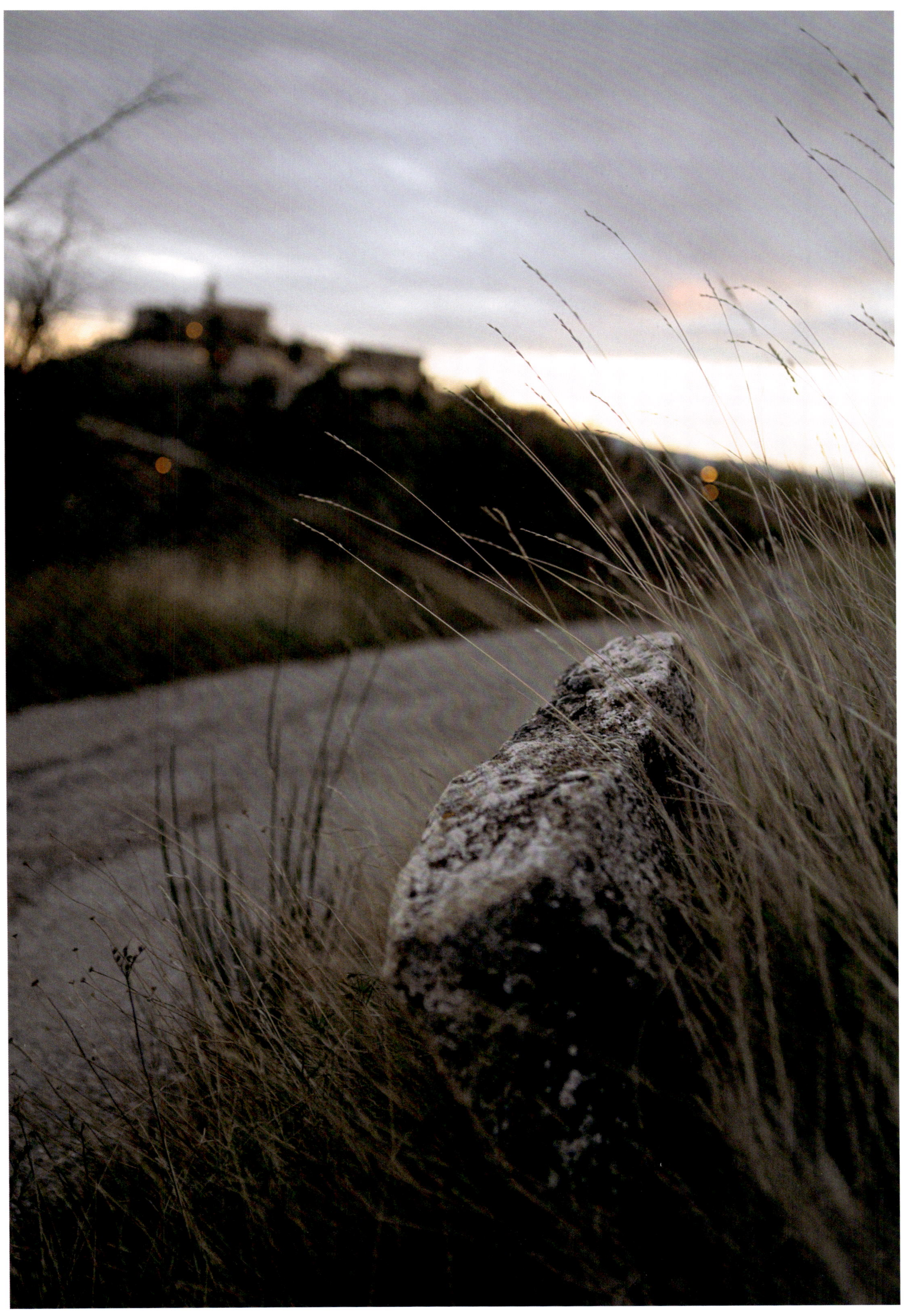

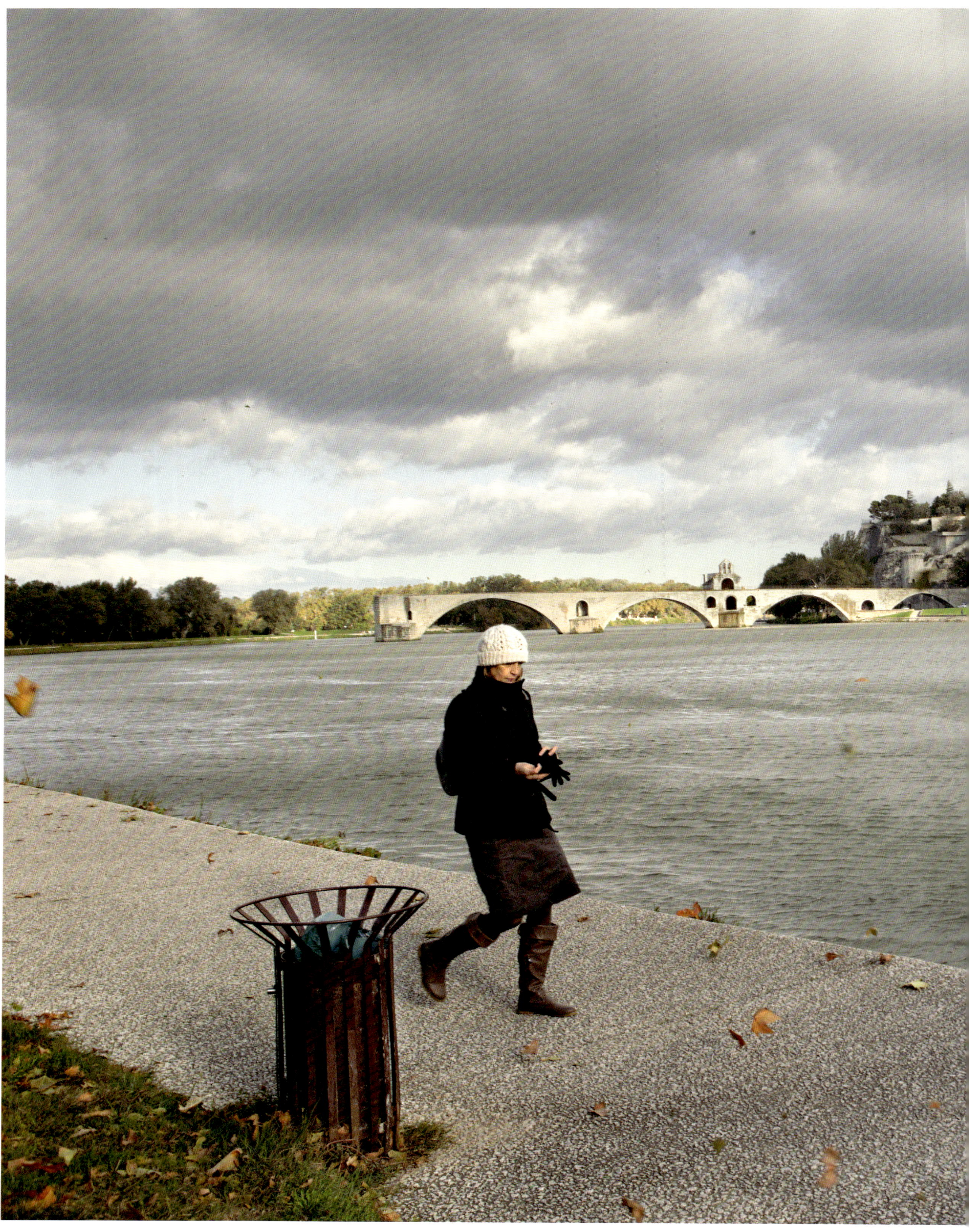

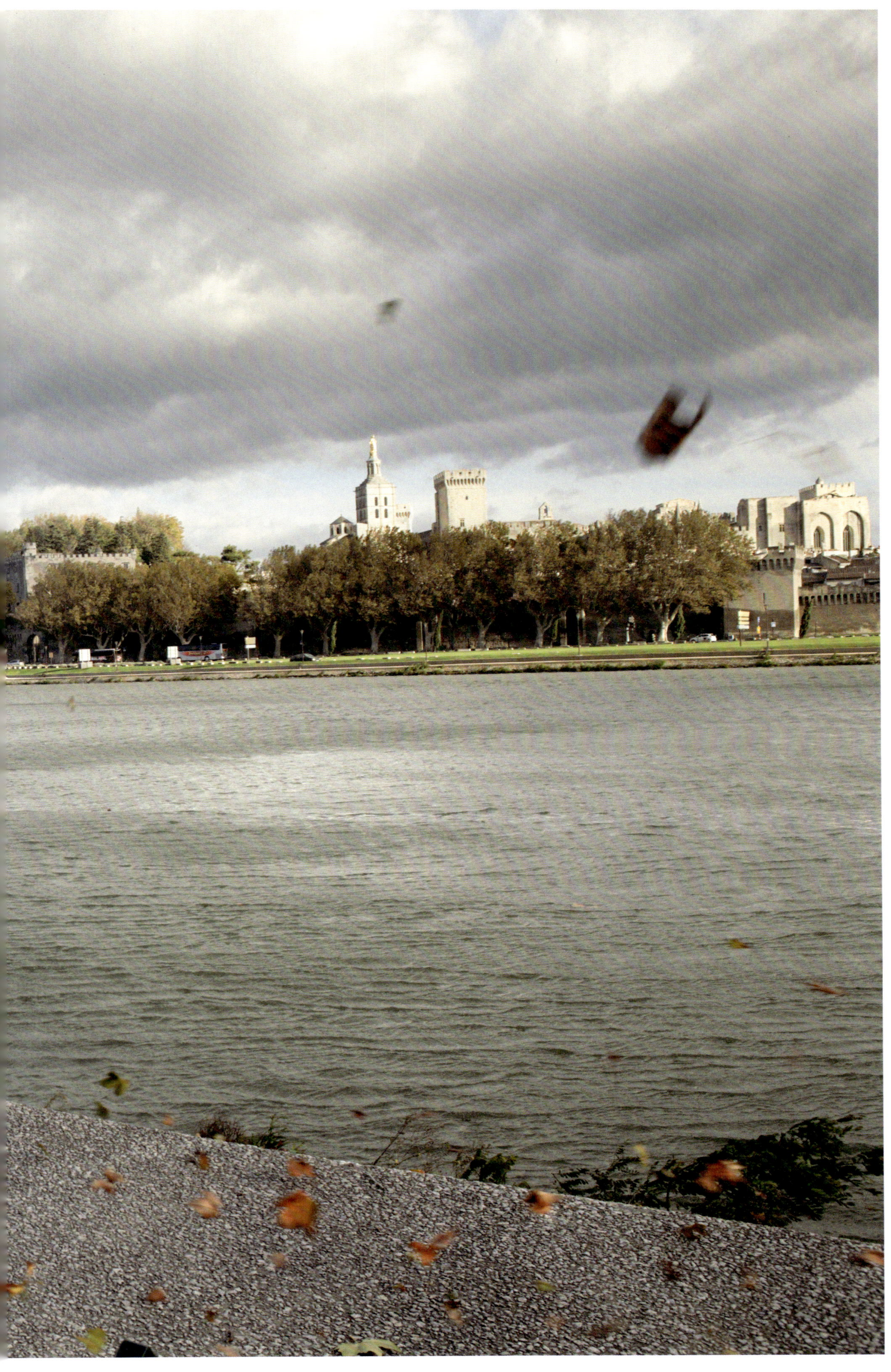

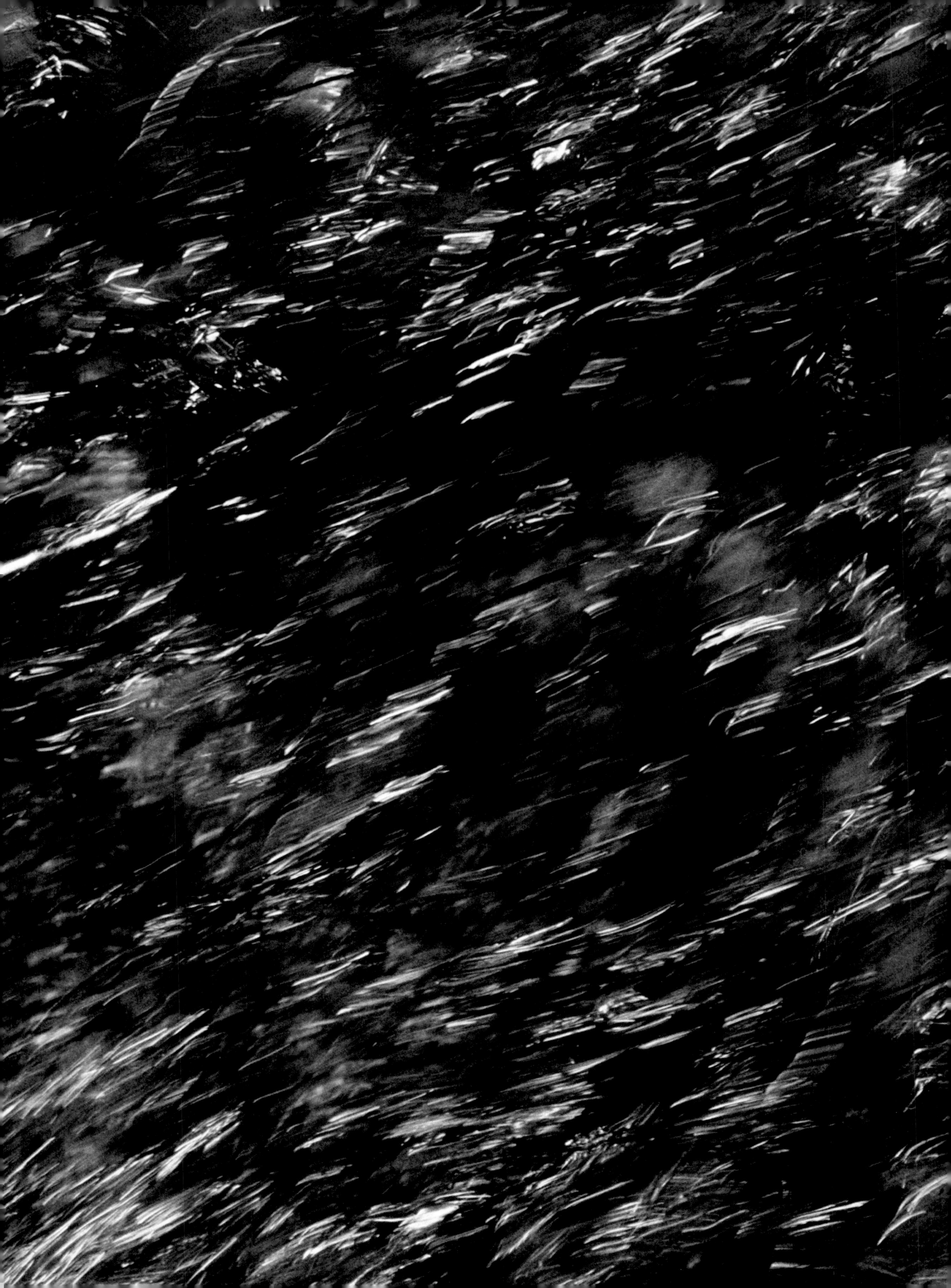

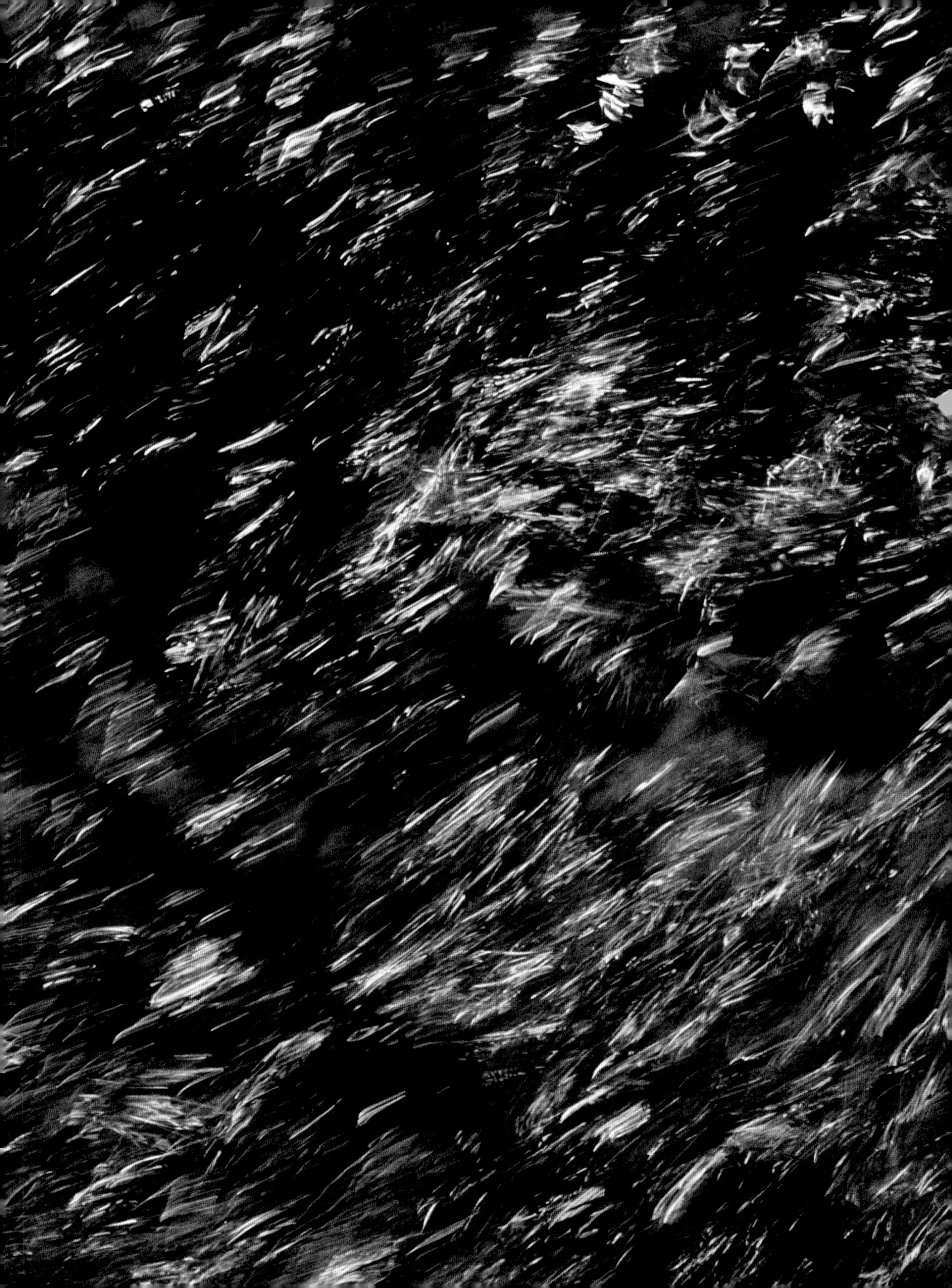

The people grew weary of being relentlessly blasted by the mistral.
One day, they captured him and locked him in a cave.
He thrashed about, demanding to be freed. "No," they said,
"you have tormented us long enough. Look at our
animals all in a state because of you. Look at our trees
felled by you. Look at our roof tiles on the ground because of you."
"You'll be sorry!" cried the wind. At first, the people relished
the quiet and the stillness. But before long, swarms of mosquitoes
began to savage them again, disease returned, and their
crops were riddled with pests. "You see," said the wind, sly as ever.
"If you let me out, I promise not to cause any more damage."
Eventually the people relented. As soon as the
mistral was released, he mercilessly punished the people.

—From a Provençal folktale

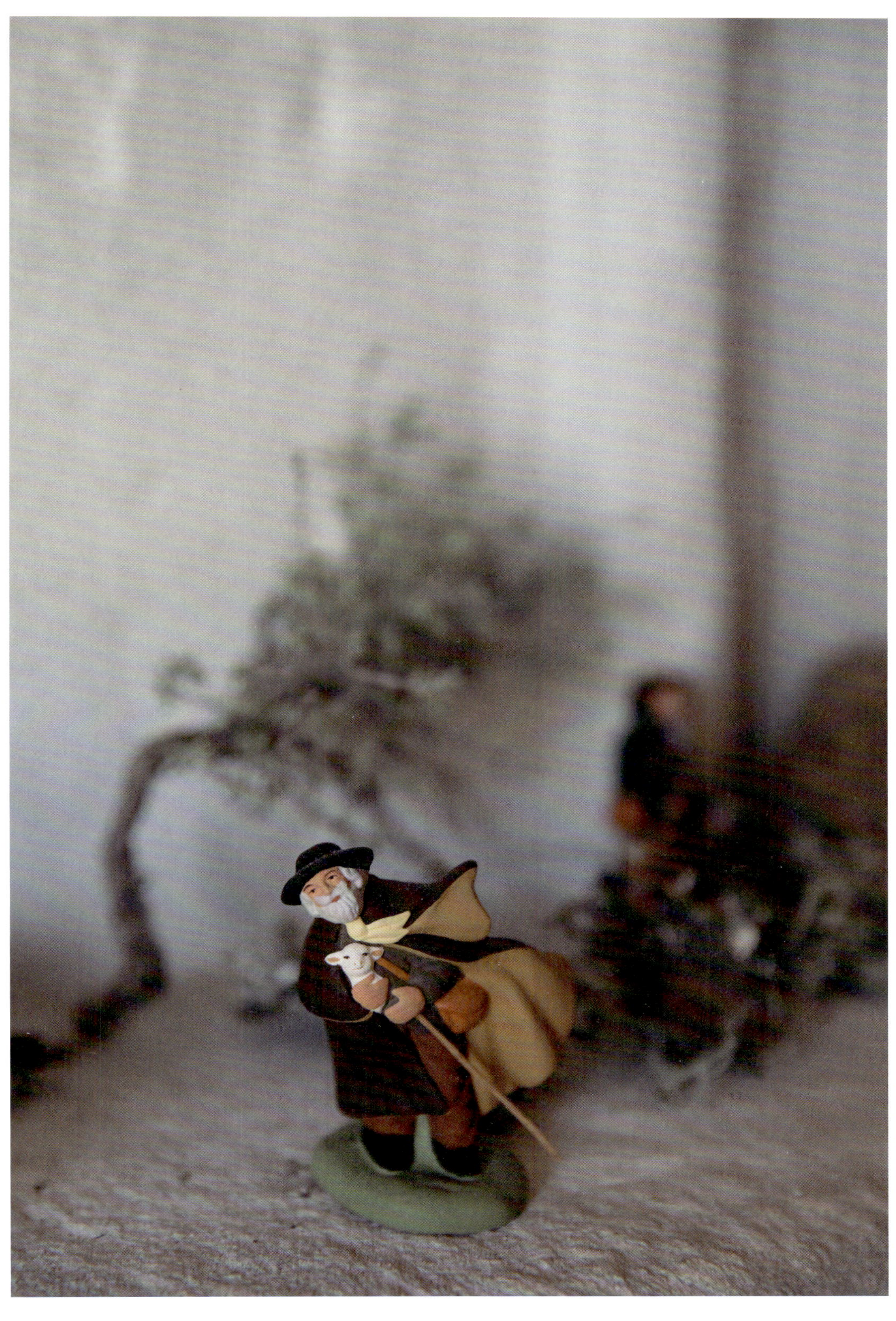

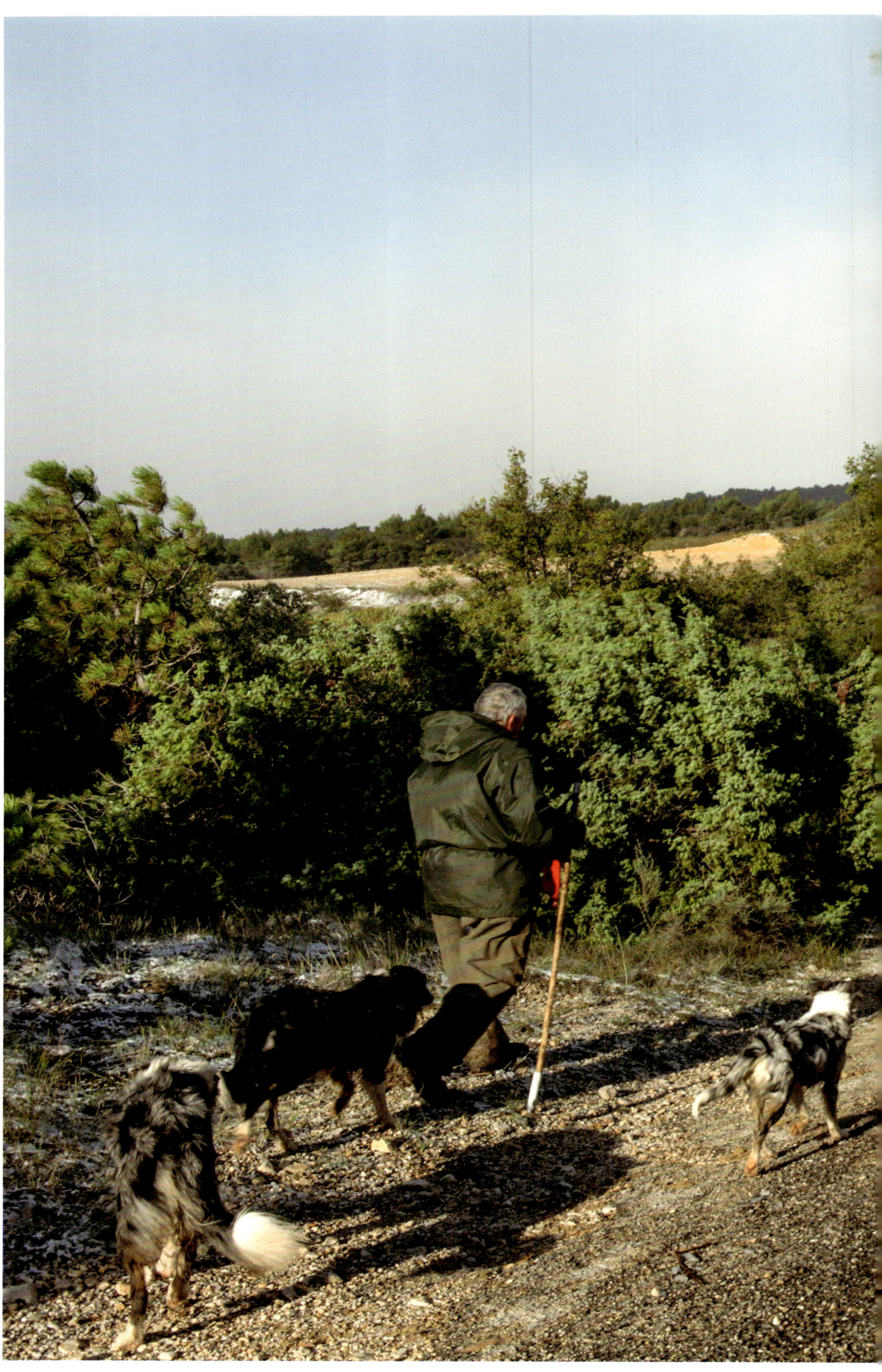

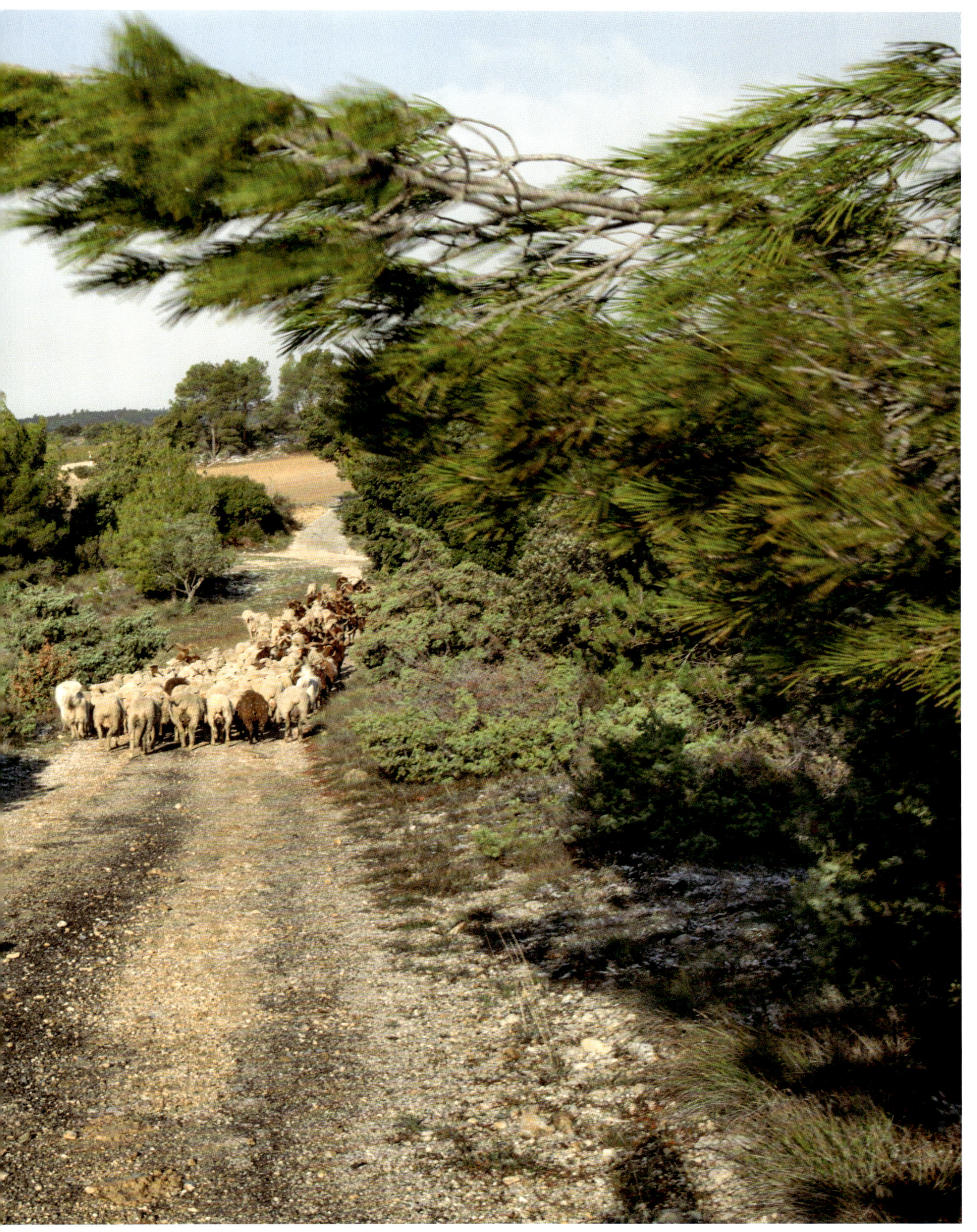

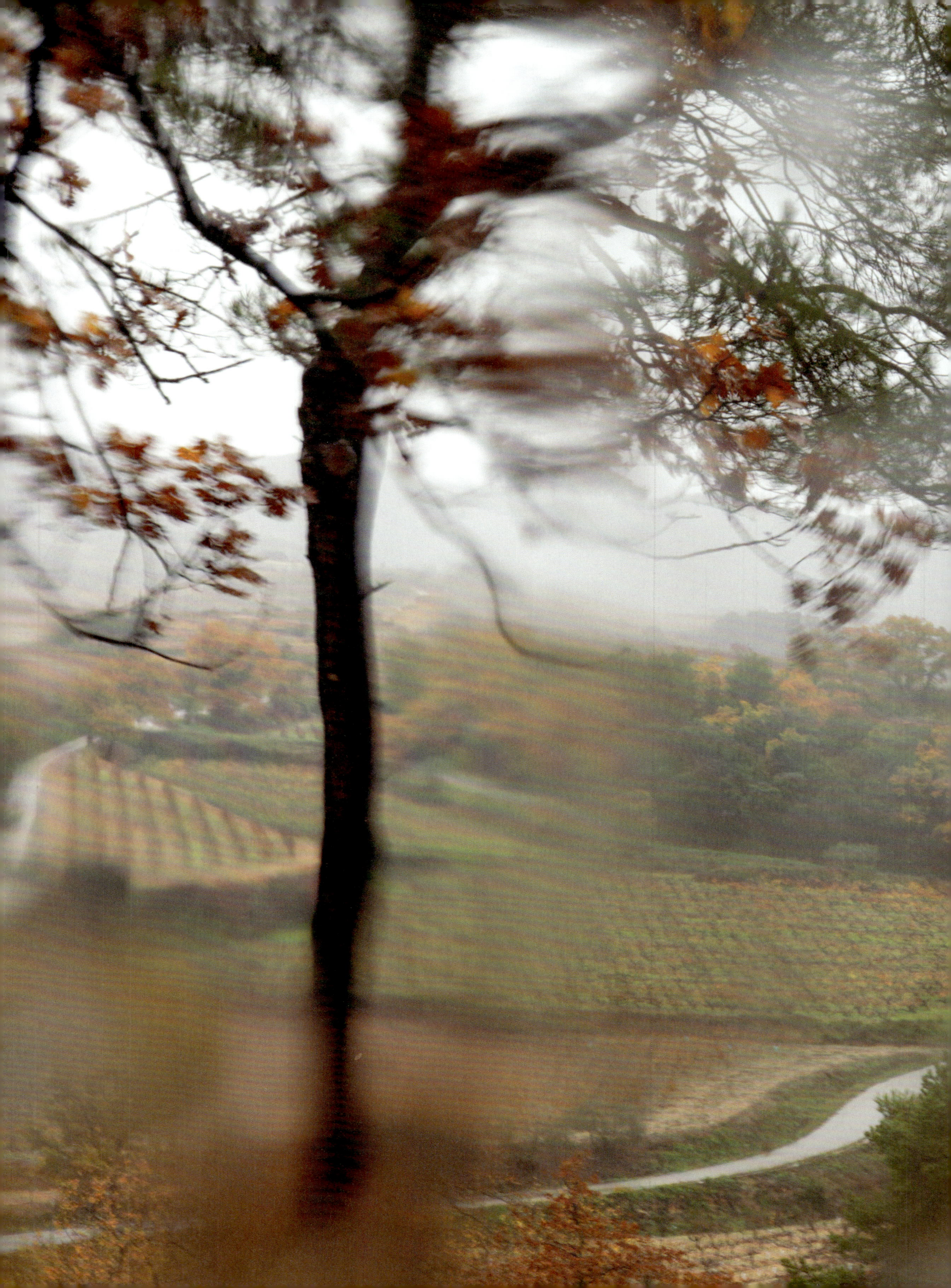

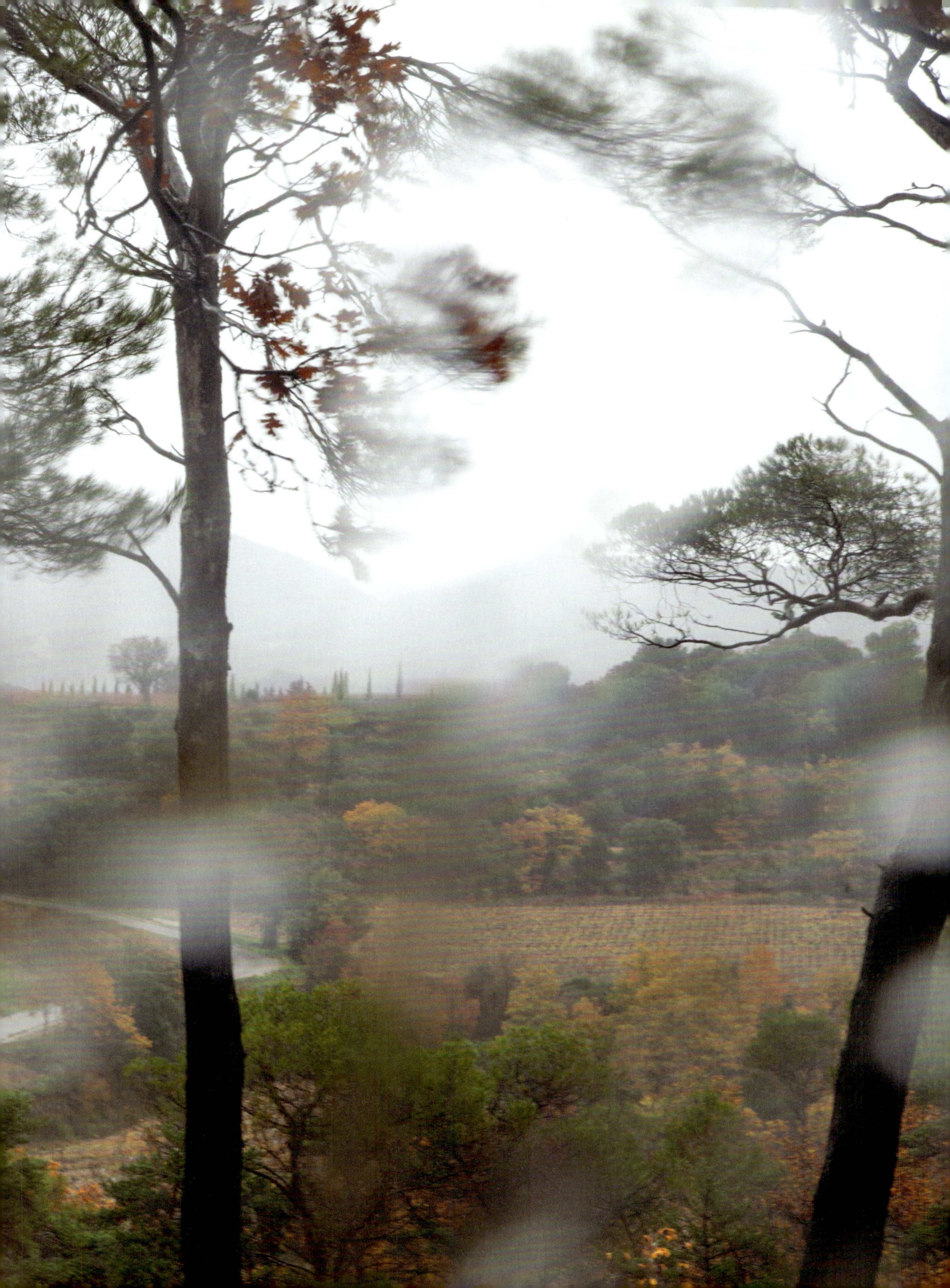

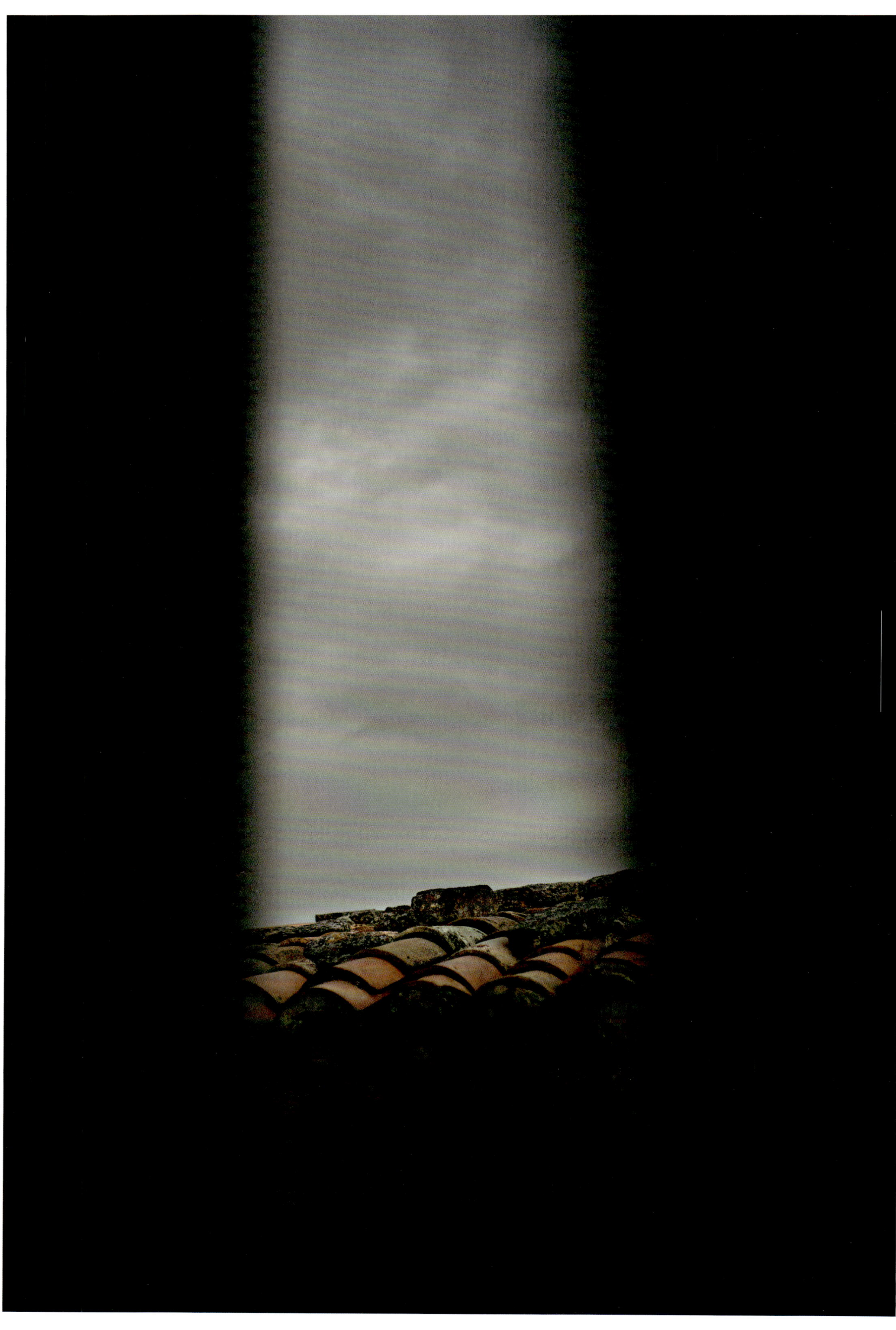

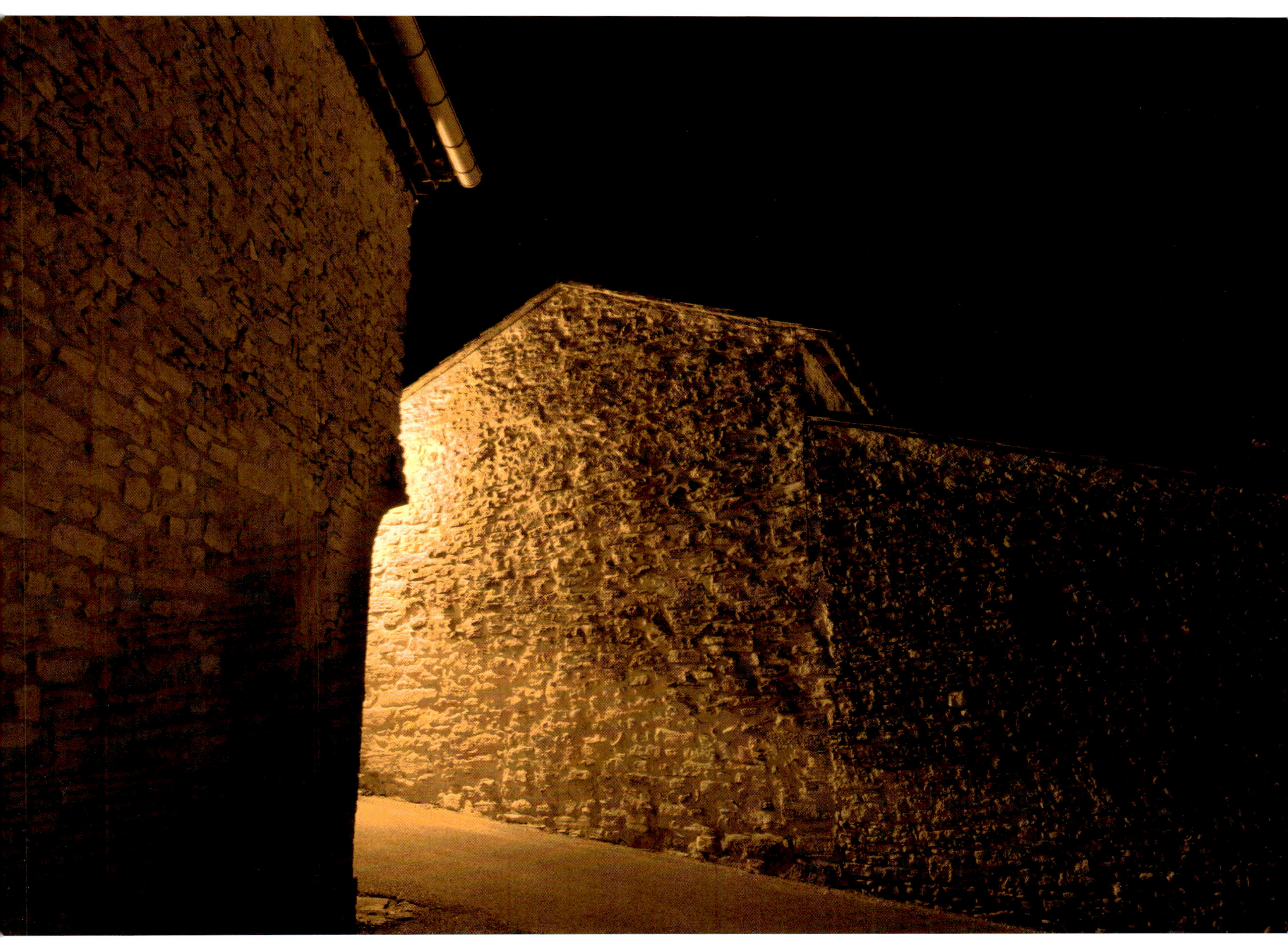

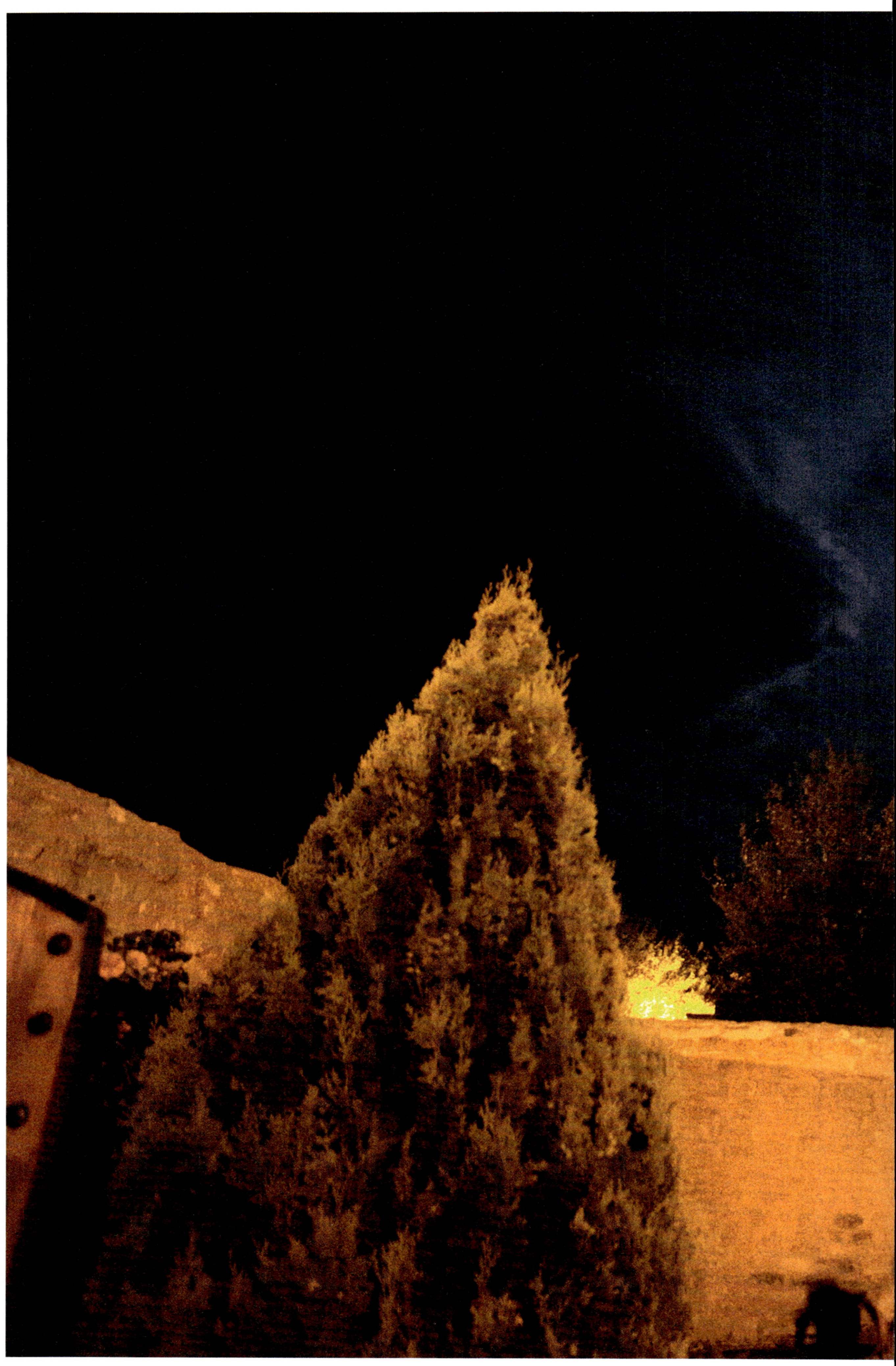

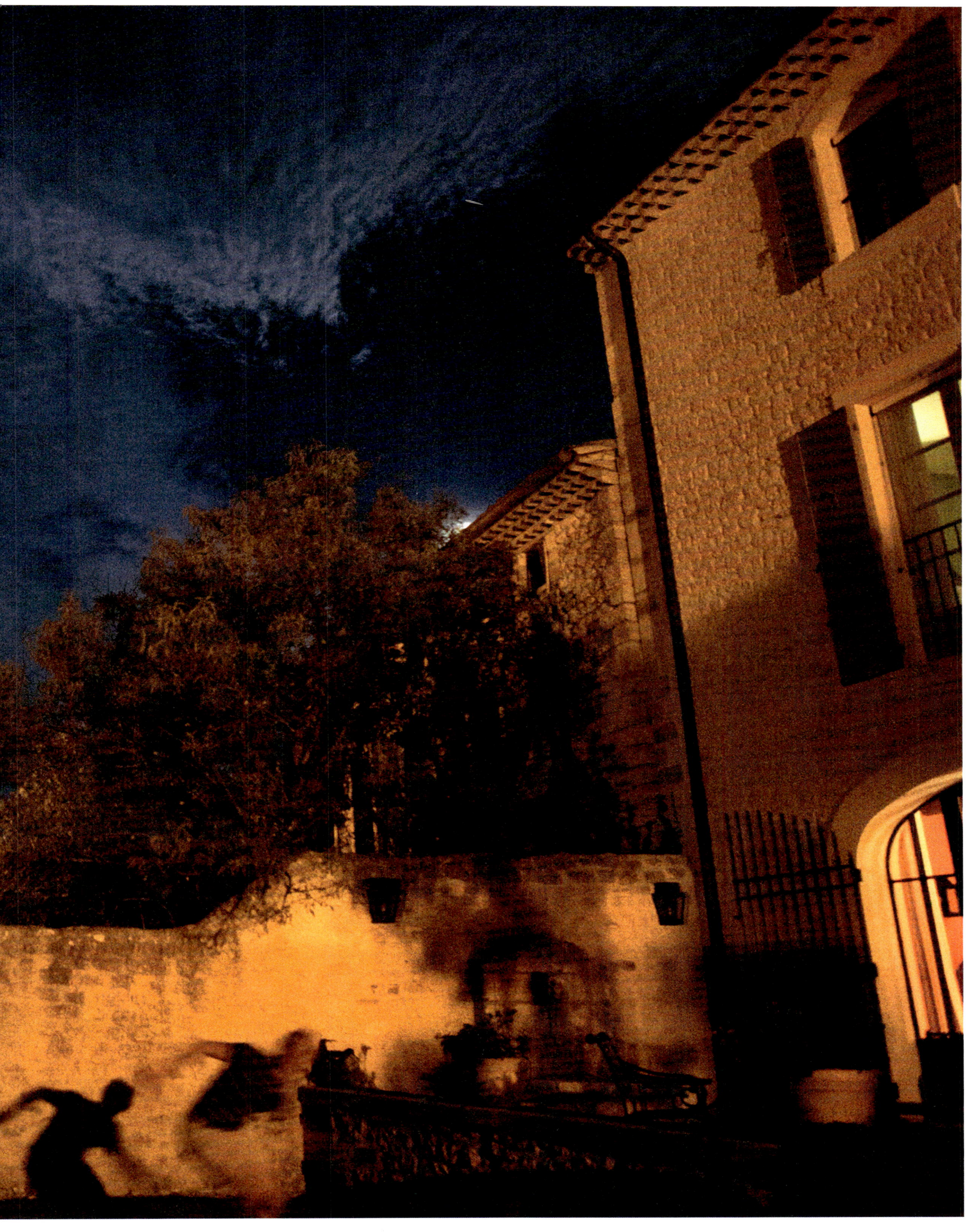

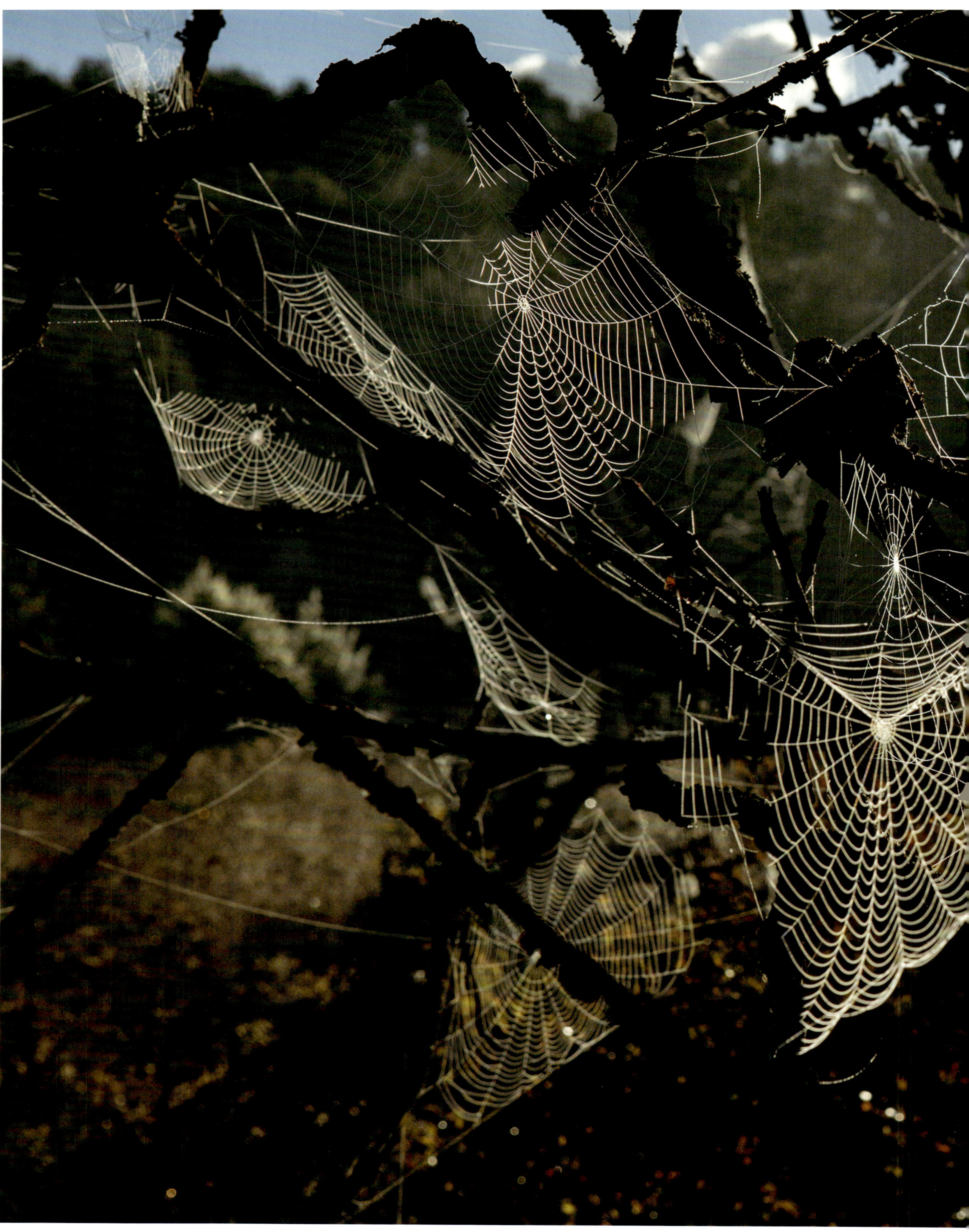

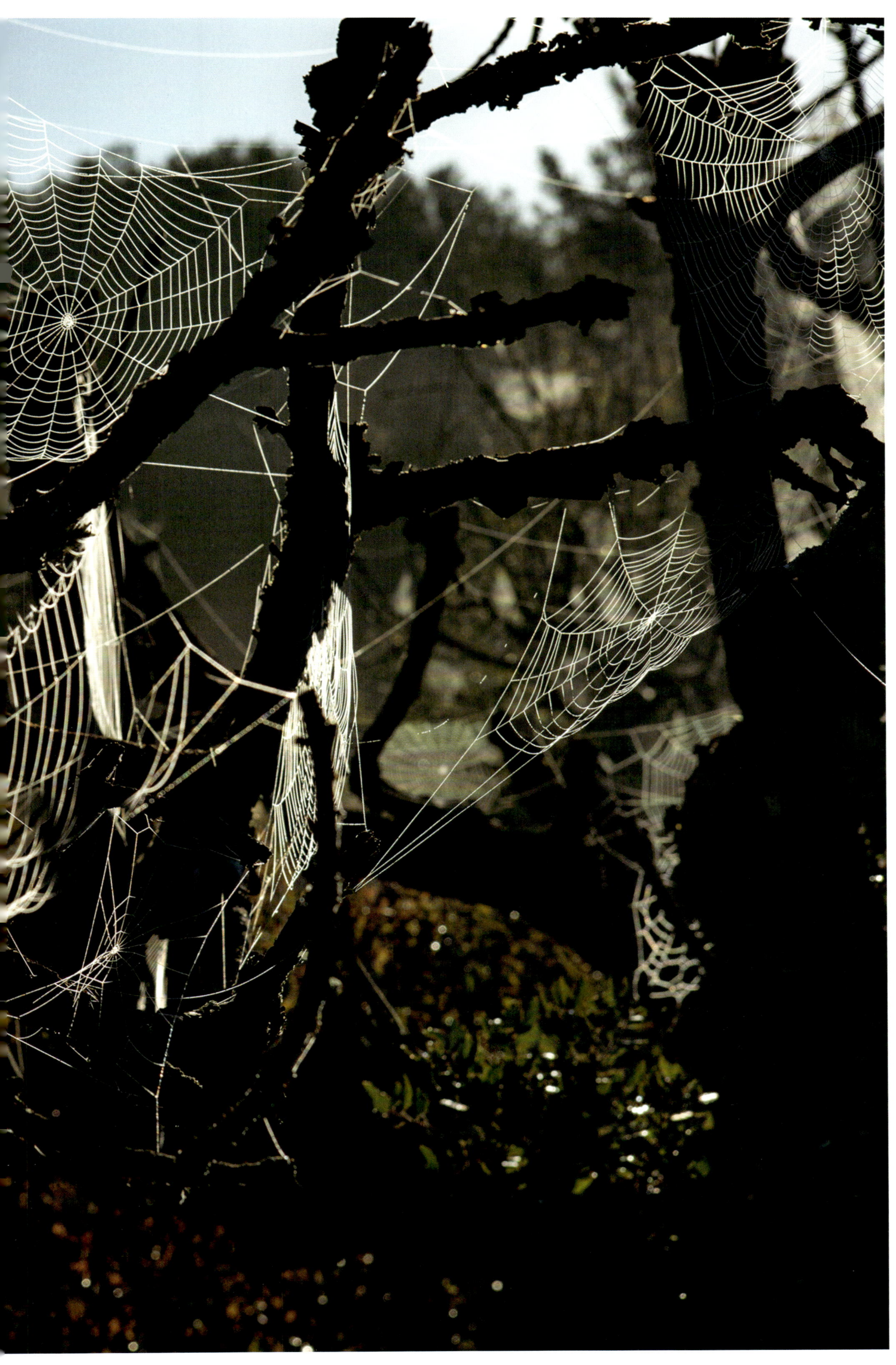

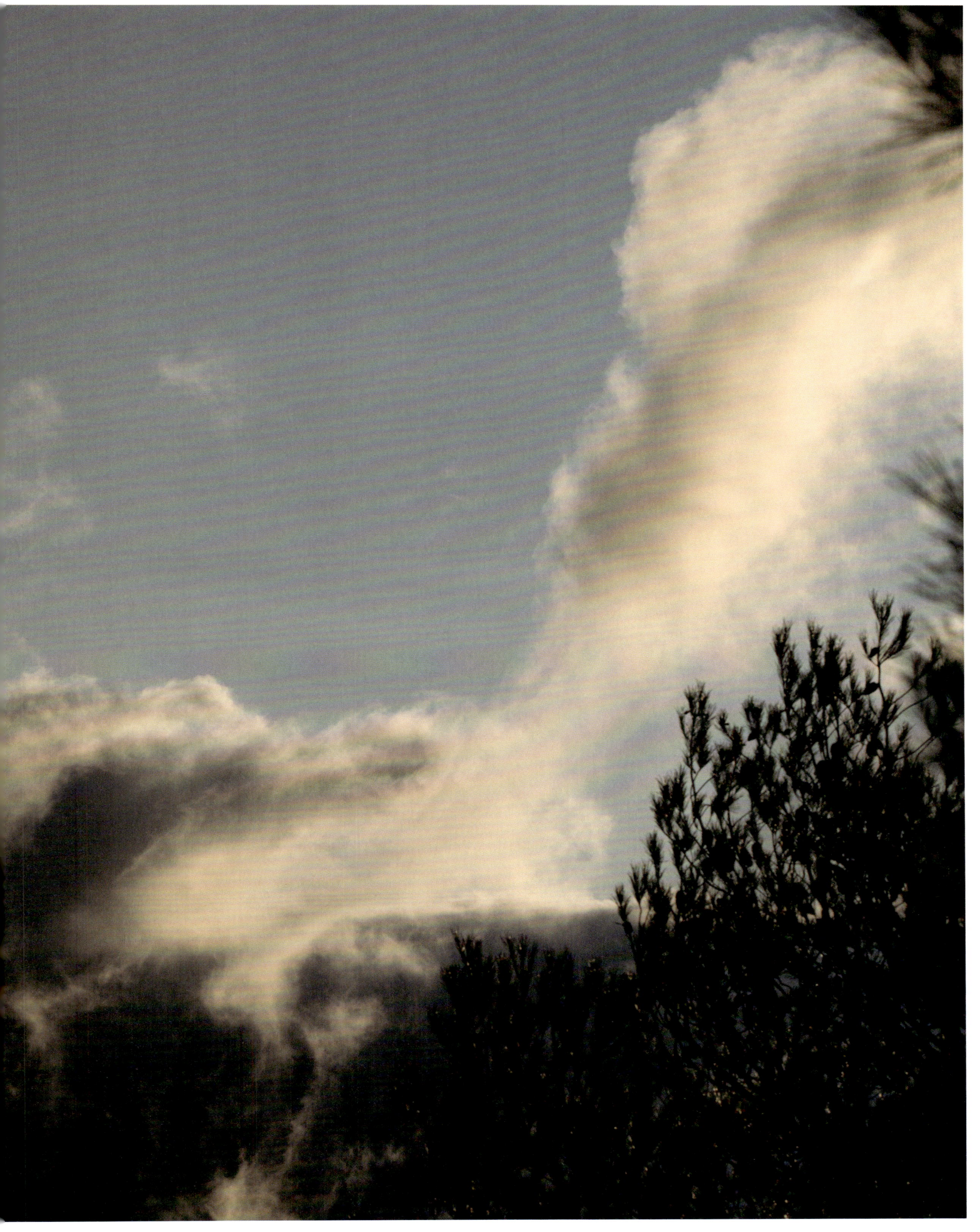

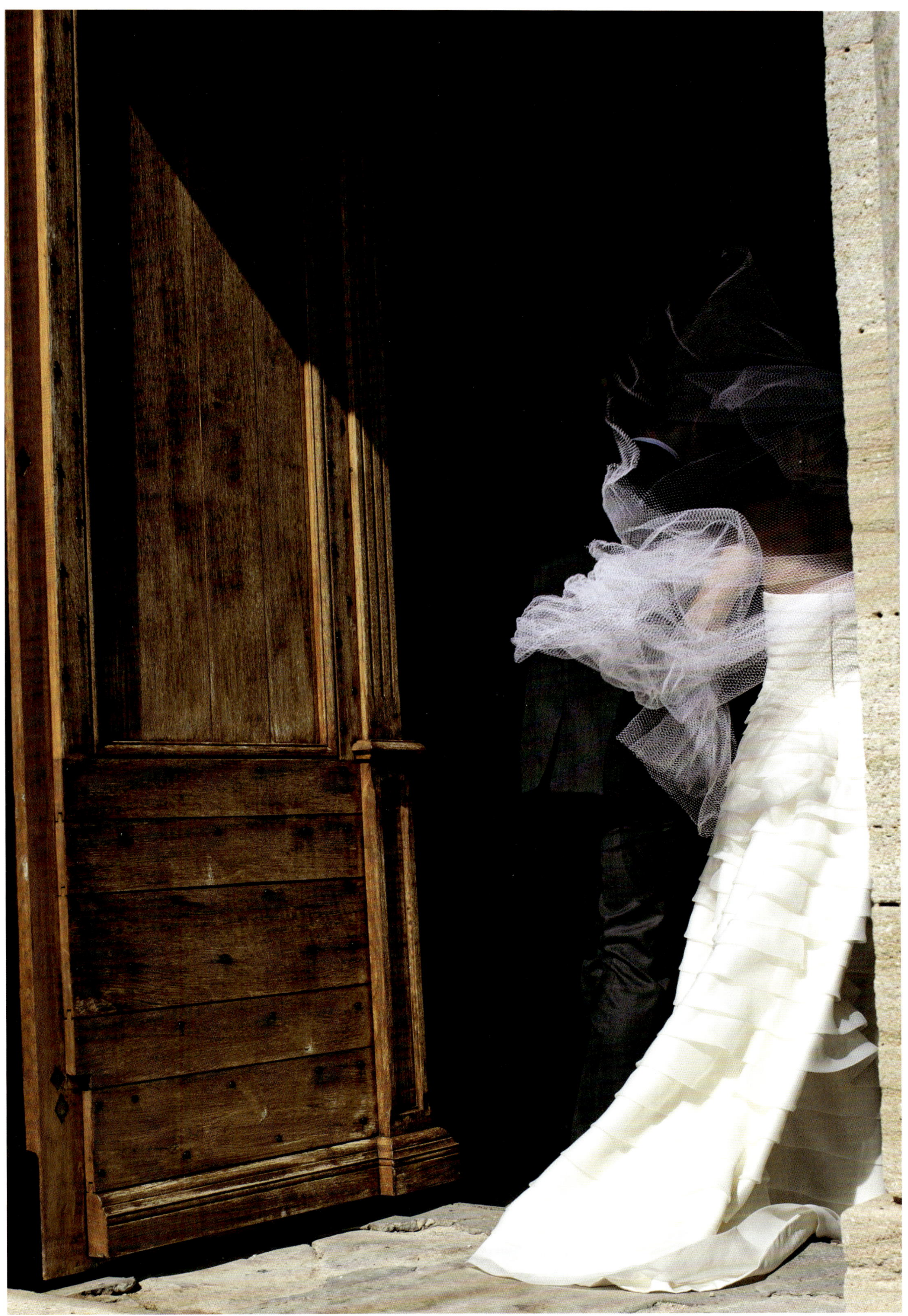

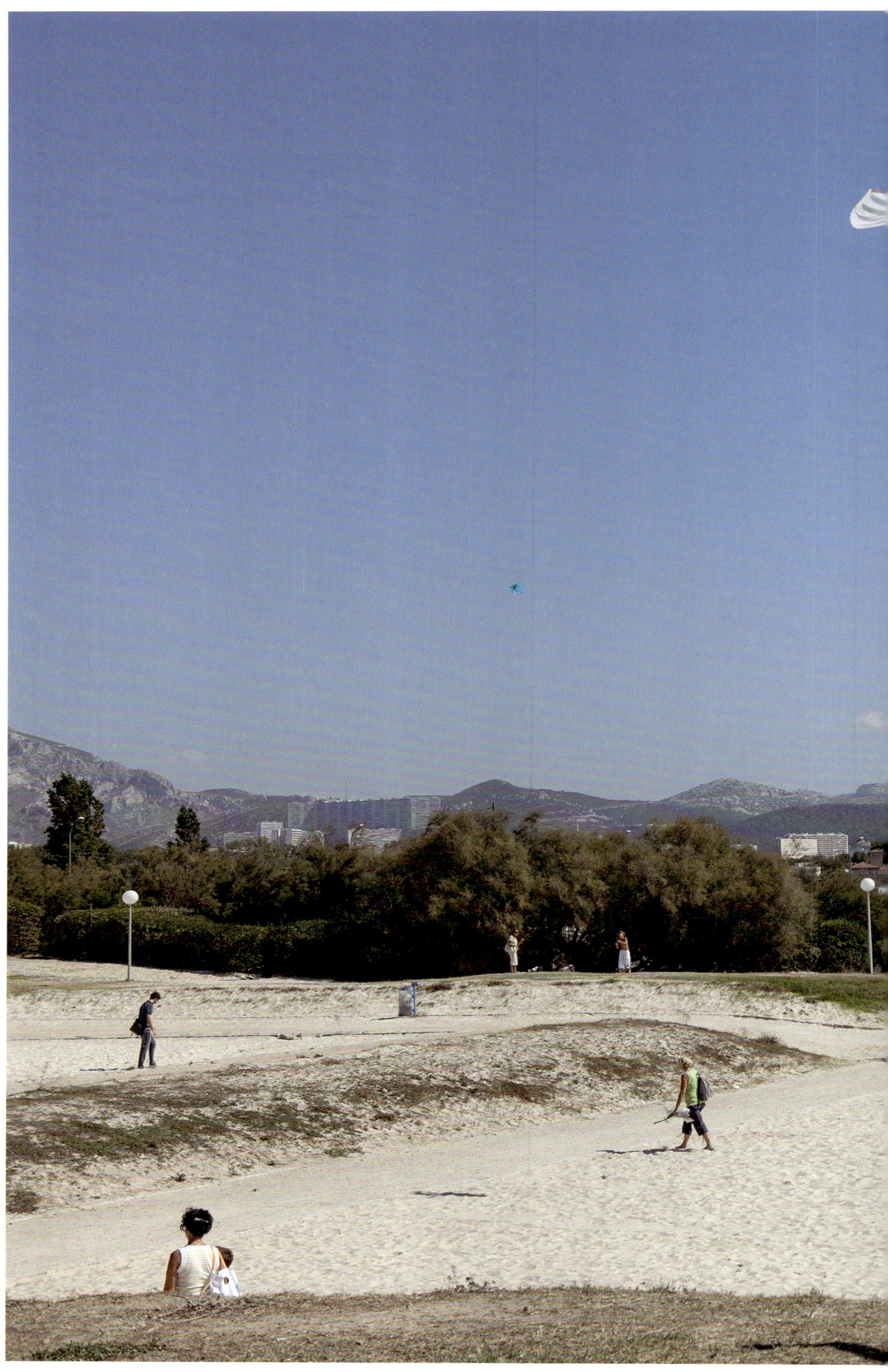

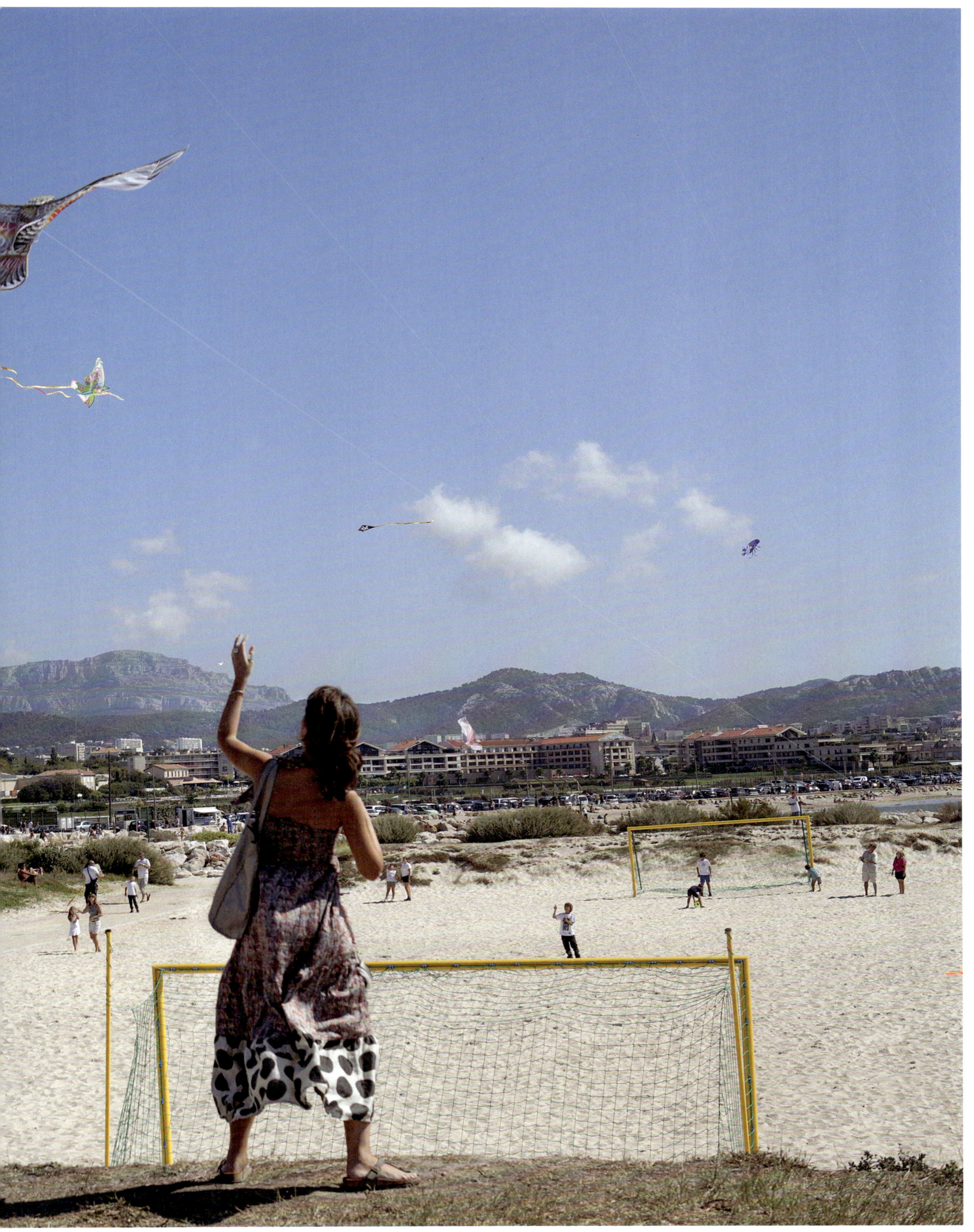

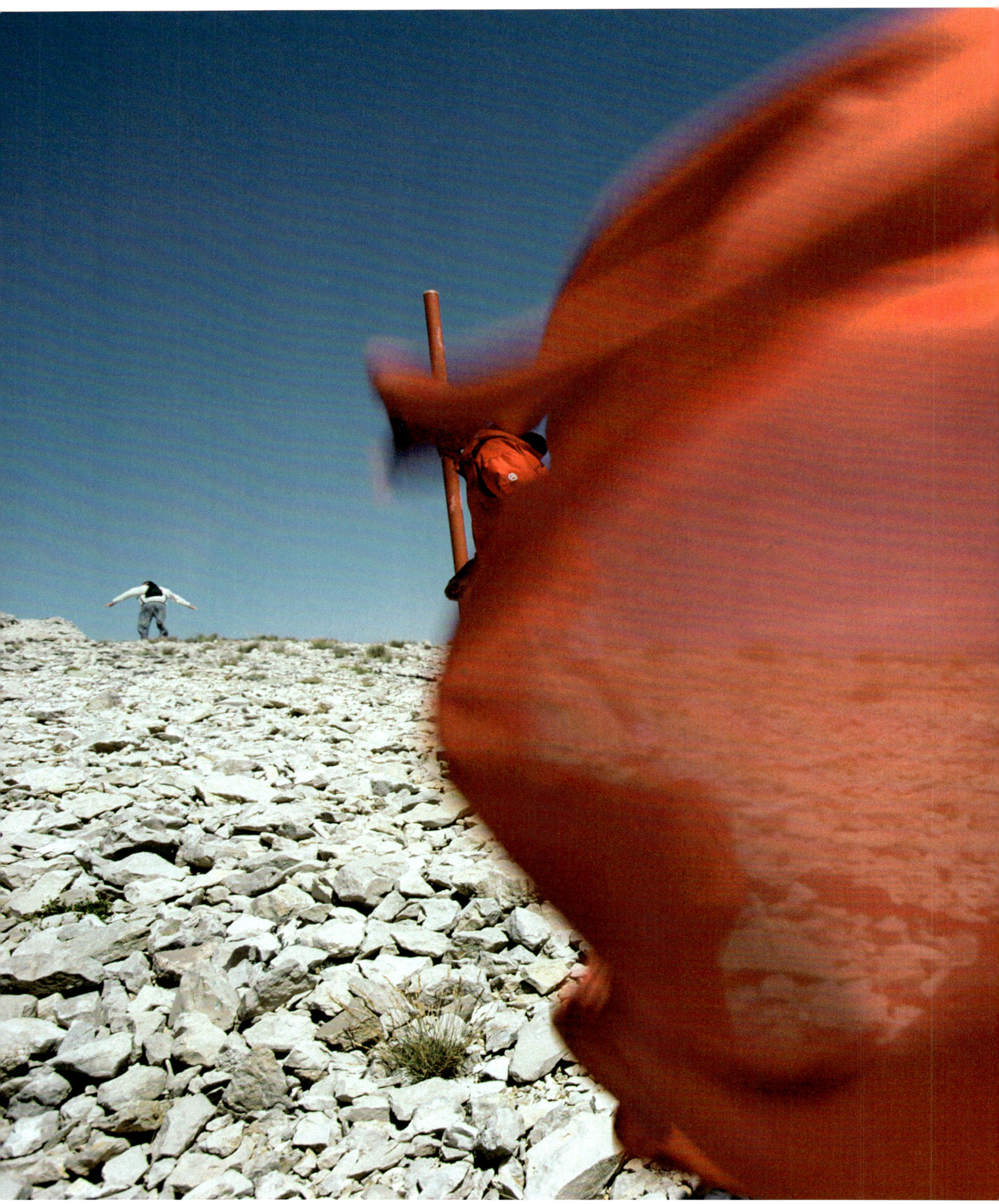

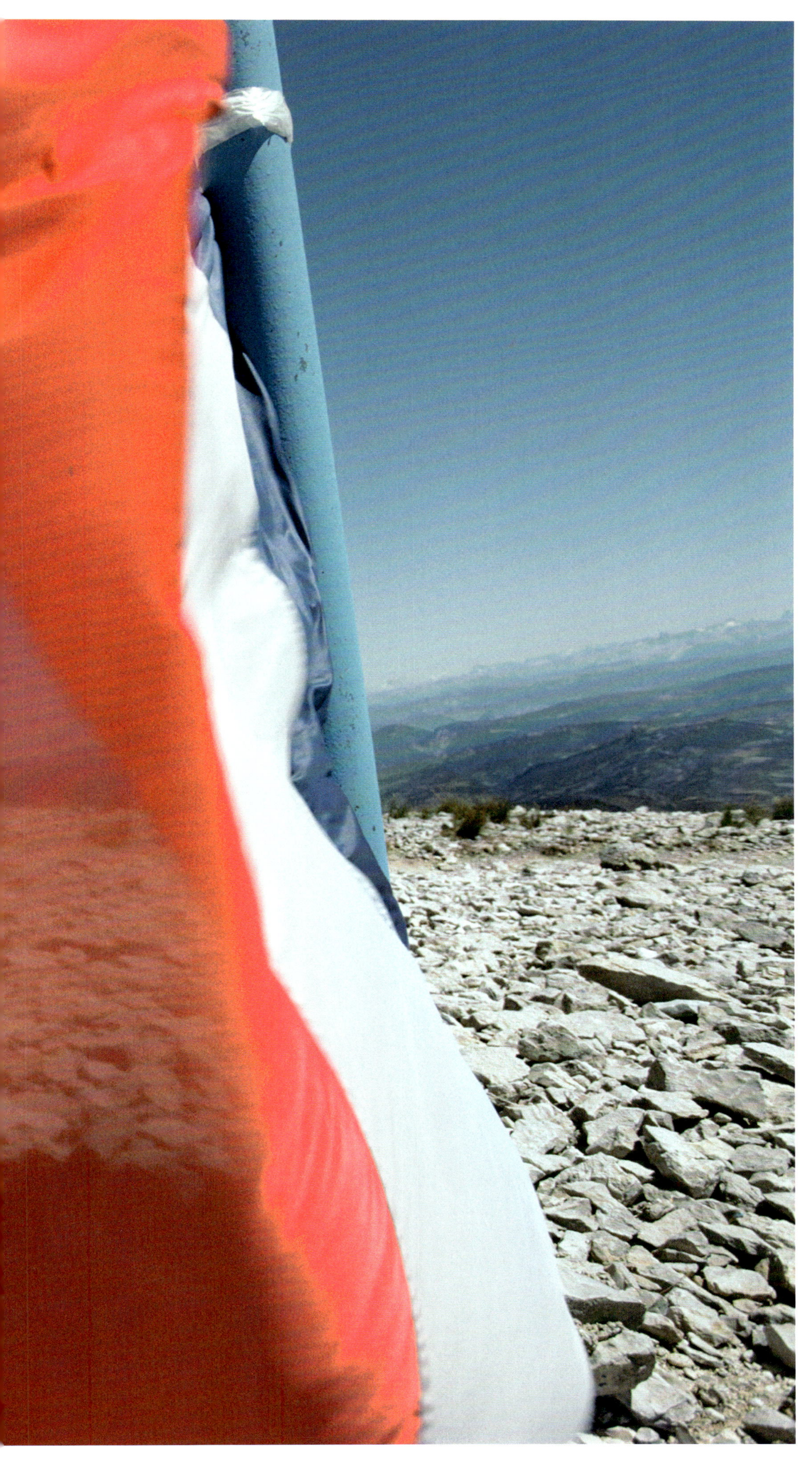

Paradoxically, the *genius loci*
of Mont Ventoux is Vinturius,
a god who does not inhabit
the mountain, a god
omnipresent in Provence,
a god whose very essence
is uprootedness, the detachment from
place, from all places—
a god who is everywhere
and nowhere.

—Allen S. Weiss,
The Wind and the Source

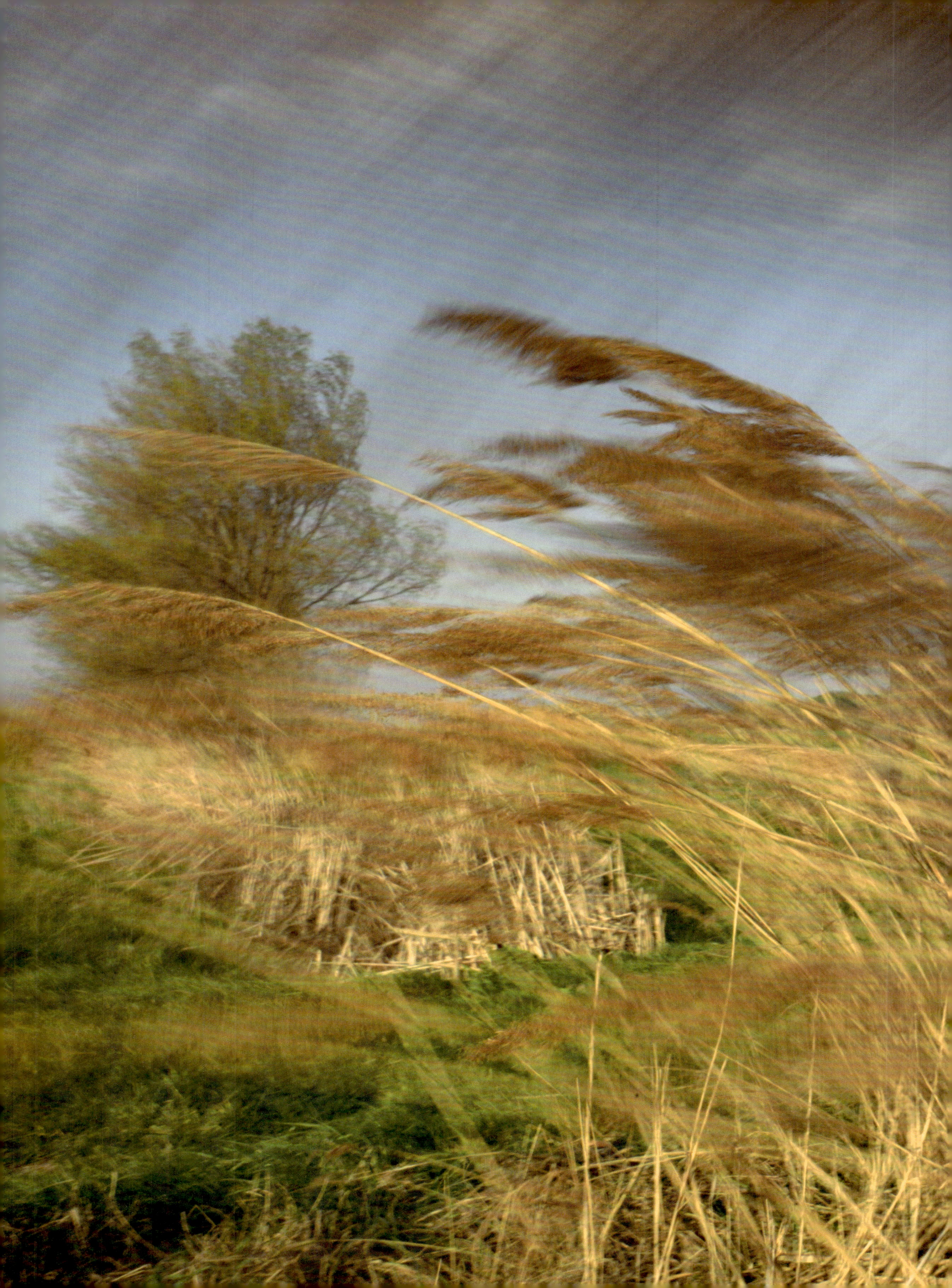

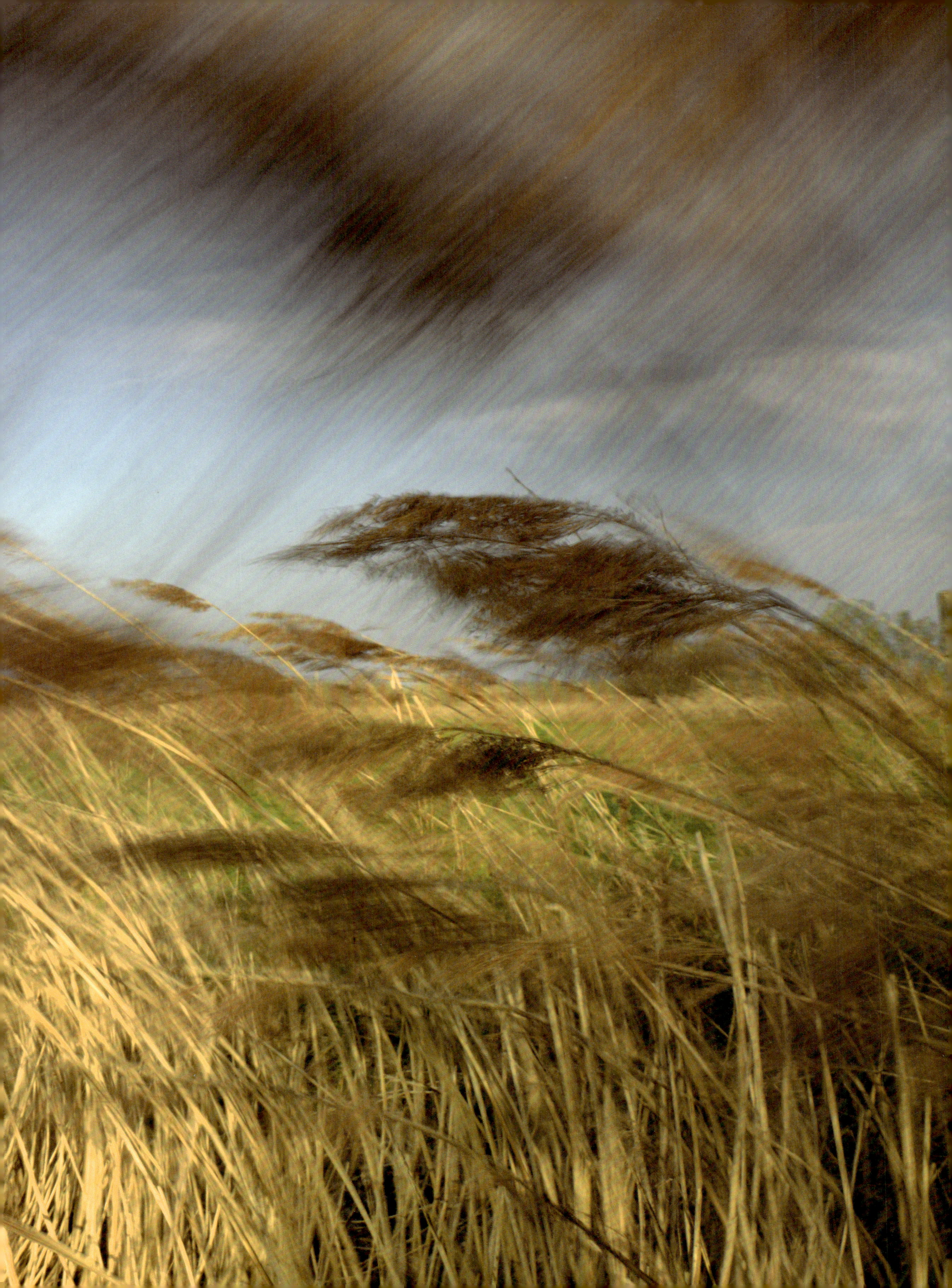

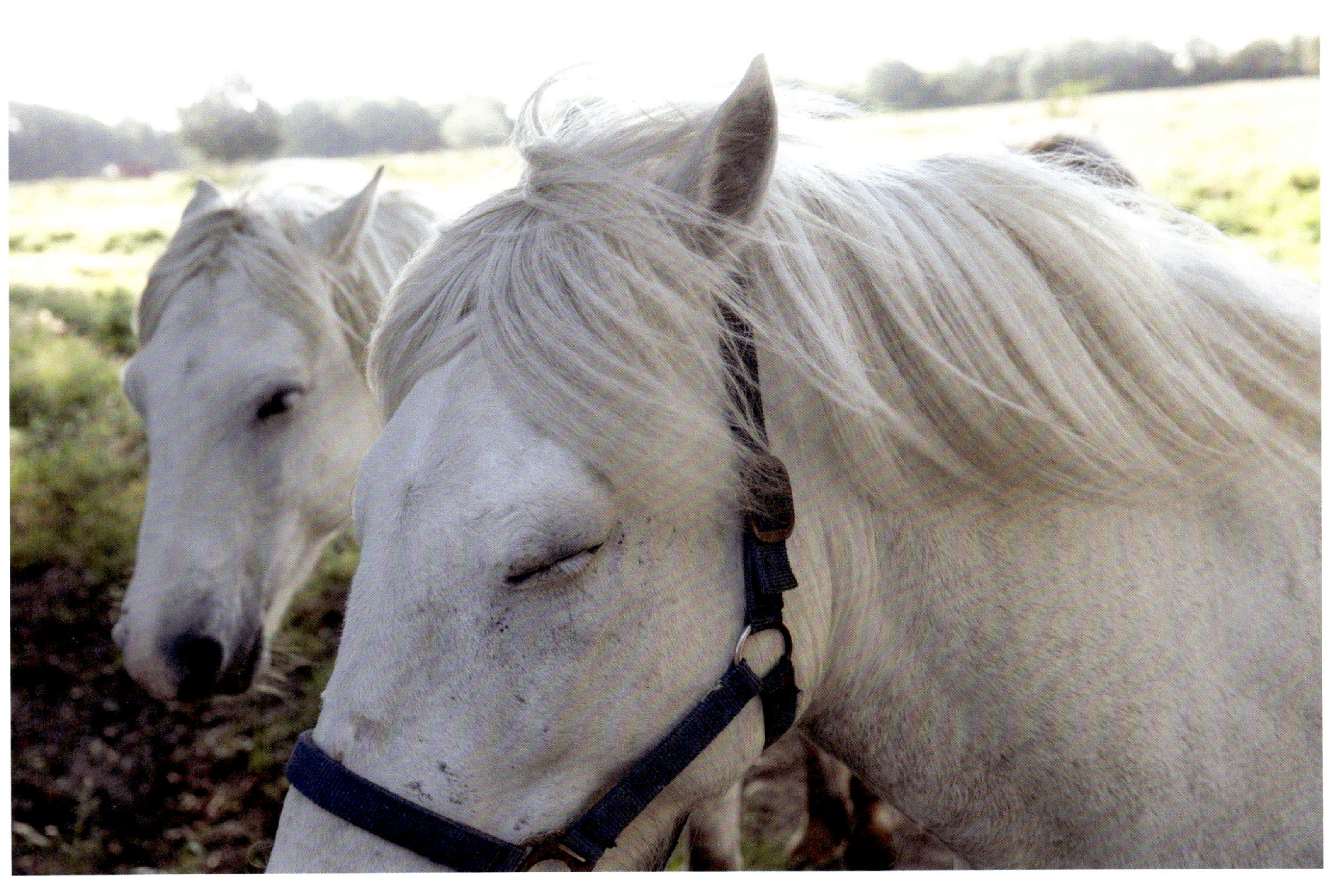

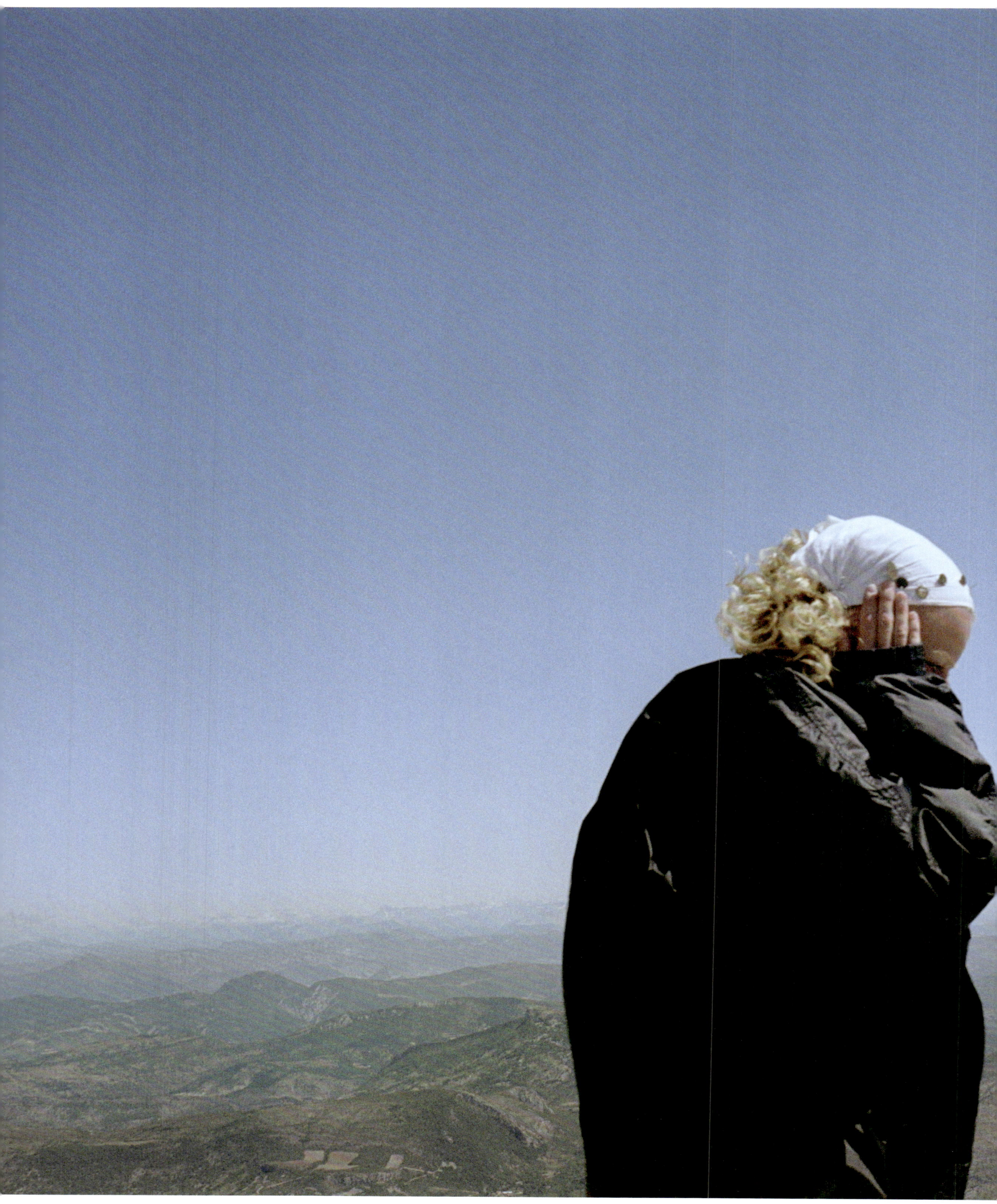

It all began that May day. The sky
was smooth as a washing stone;
the mistral had scrubbed it blue;
the sun spurted out from all sides;
things no longer had shadows;
the mystery was there, against the skin;
this wind of perdition
tore words from the lips and carried them
off into other worlds.

Tout est venu de ce jour de mai: le ciel
était lisse comme une pierre de lavoir;
le mistral y écrasait du
bleu à pleine main; le soleil giclait de
tous les côtés; les choses n'avaient
plus d'ombre;
le mystère était là, contre la peau;
ce vent de perdition
arrachait les mots aux lèvres et les
emportait dans les autres mondes.

—Jean Giono, *The Serpent of Stars*

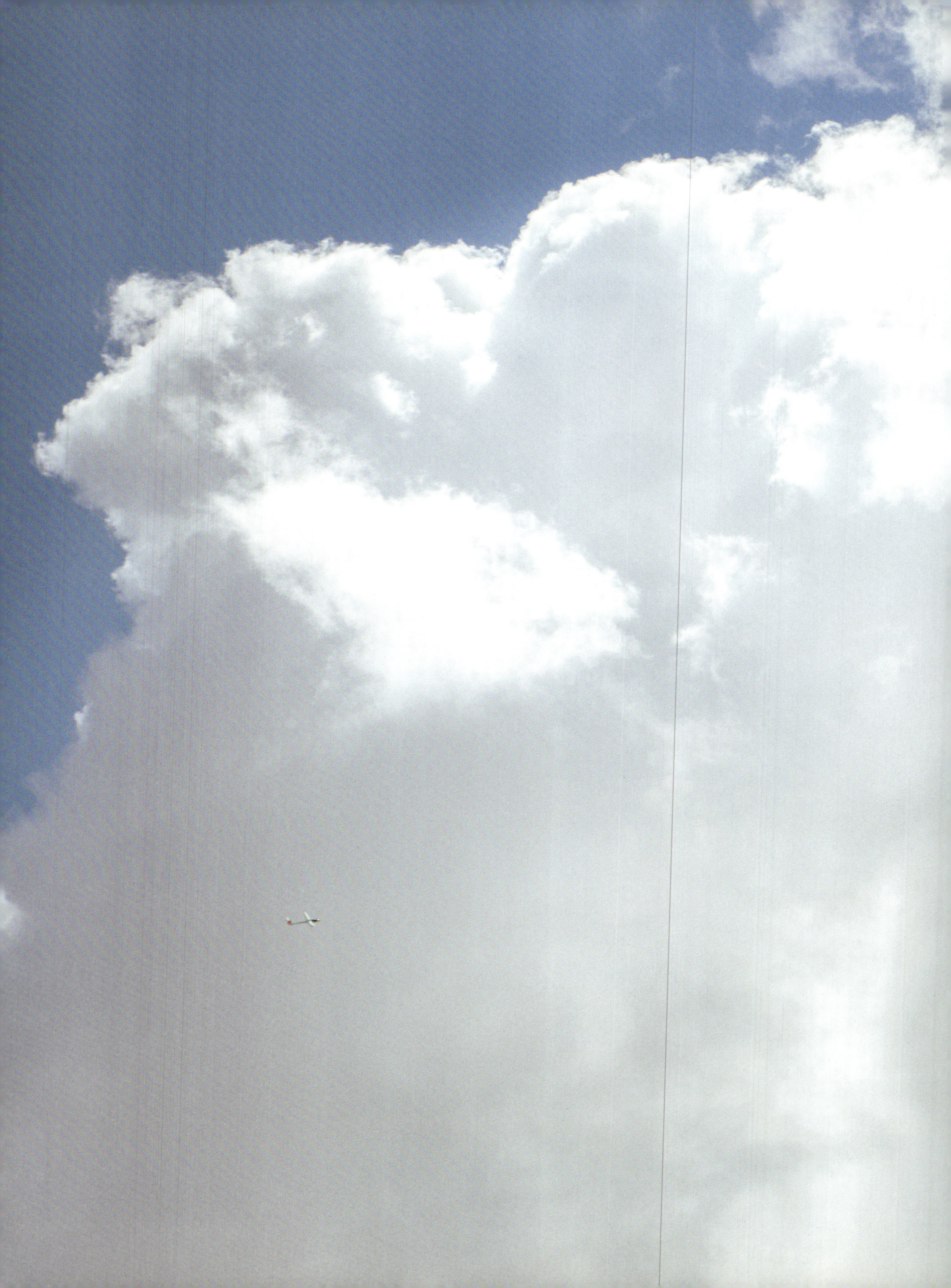

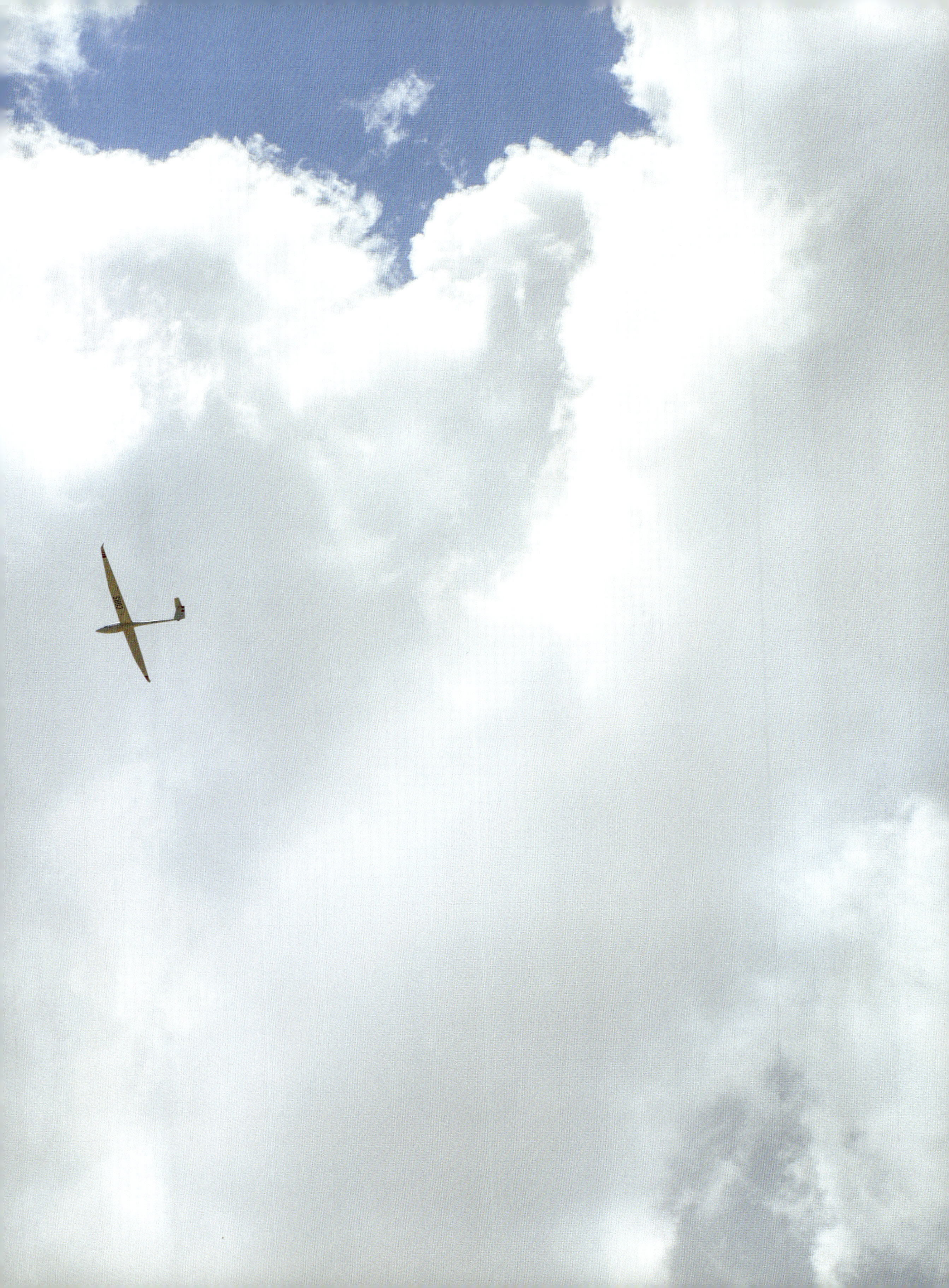
CORS

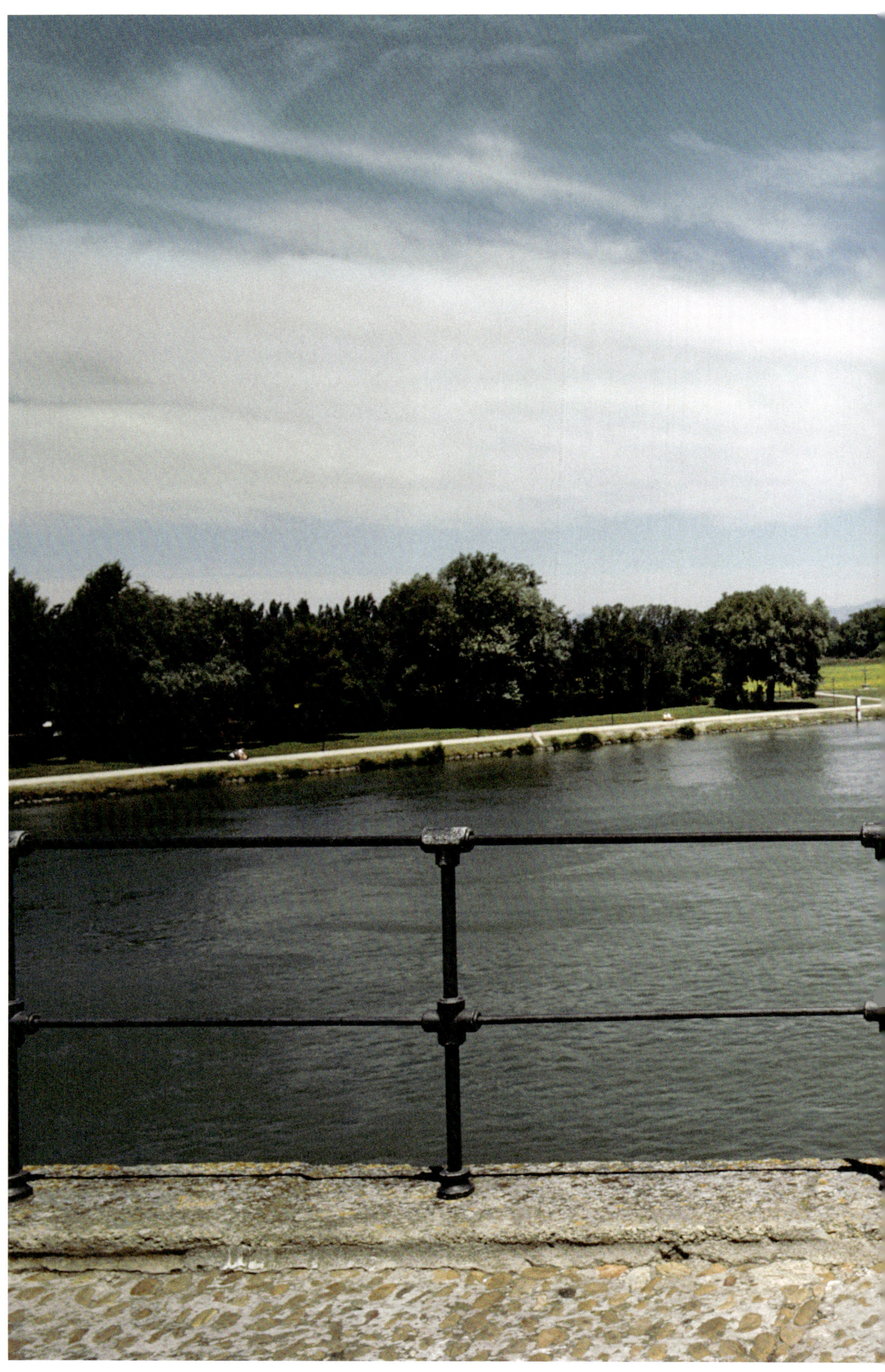

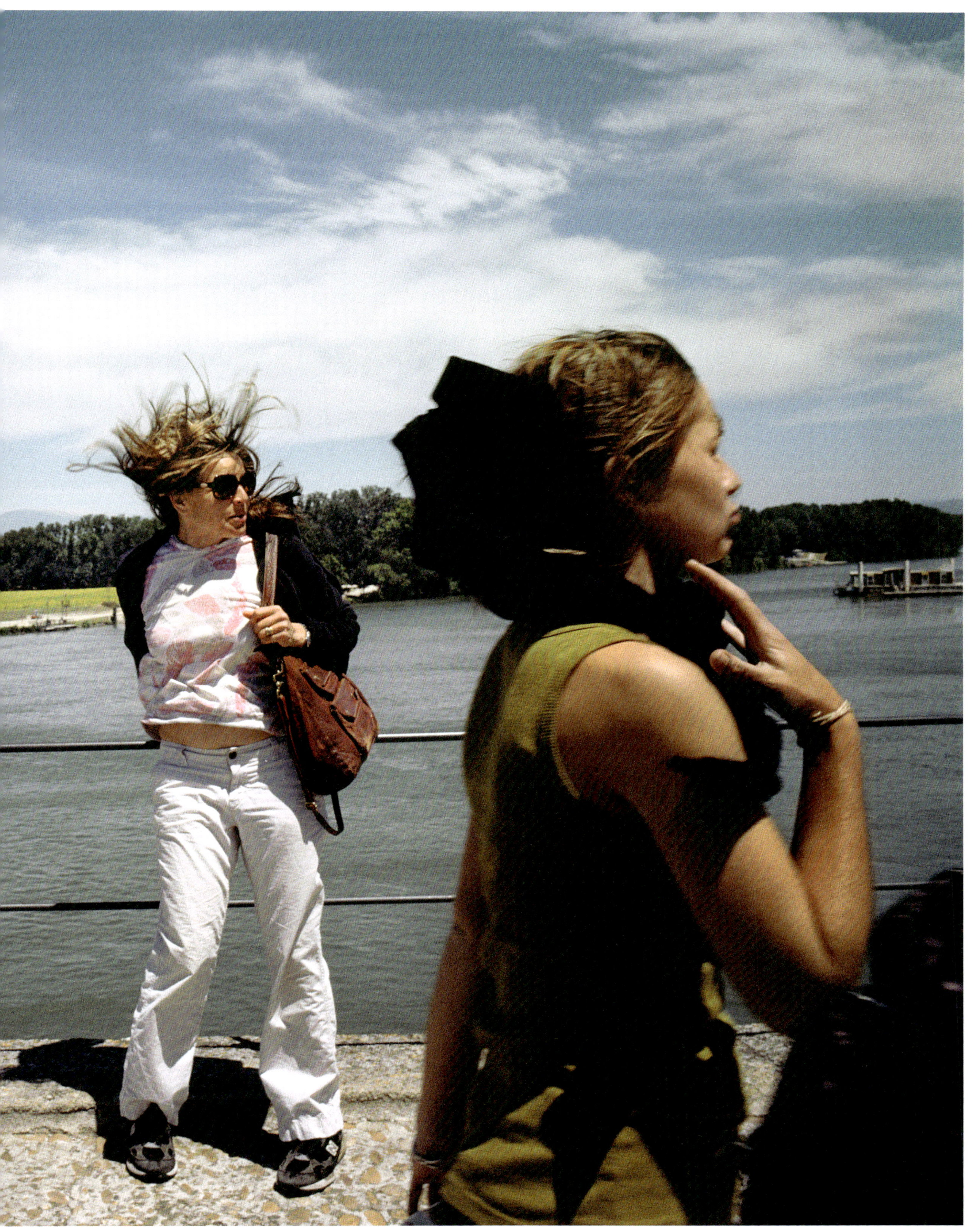

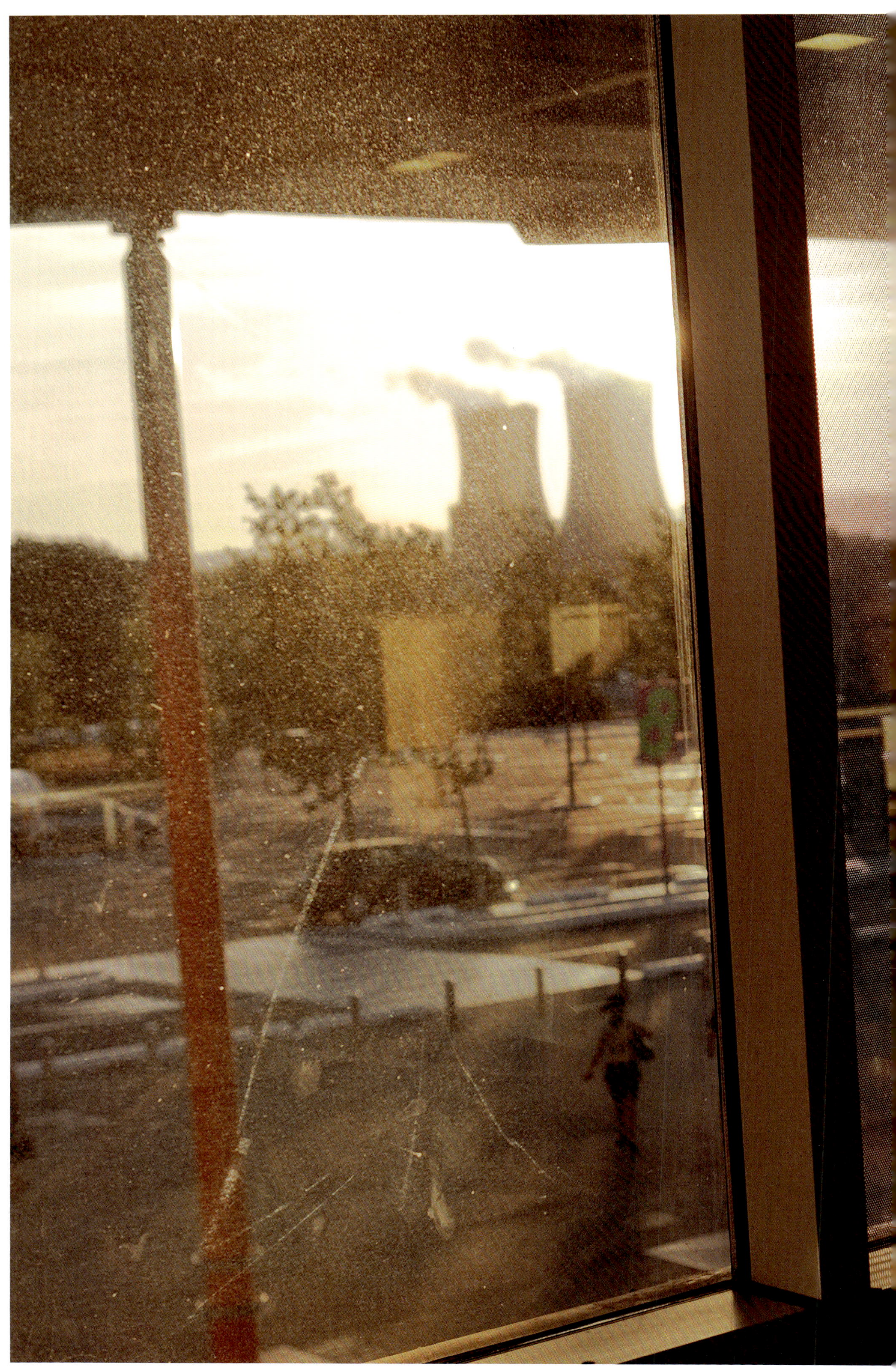

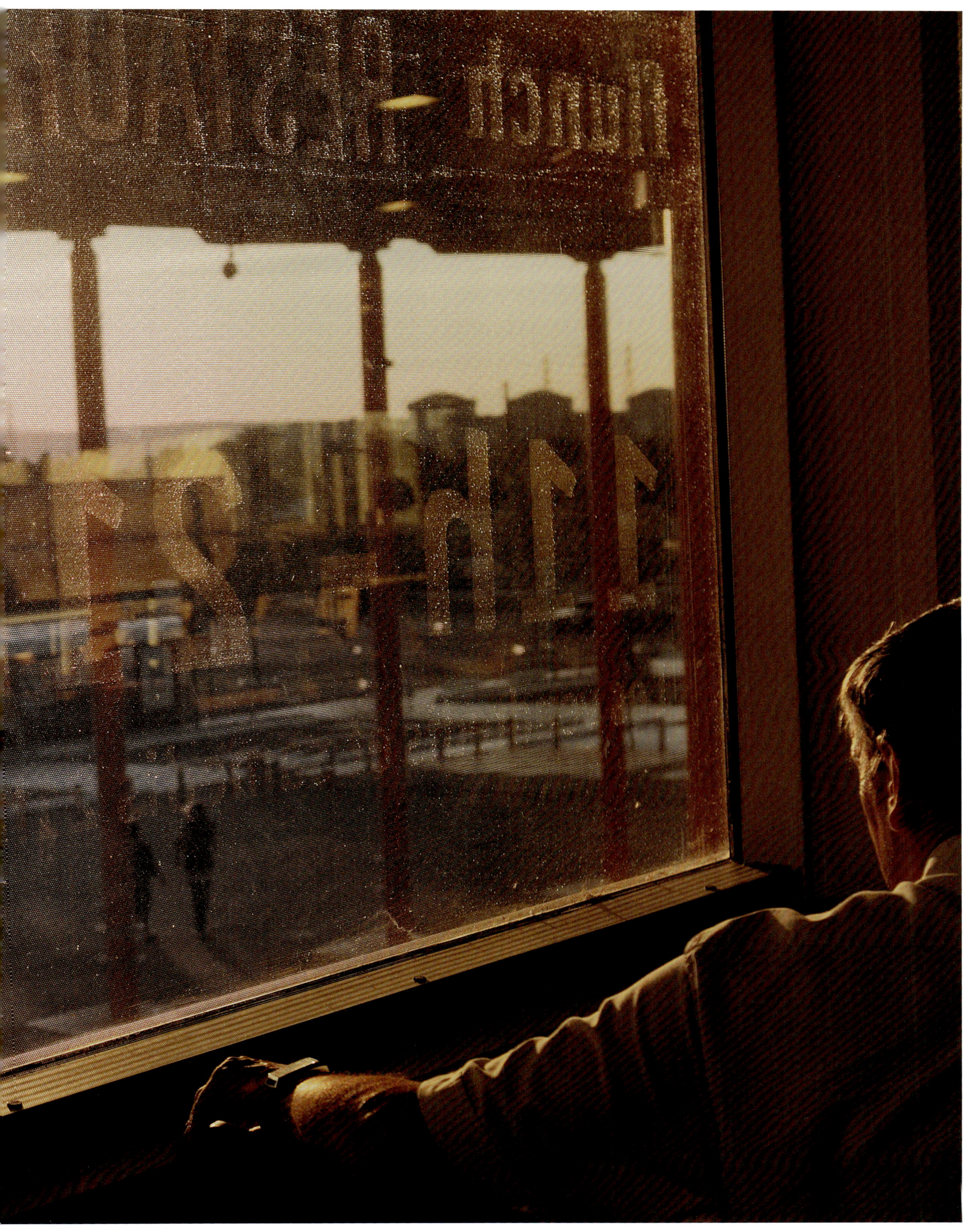

For the past three days, the mistral had been blowing. And now it raged, a furious whirlwind, and beat against the house, rattling it from garret to cellar, day after day, night after night, without a moment's cessation. The tiles blew off, the shutter fasteners were ripped out, while the wind, entering through the crevices, moaned and sobbed wildly throughout the house; and the doors, if they were left open for a moment, through forgetfulness, slammed to with a noise like the report of a cannon. It was as if they were withstanding a siege, among the clamor and anguish.

Depuis trois jours déjà, le mistral soufflait. Et c'était une rage, une trombe furieuse, continue, qui flagellait la maison, l'ébranlait des caves aux greniers, pendant des jours, pendant des nuits, sans un arrêt. Les tuiles volaient, les ferrures des fenêtres étaient arrachées; tandis que, par les fentes, à l'intérieur, le vent pénétrait, en un ronflement éperdu de plainte, et que les portes, au moindre oubli, se refermaient avec des retentissements de canon. On aurait dit tout un siège à soutenir, au milieu du vacarme et de l'angoisse.

—Émile Zola, *Doctor Pascal*

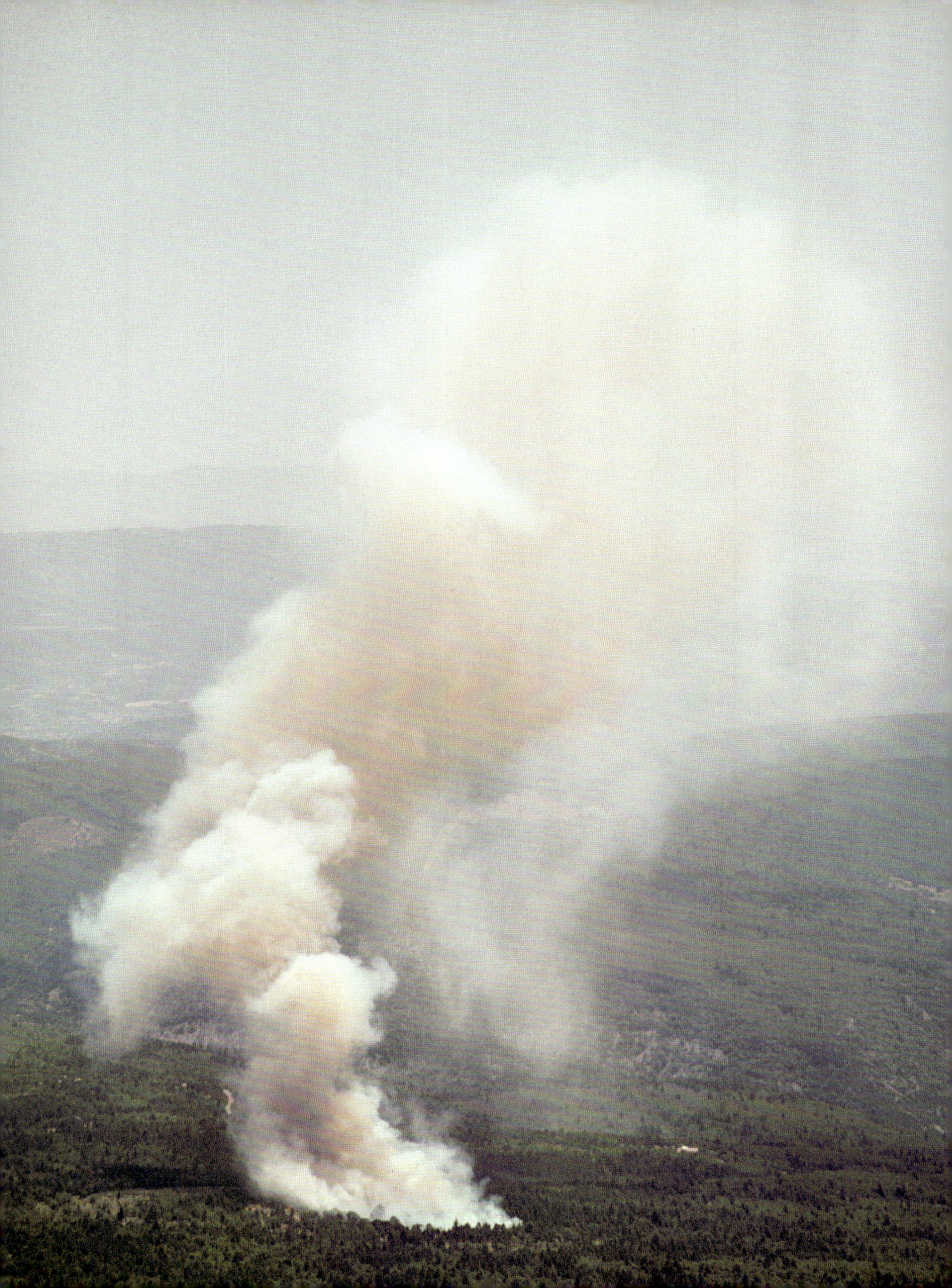

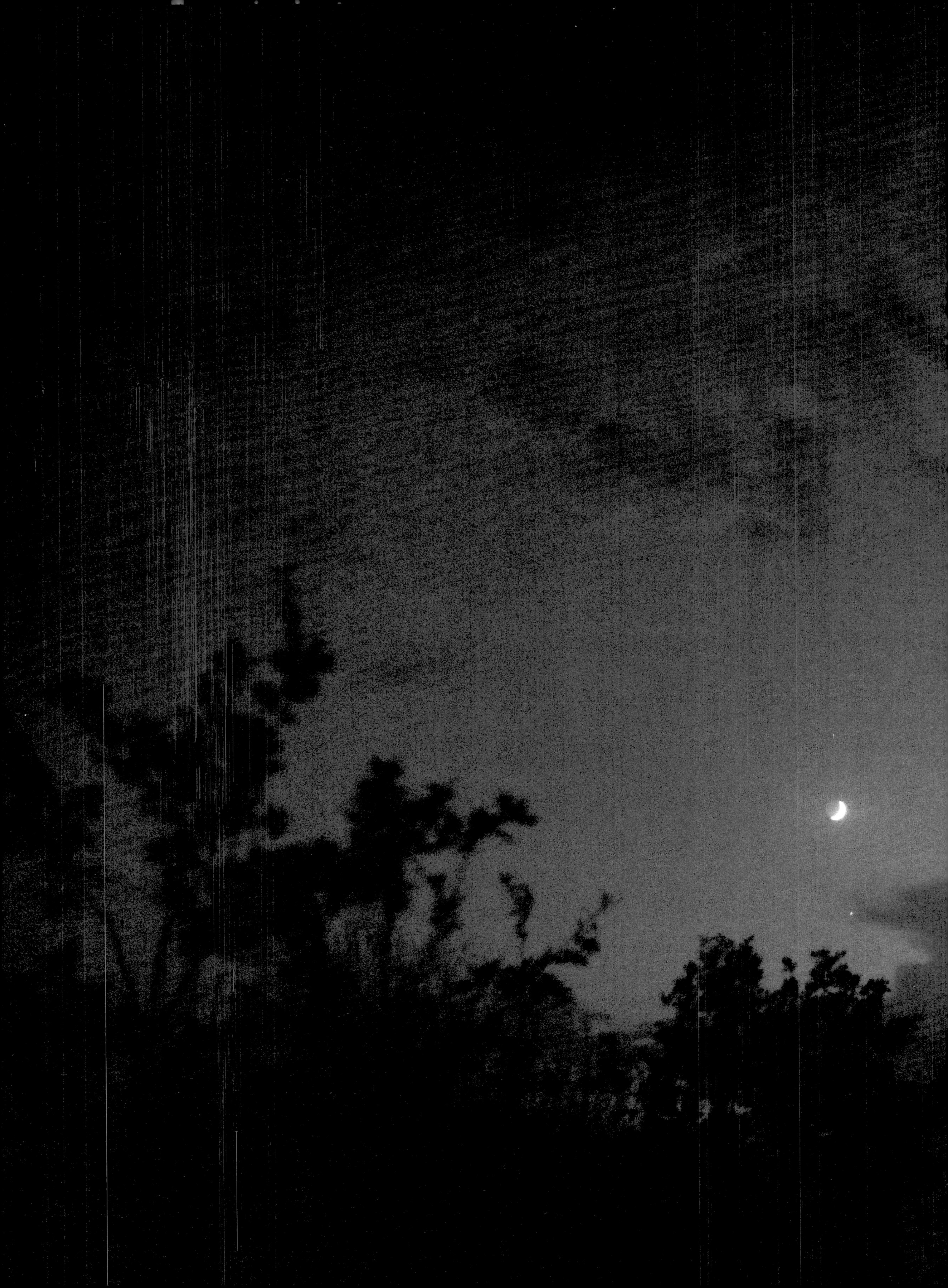

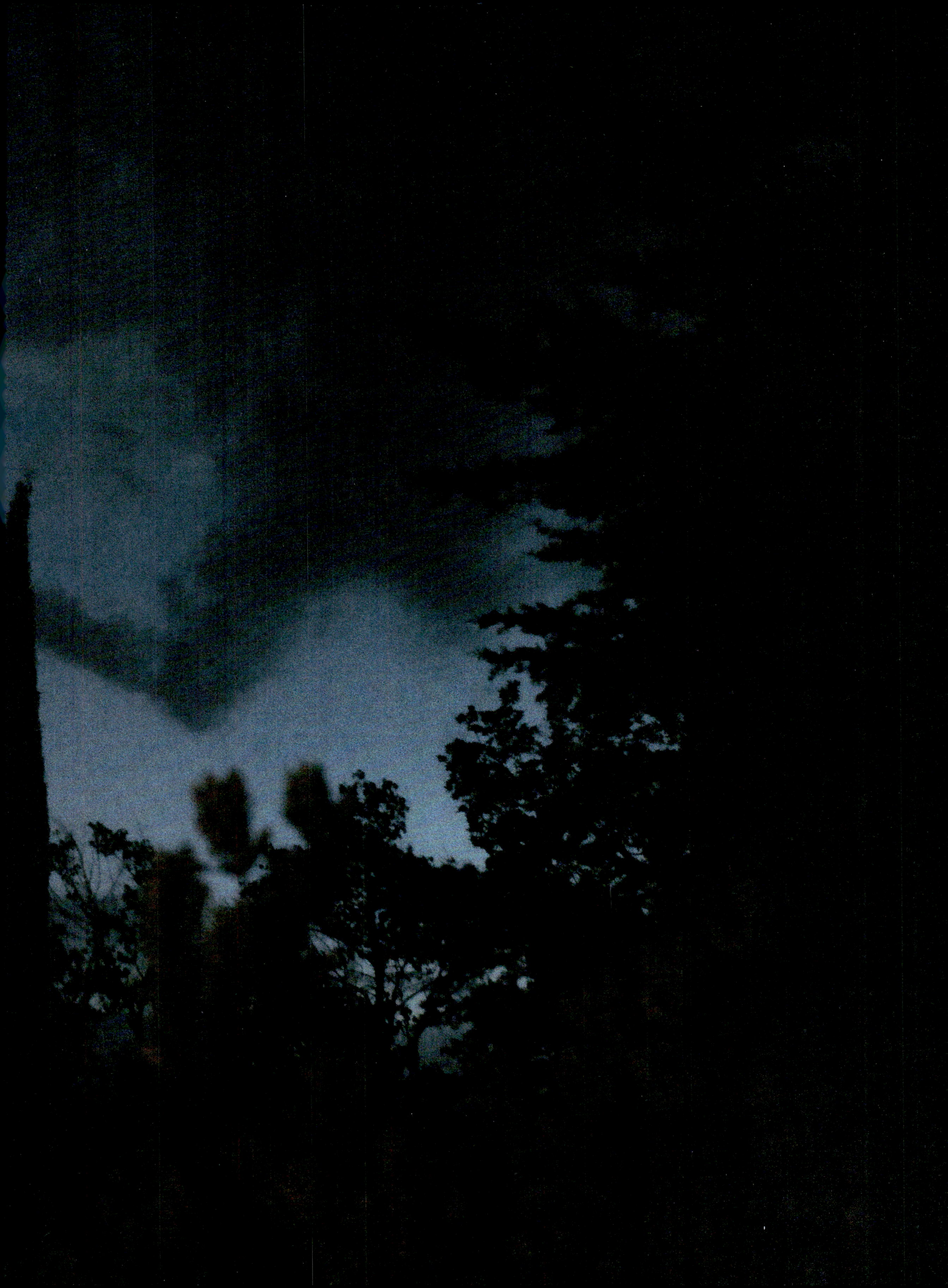

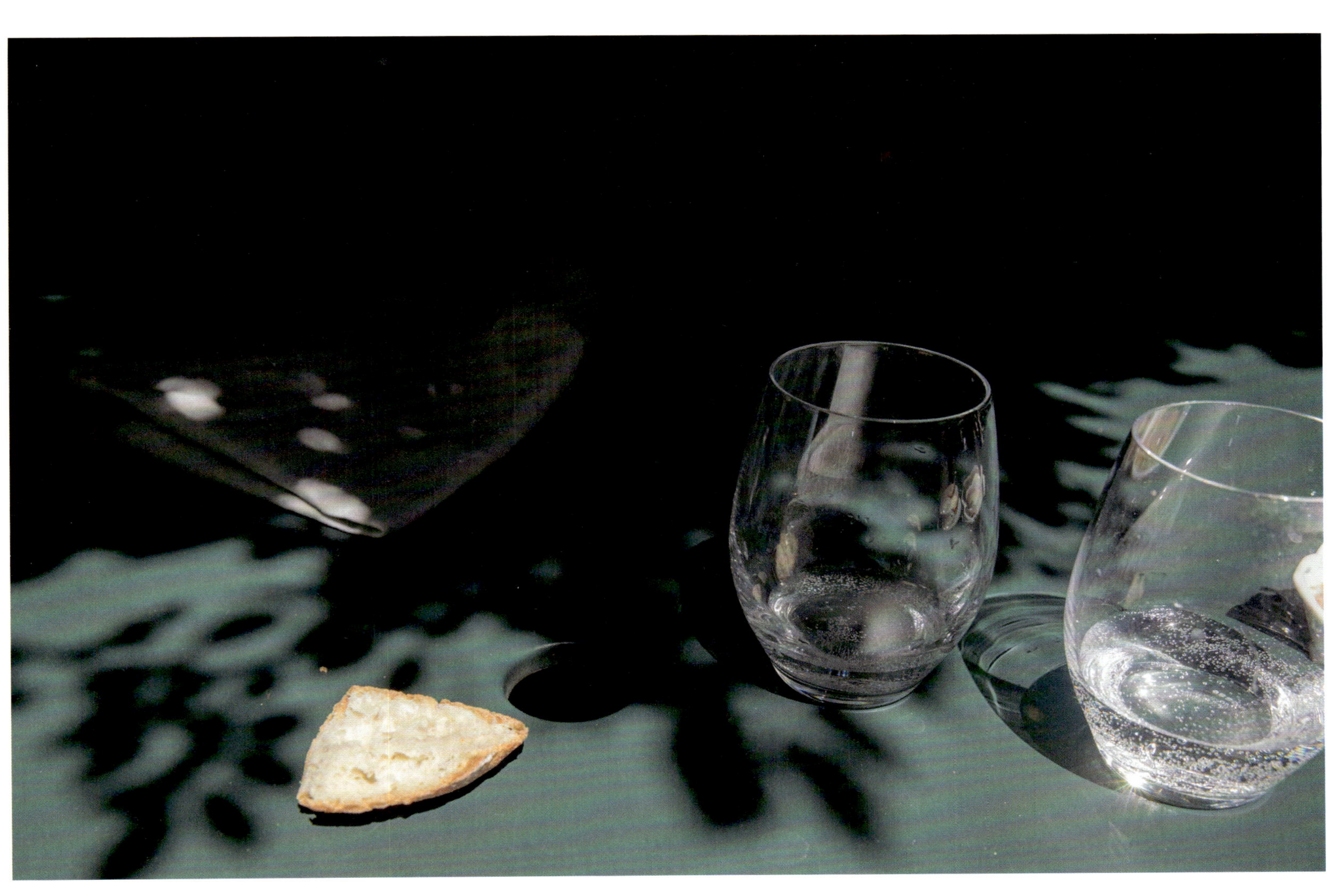

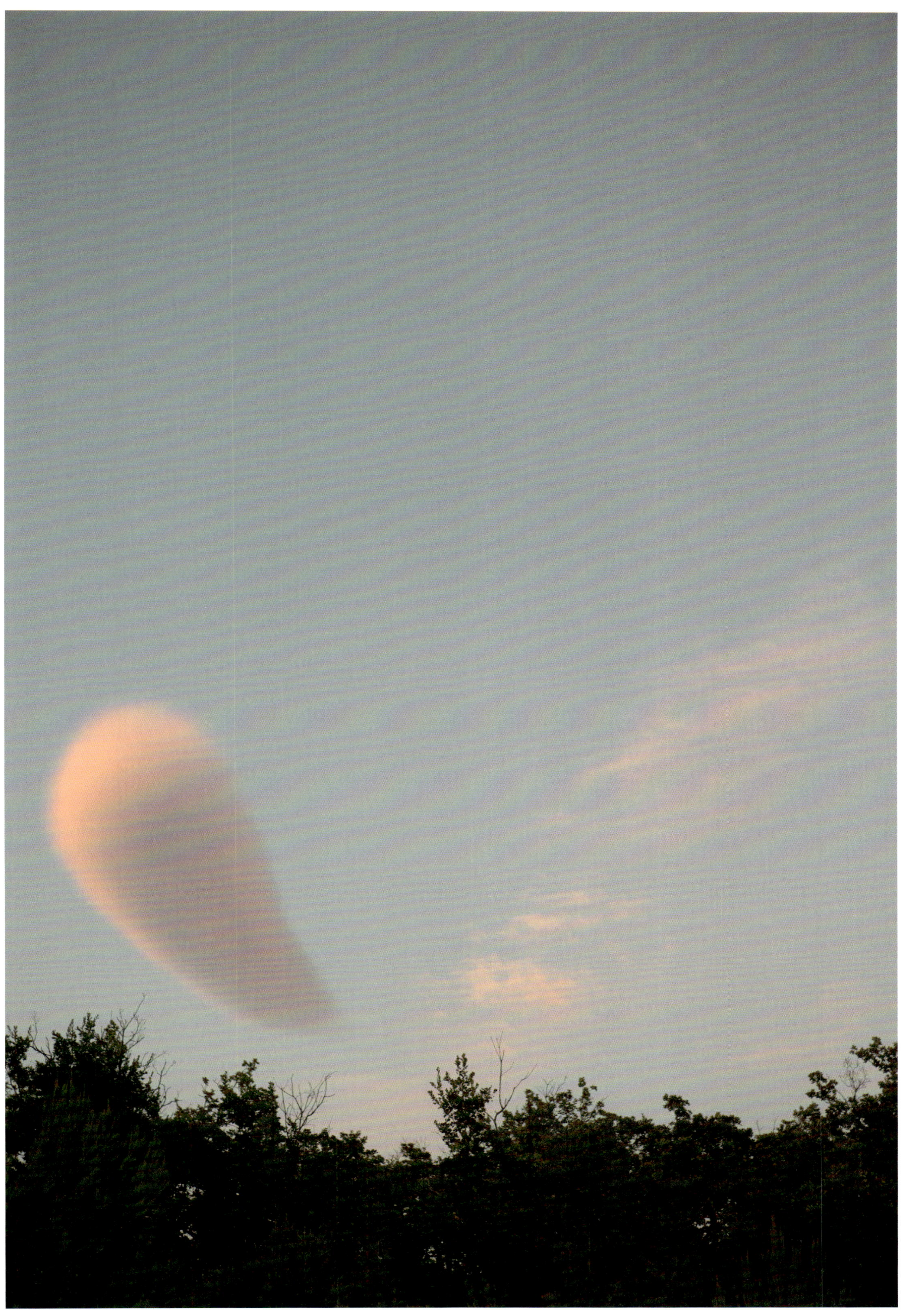

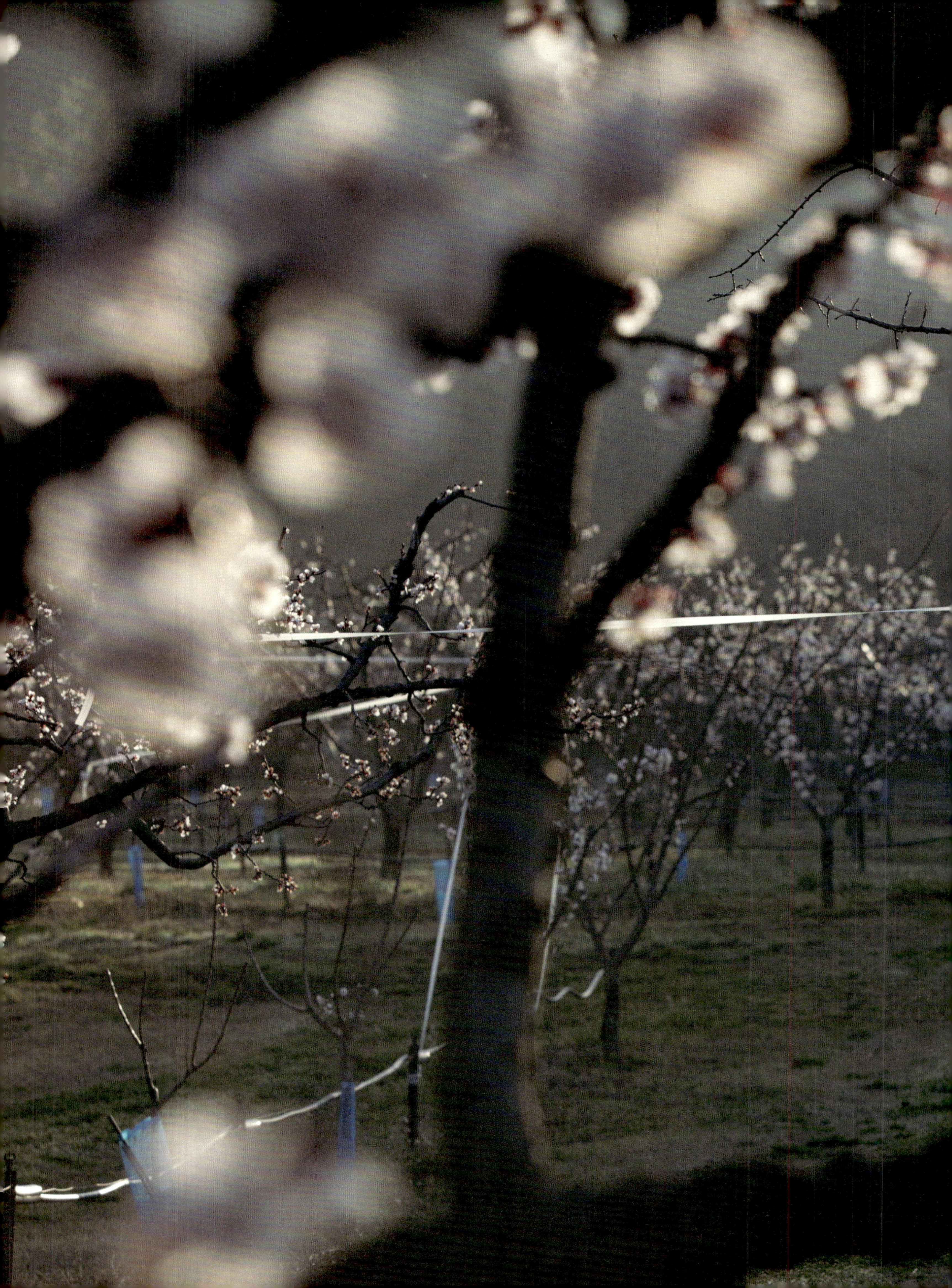

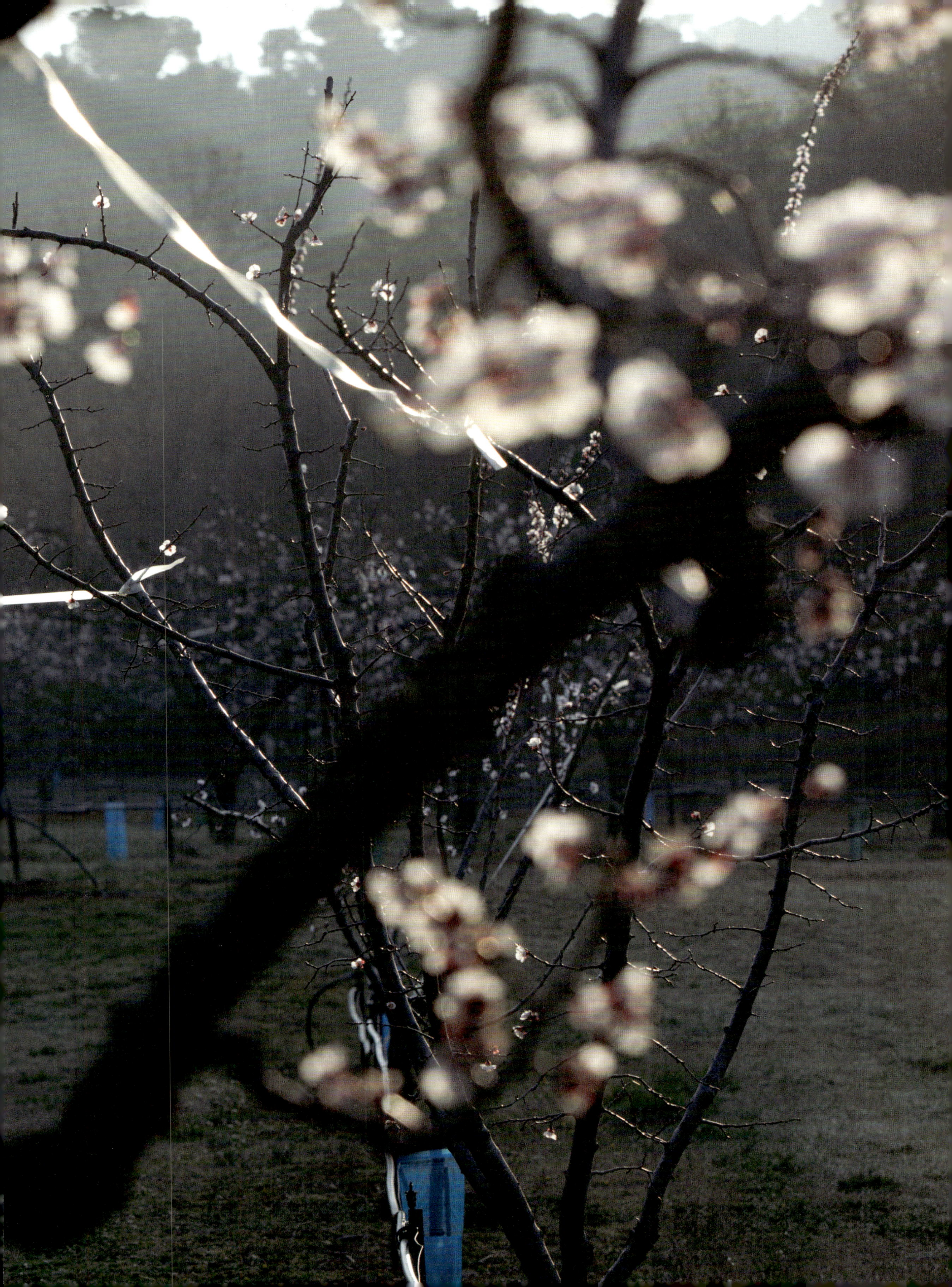

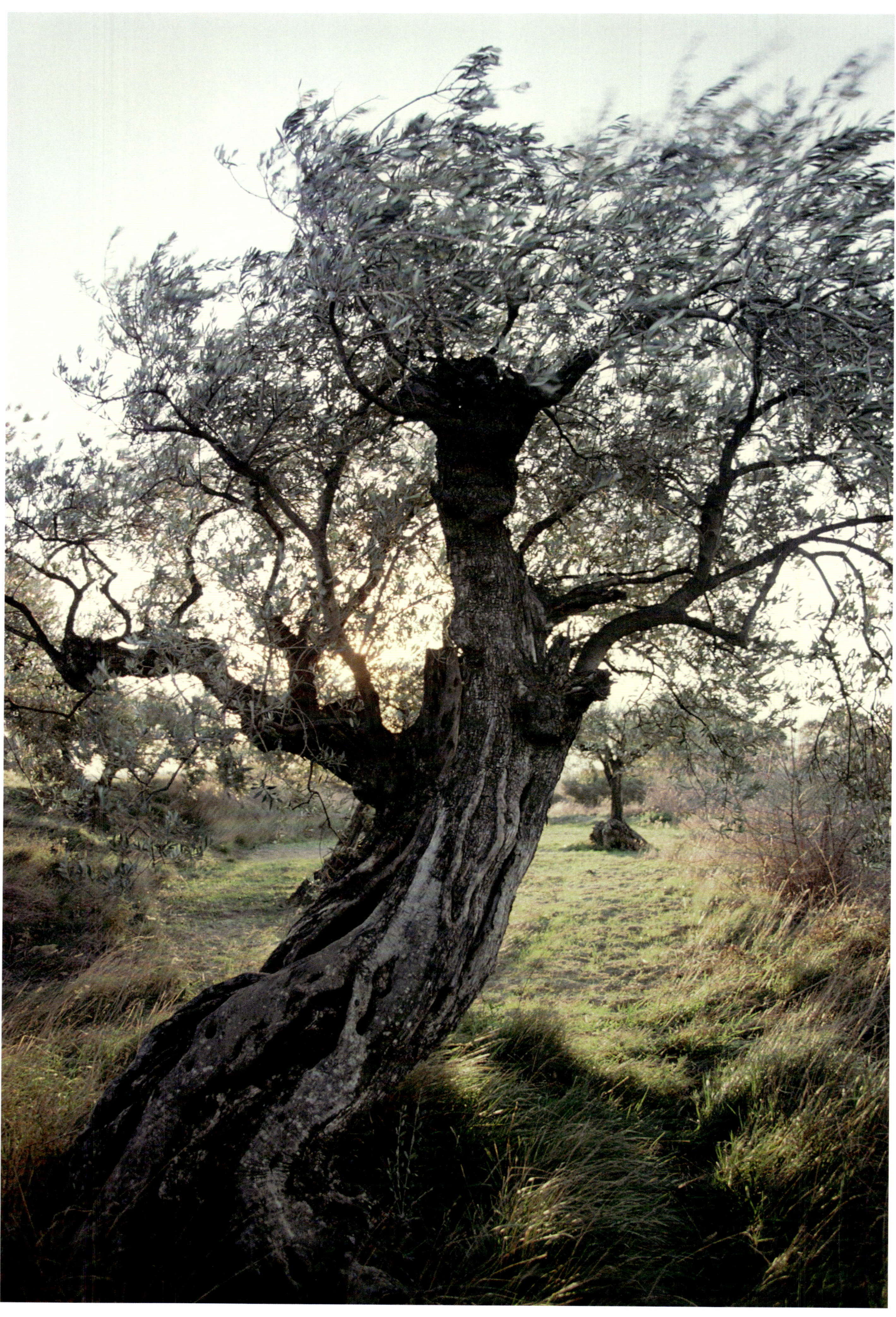

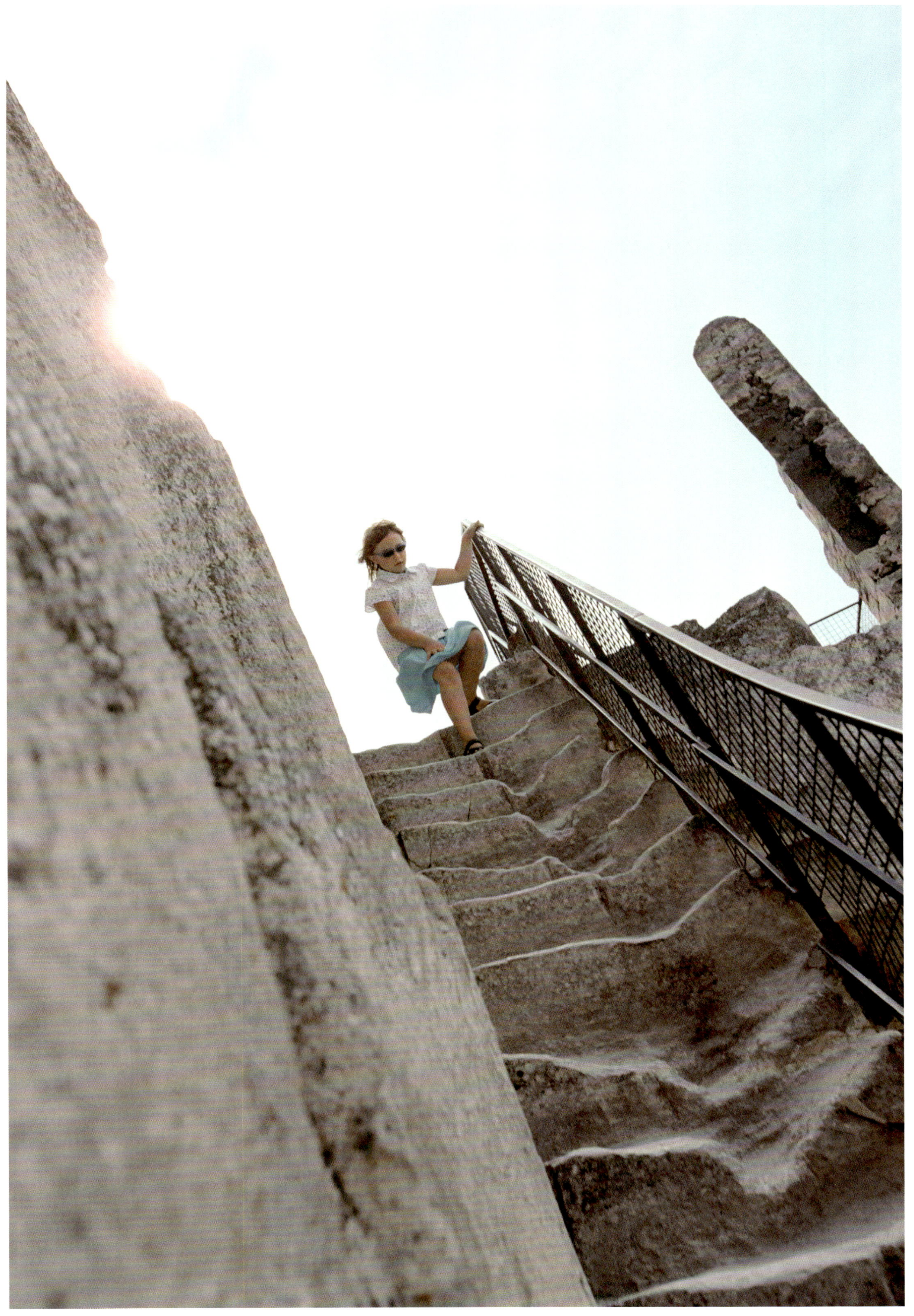

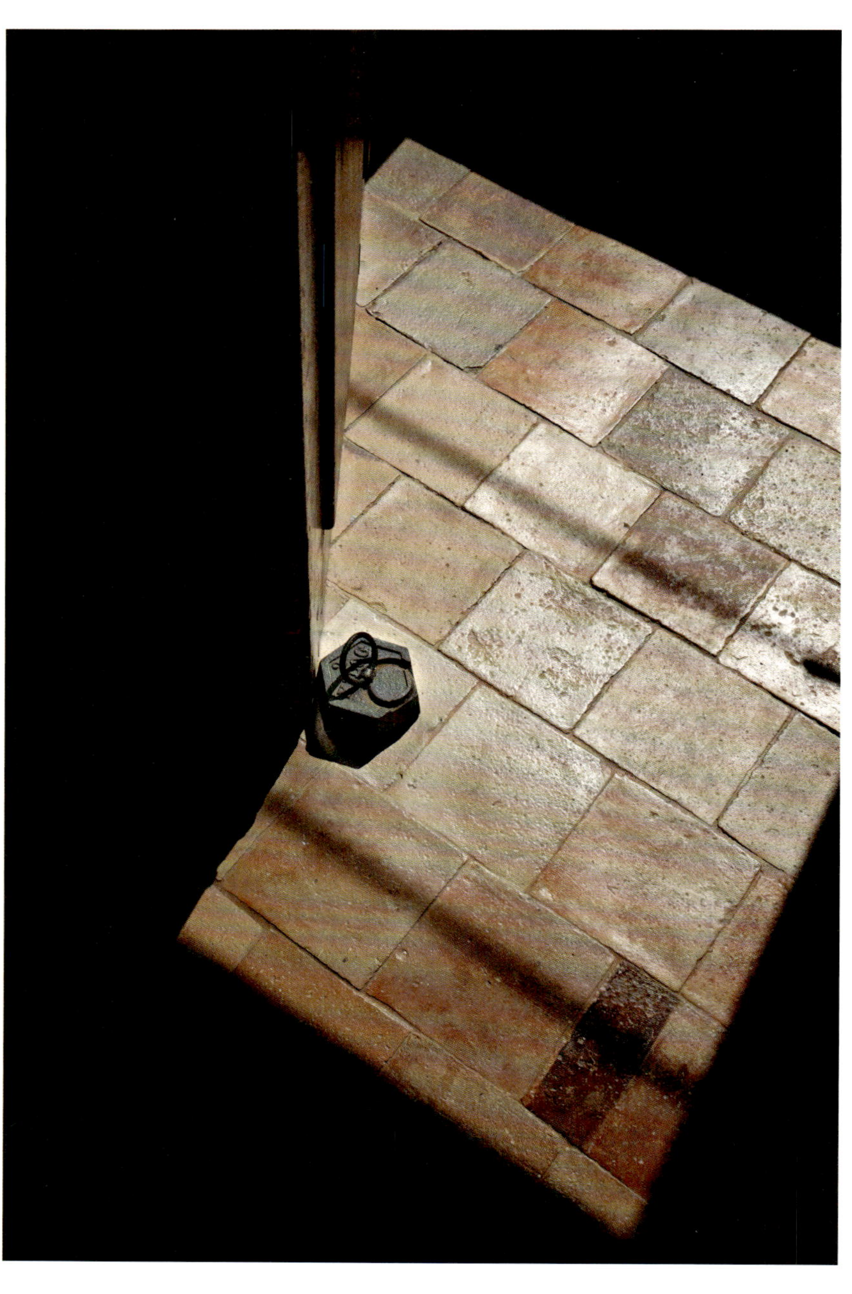

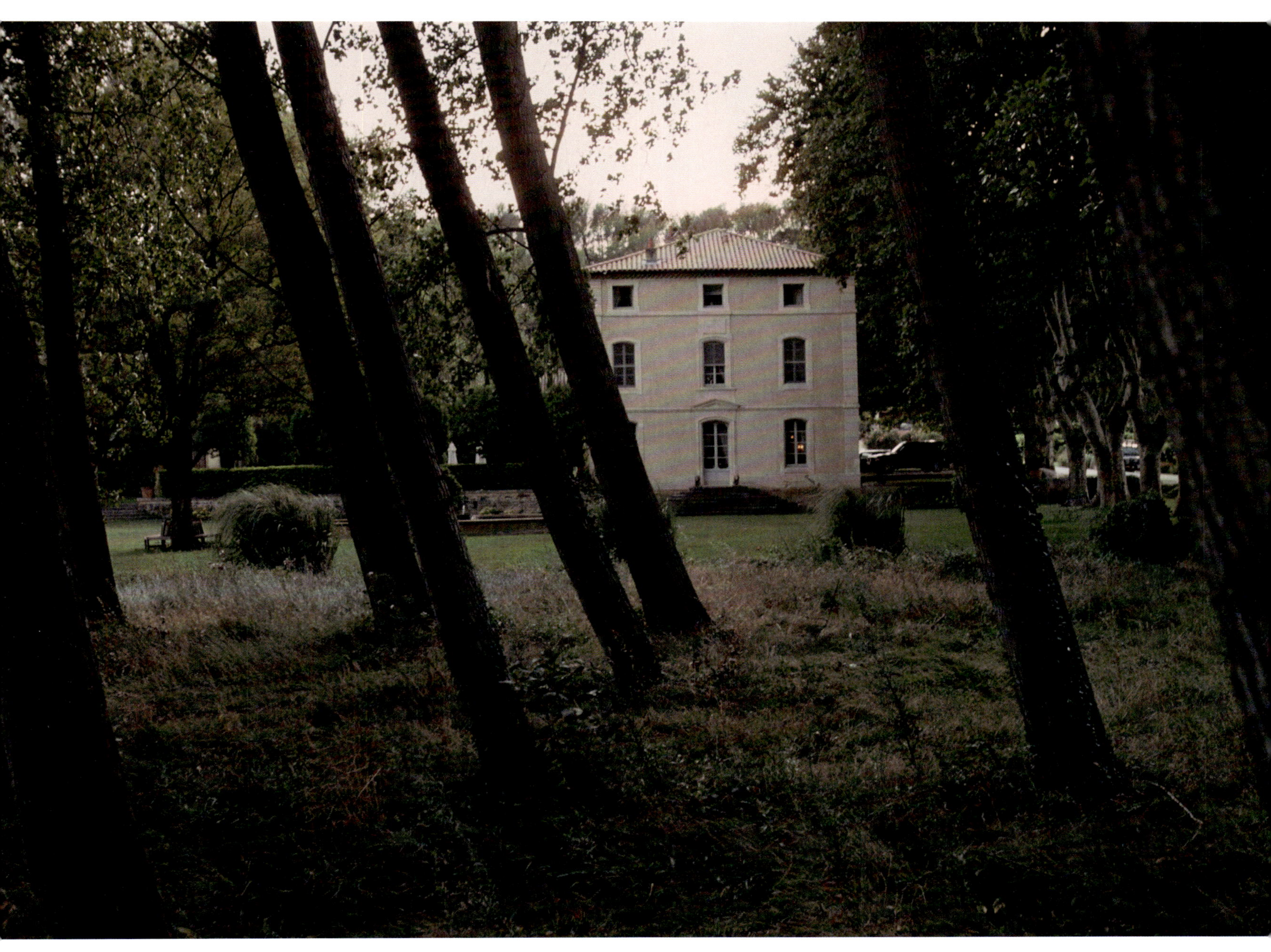

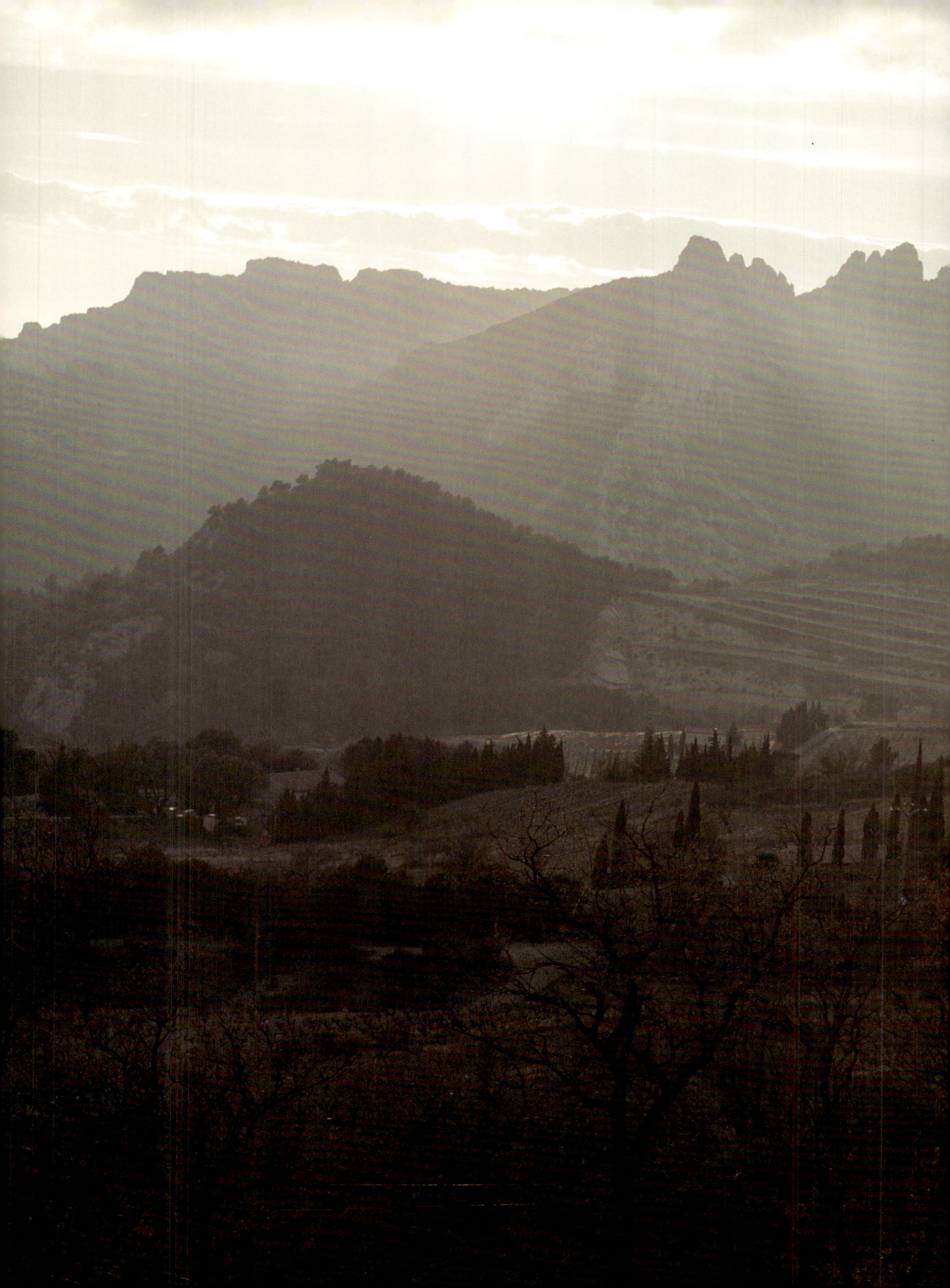

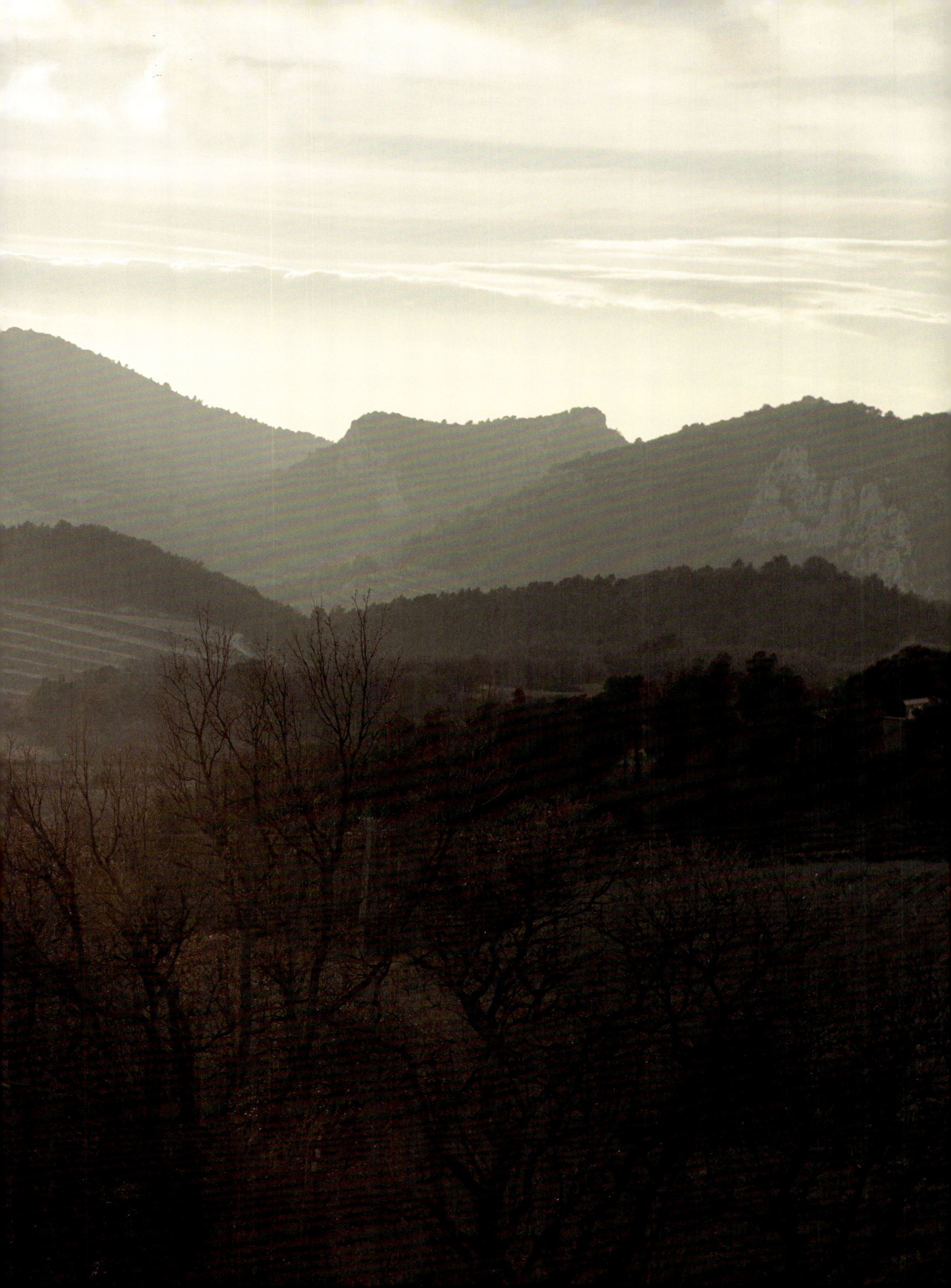

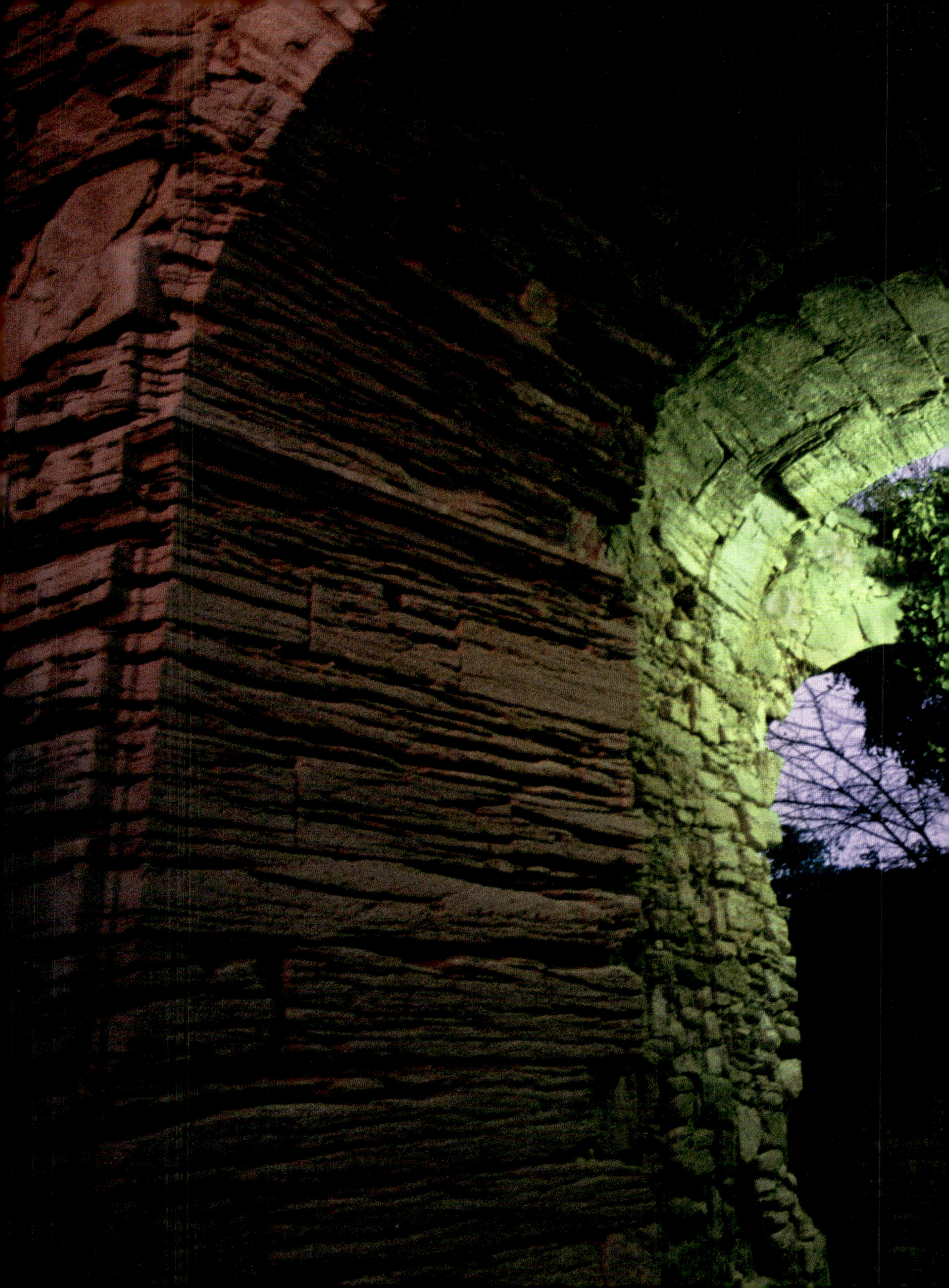

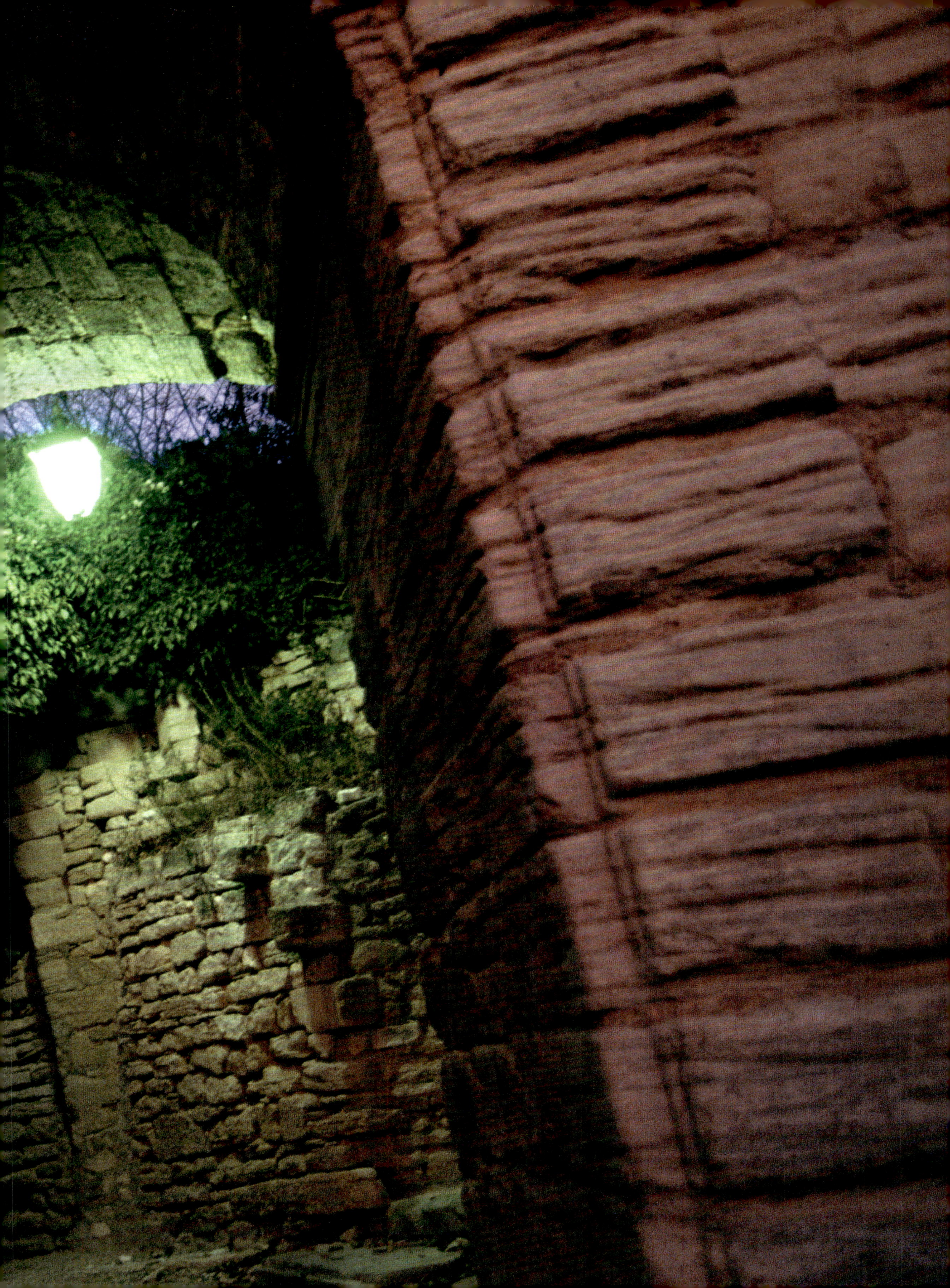

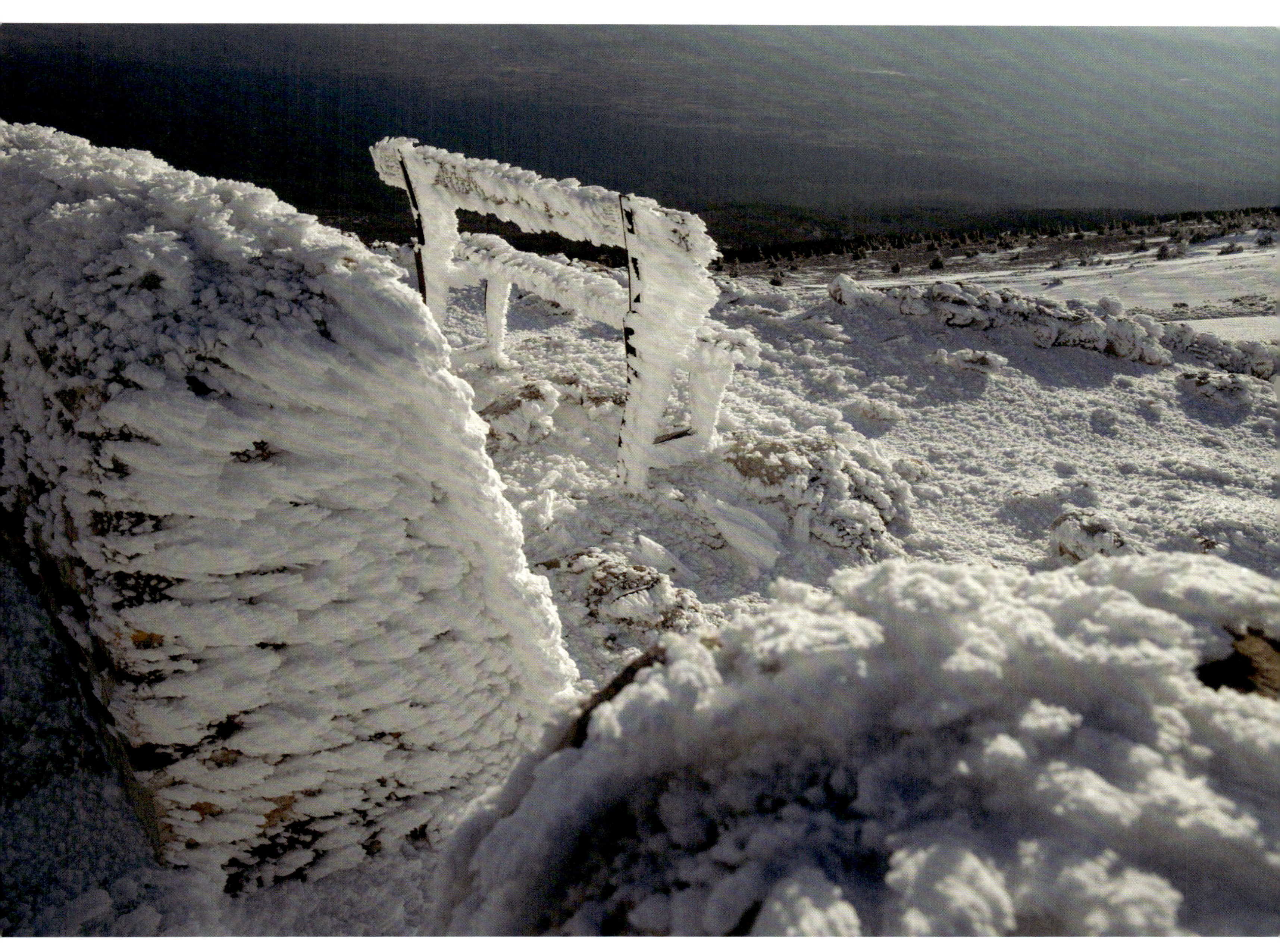

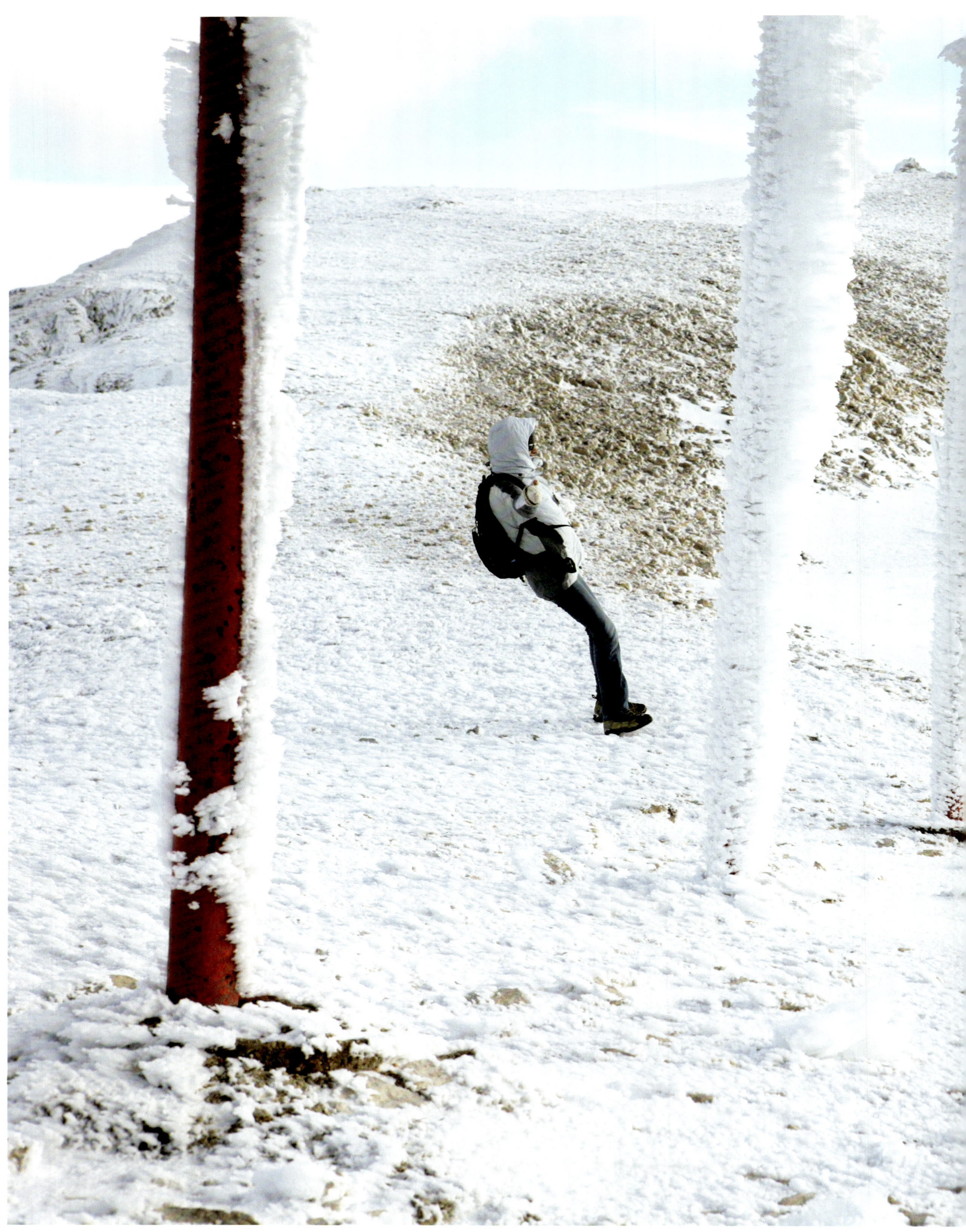

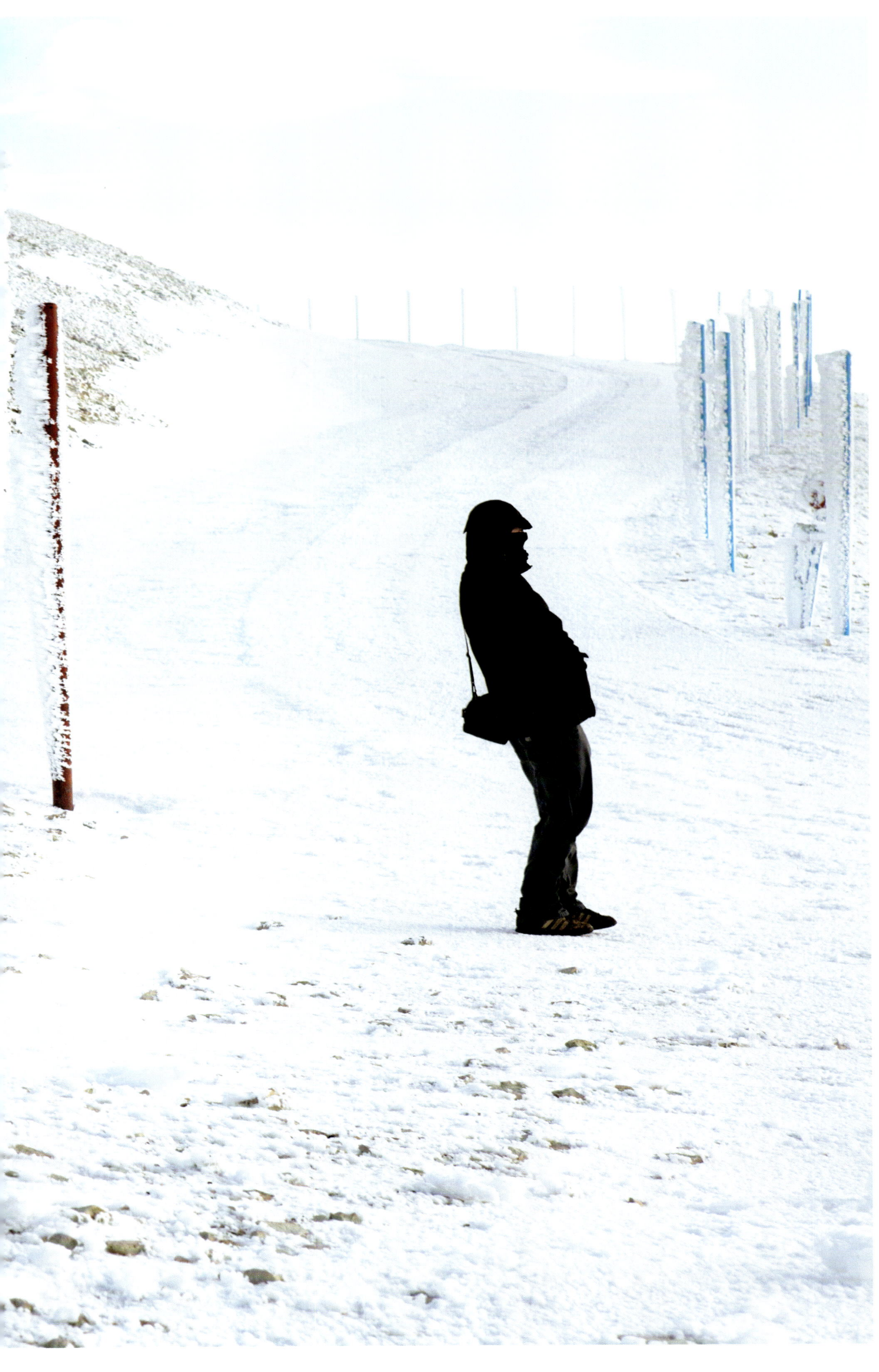

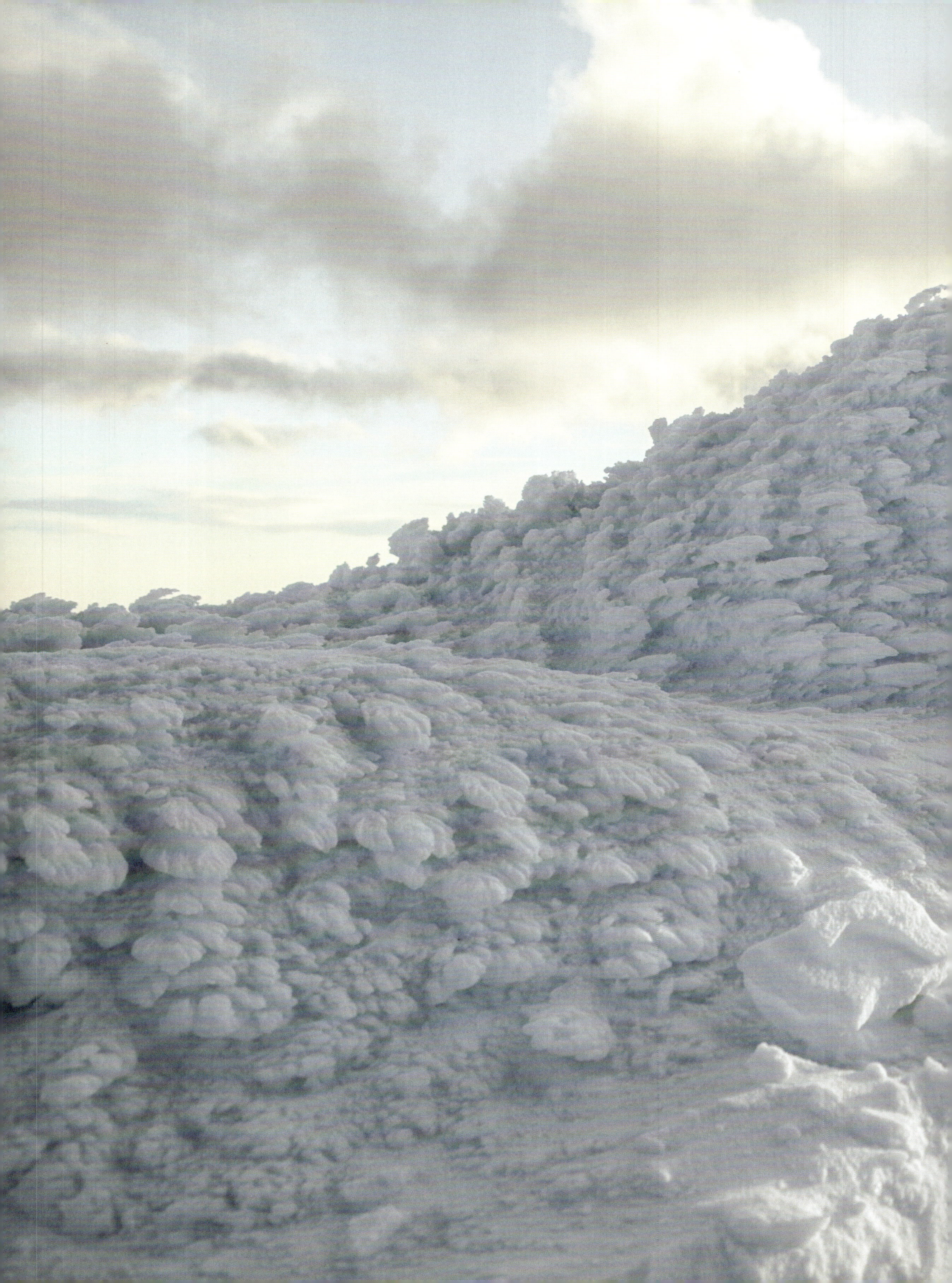

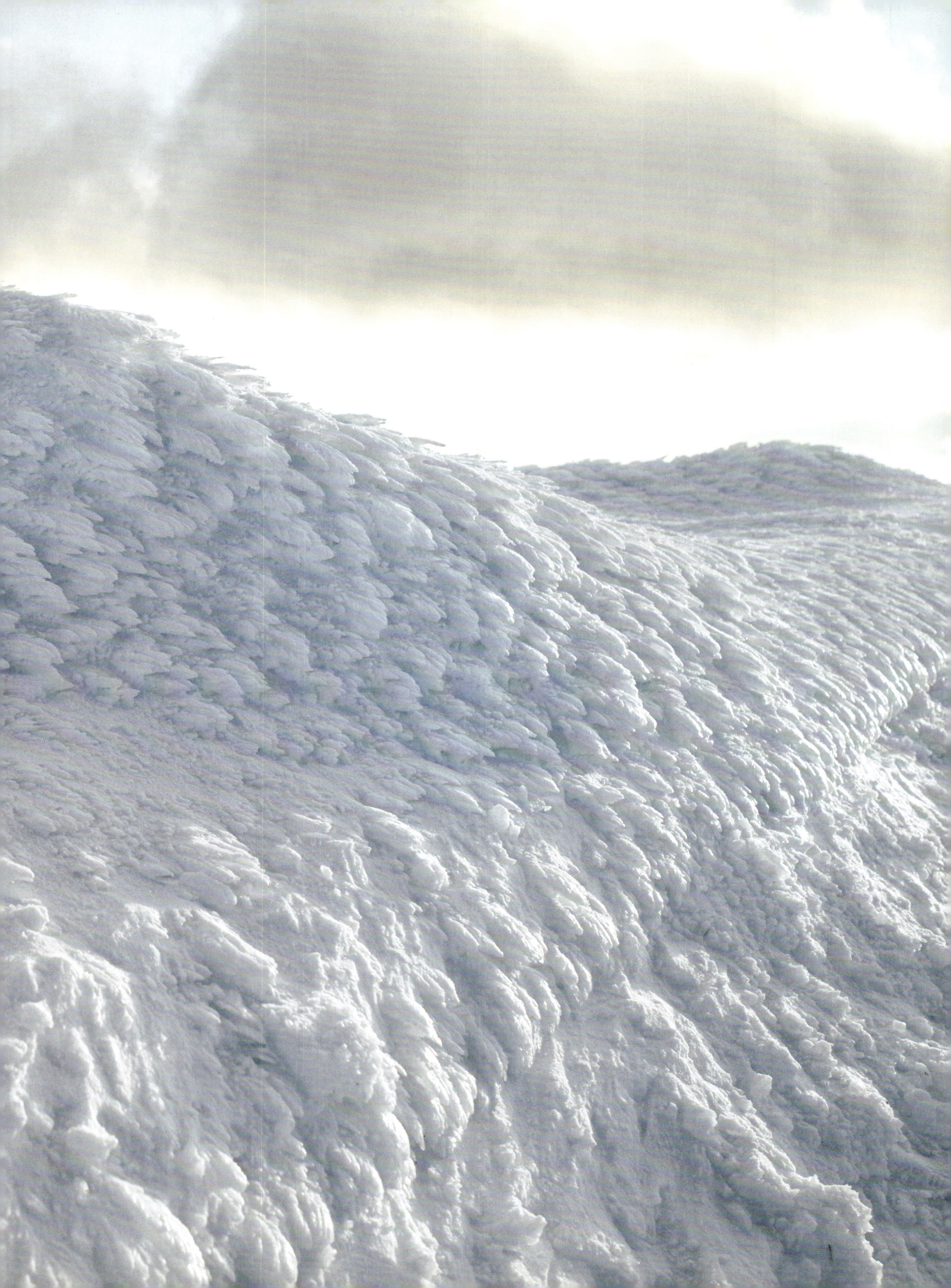

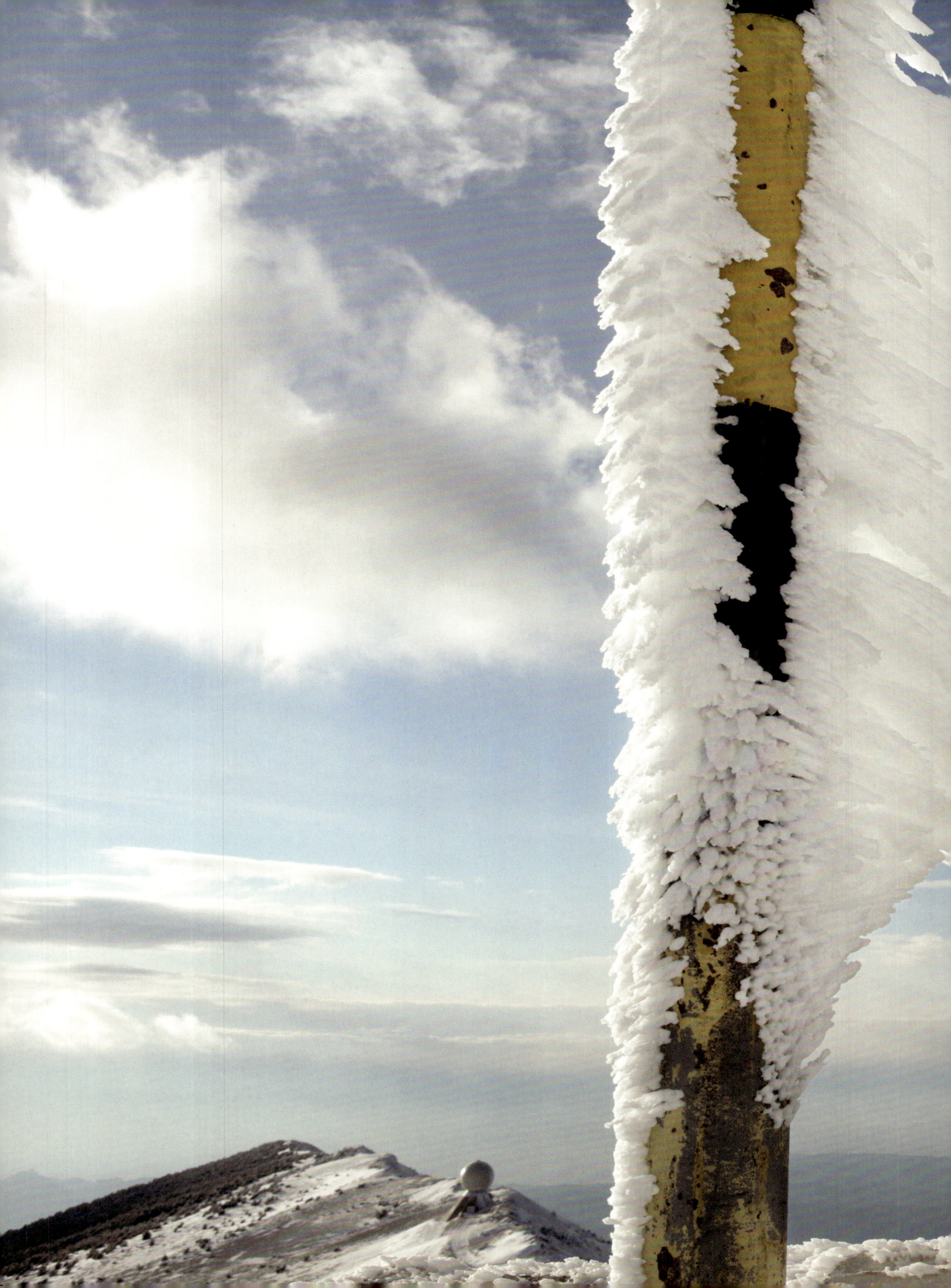

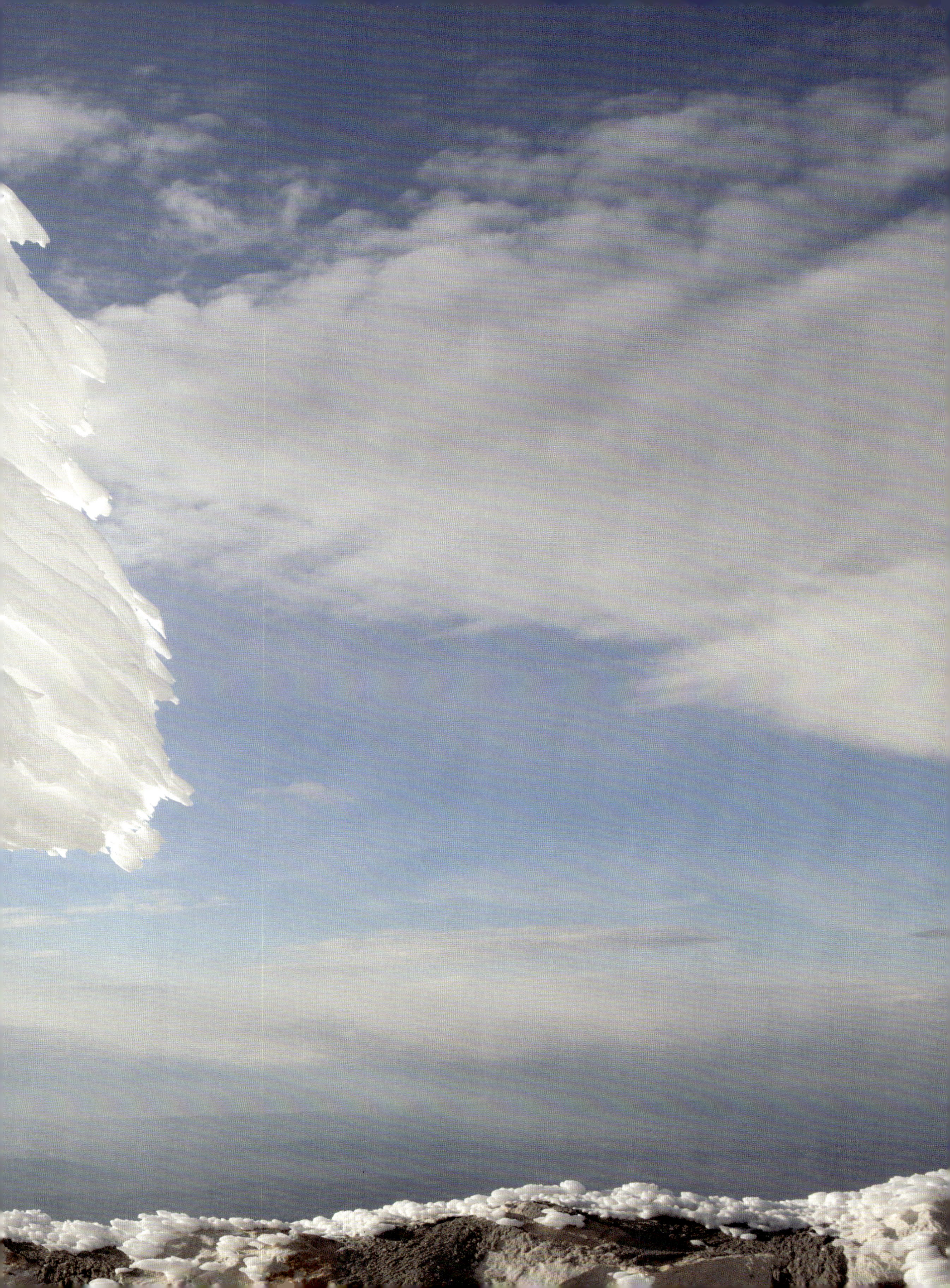

It was a fine June day, brilliant
with sunlight, but over this
unsheltered land, high in the sky,
the wind blew with unendurable
ferocity. It growled over the
carcasses of the houses
like a lion disturbed at its meal.

C'était un beau jour de juin
avec grand soleil, mais sur ces
terres sans abri et hautes dans le ciel,
le vent soufflait avec une
brutalité insupportable. Ses
grondements dans les carcasses
des maisons étaient ceux d'un fauve
dérangé dans son repas.

—Jean Giono,
The Man Who Planted Trees

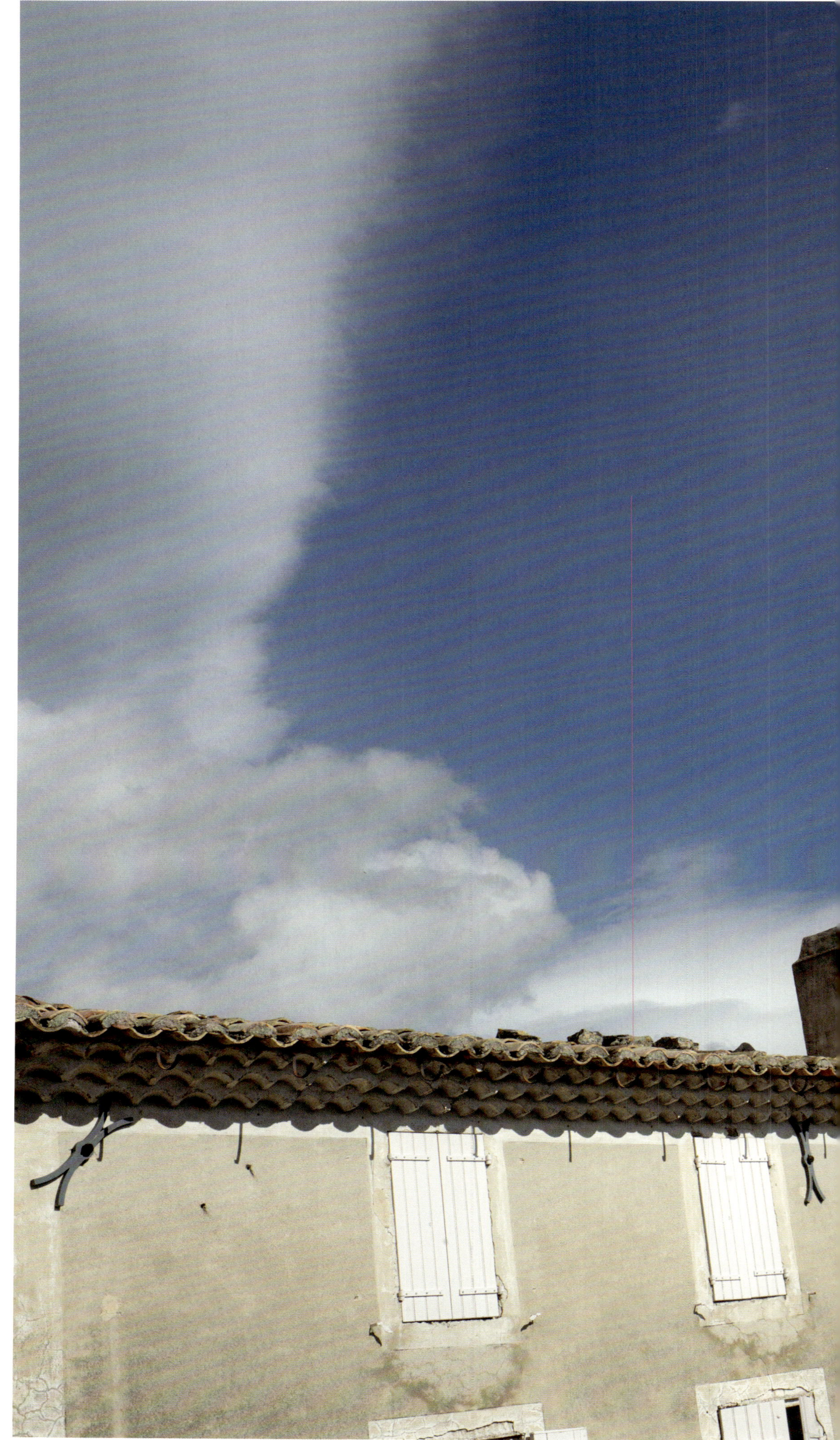

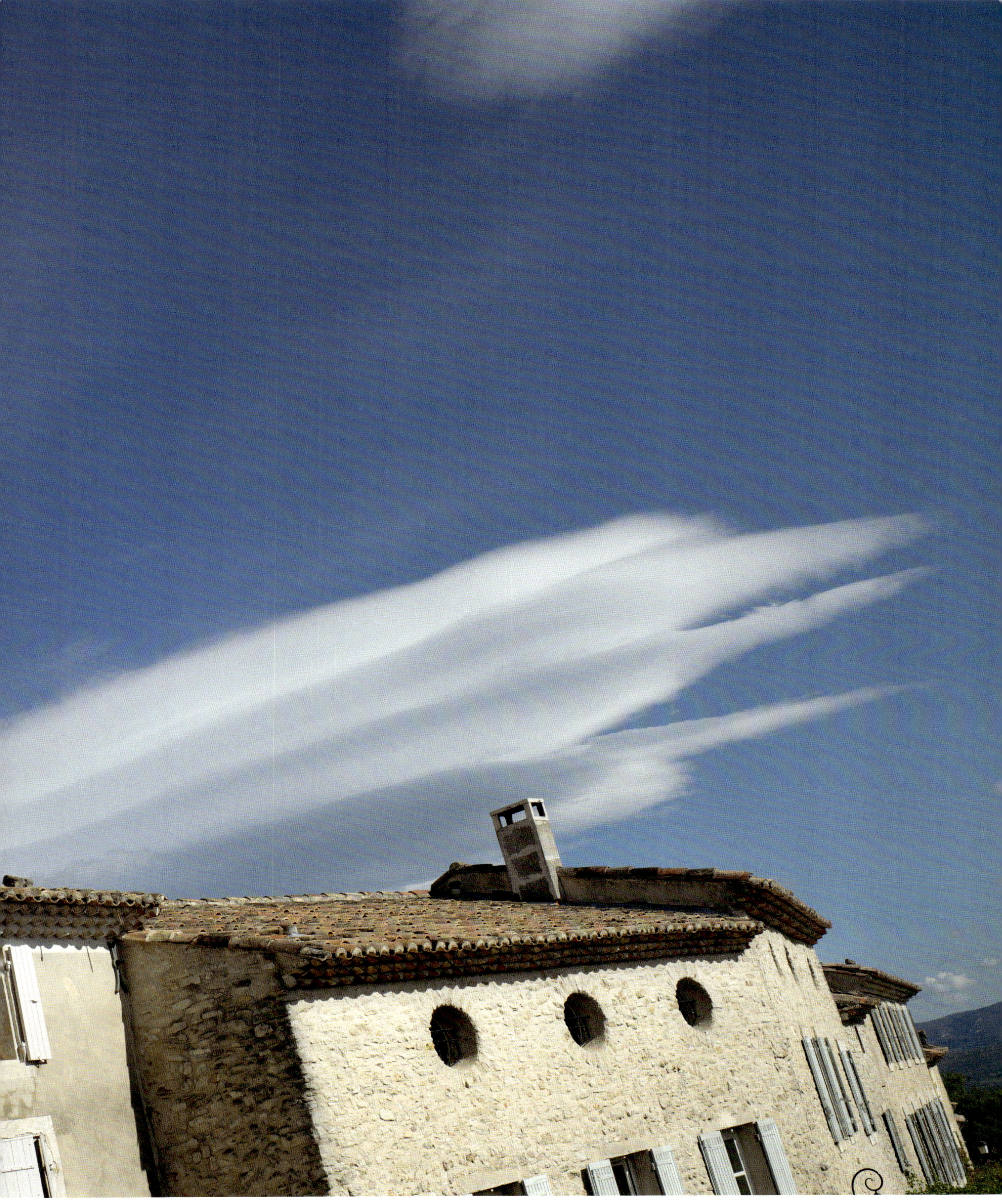

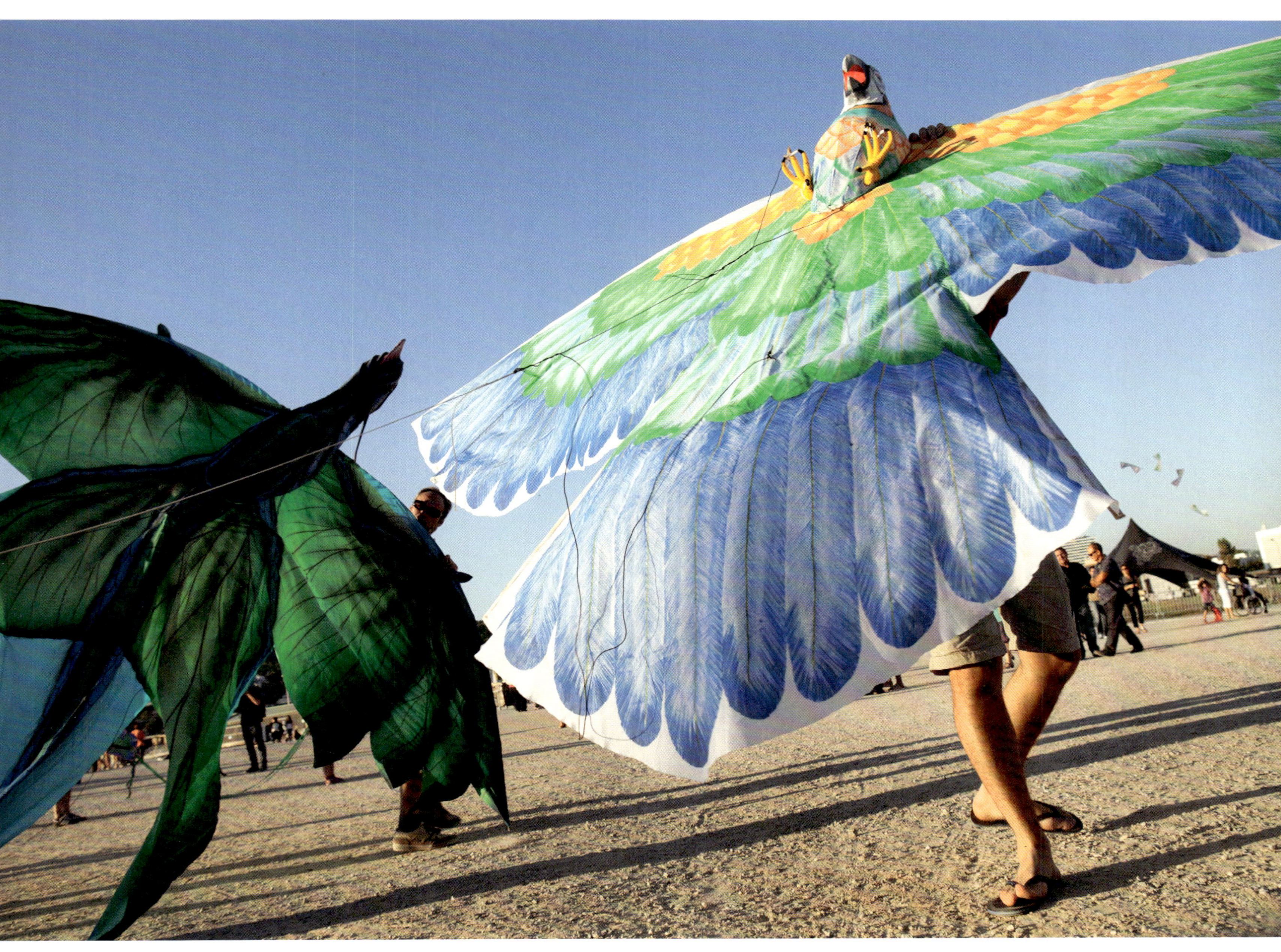

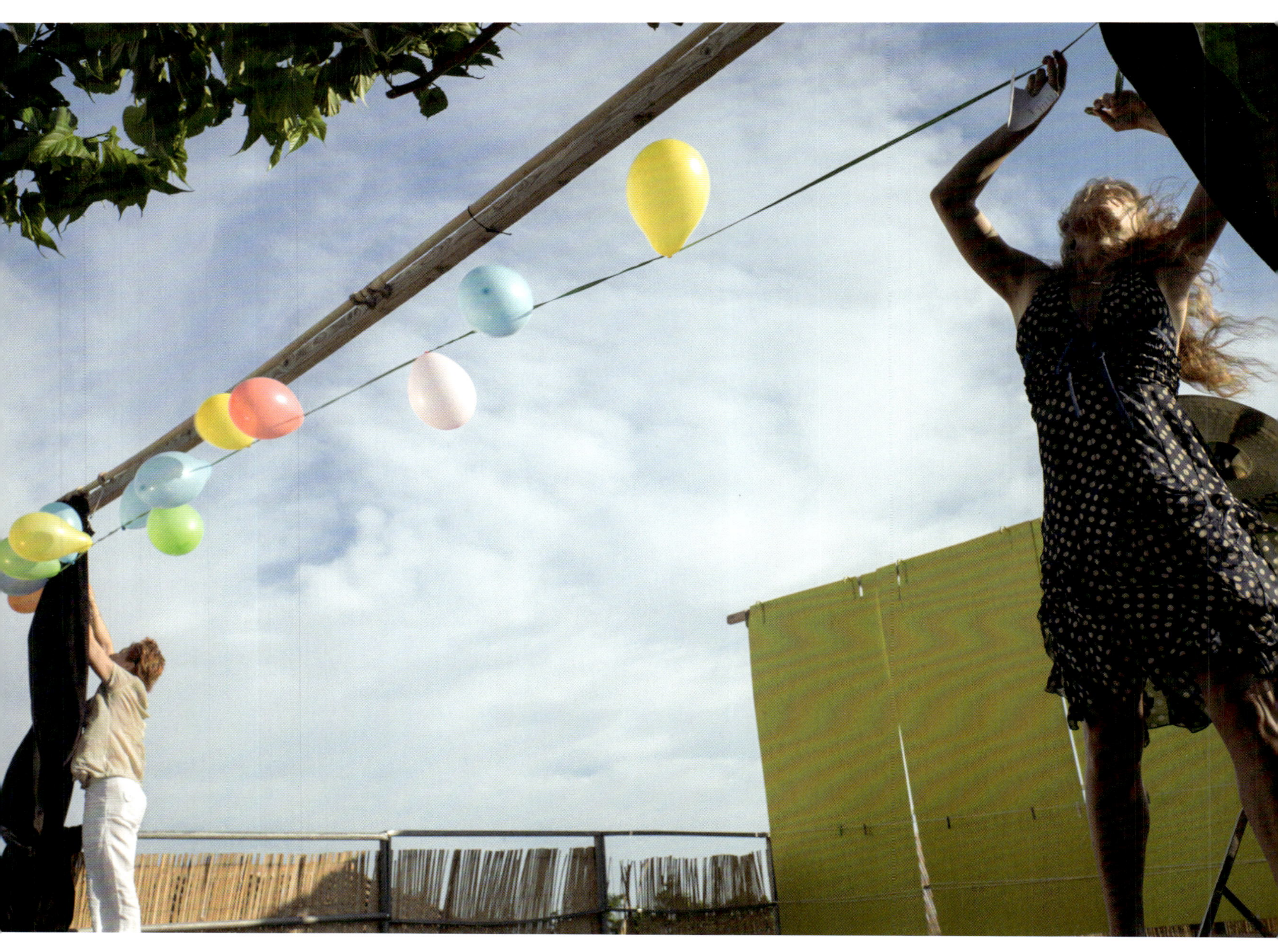

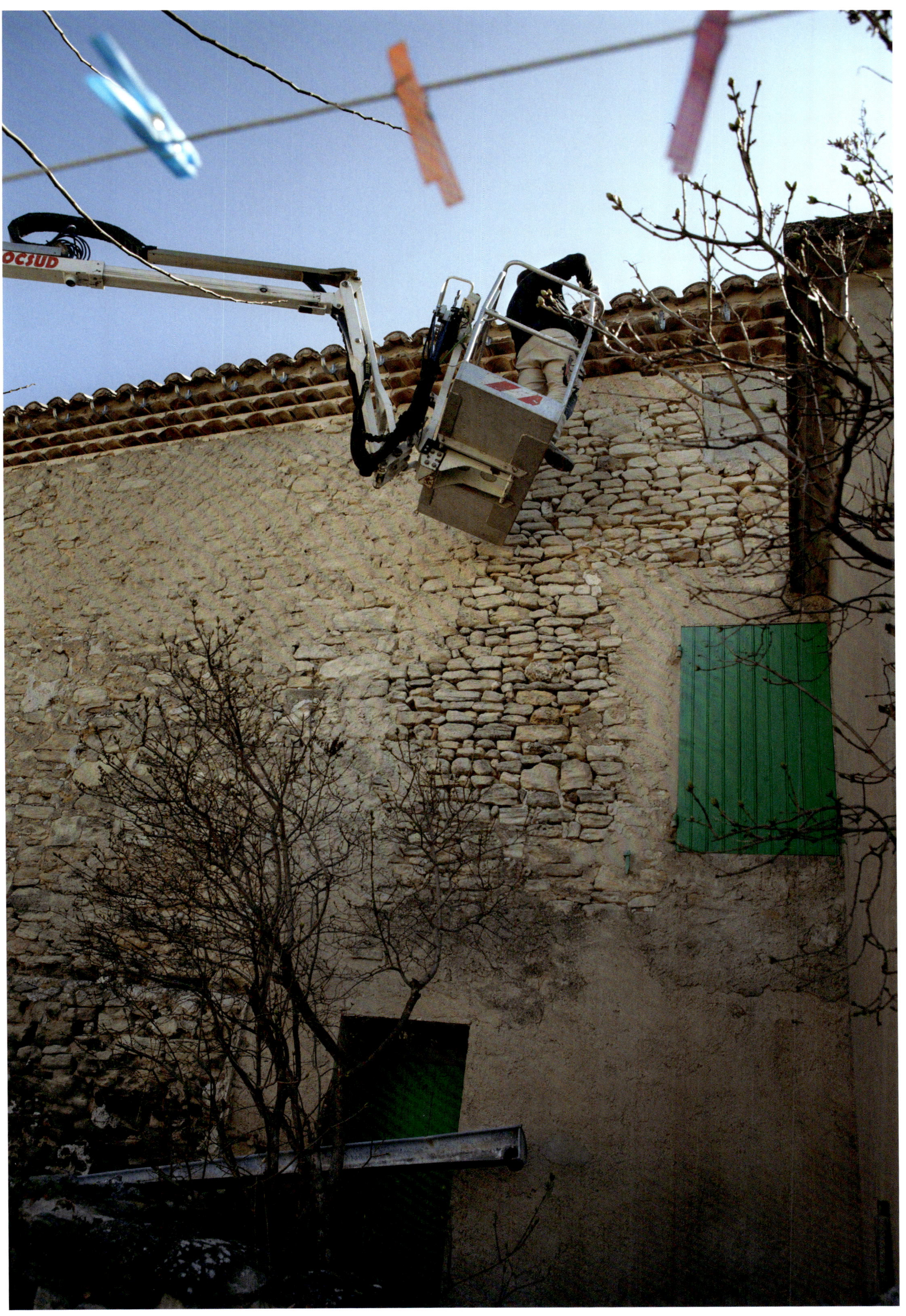
OCSUD

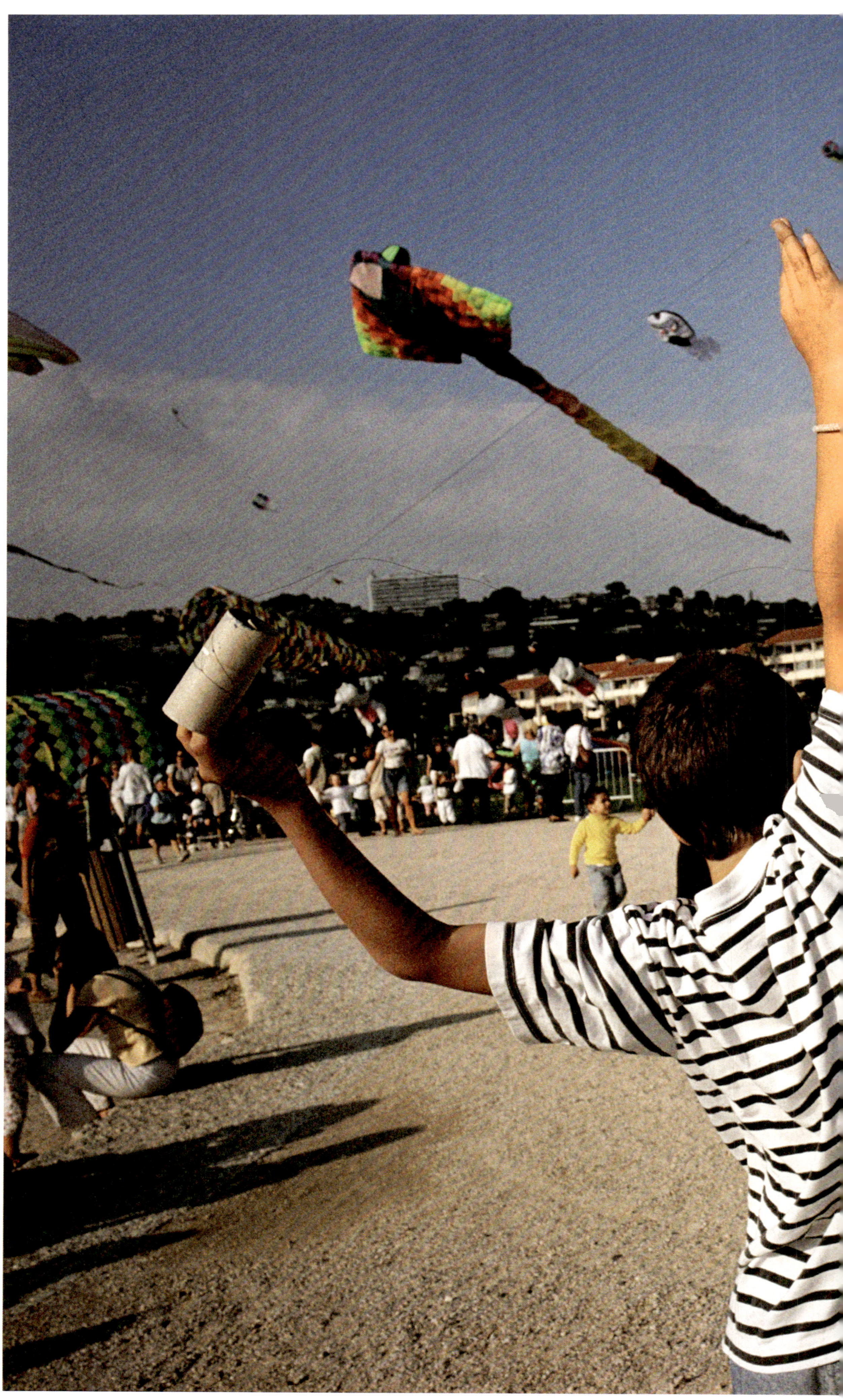

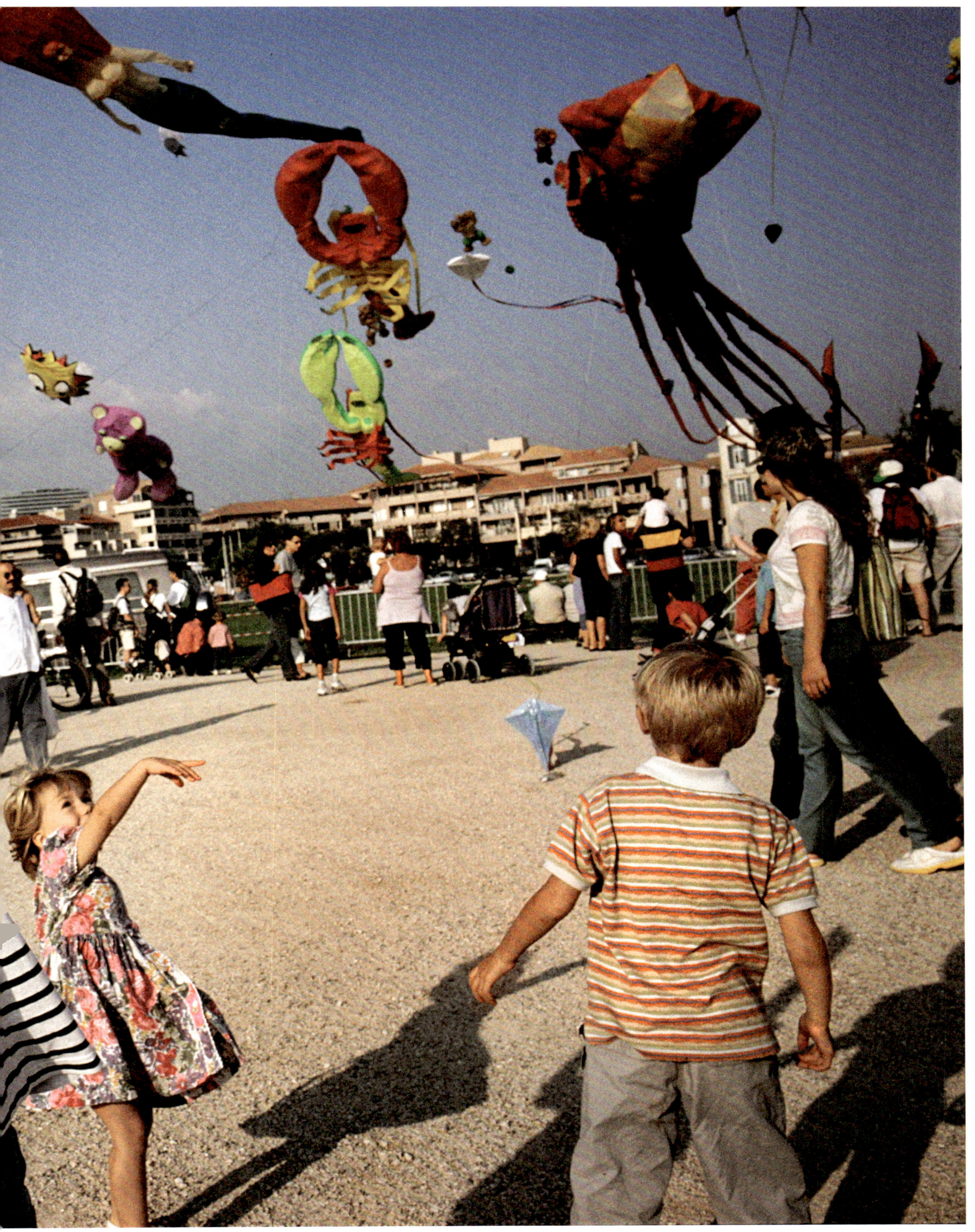

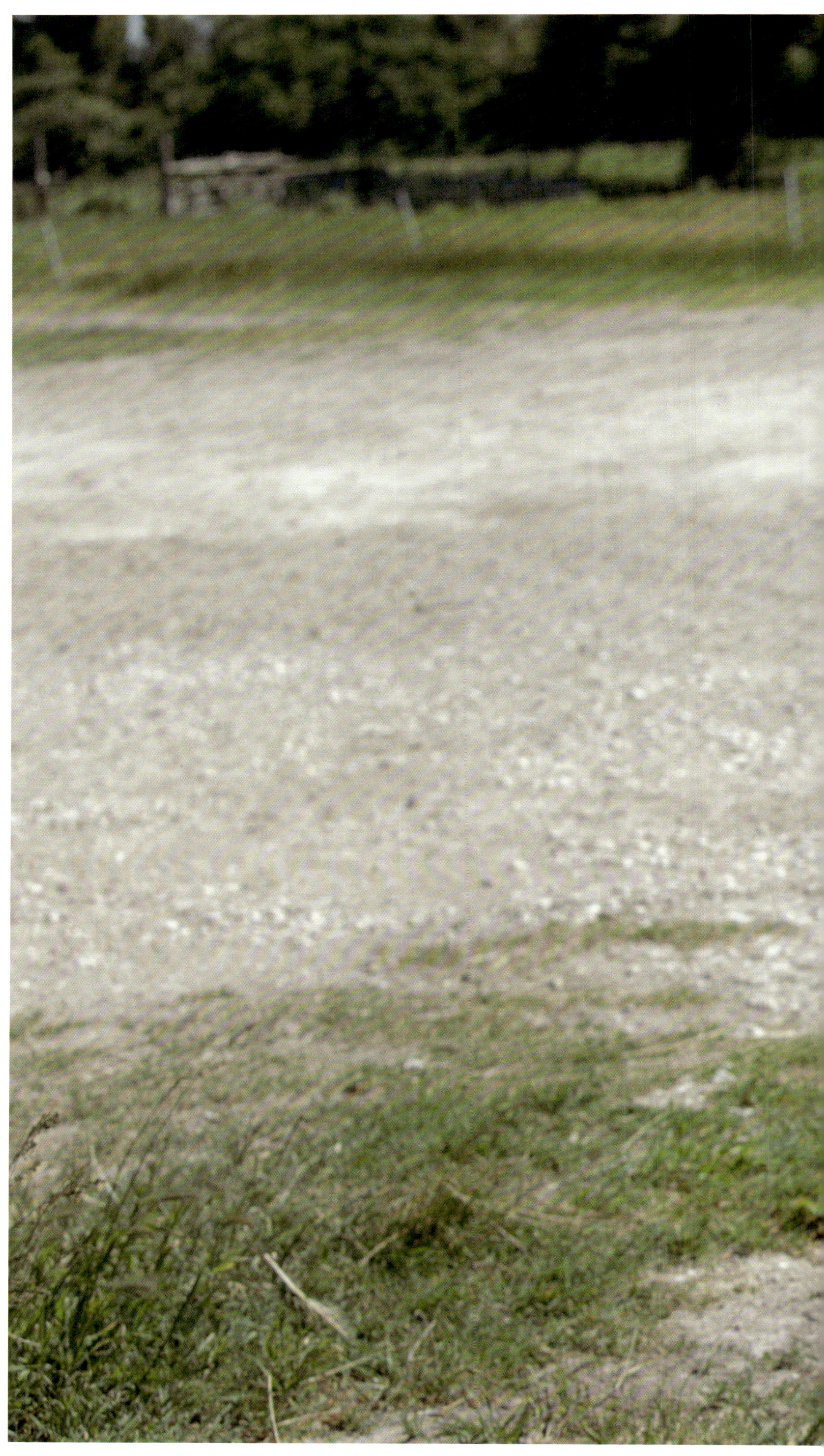

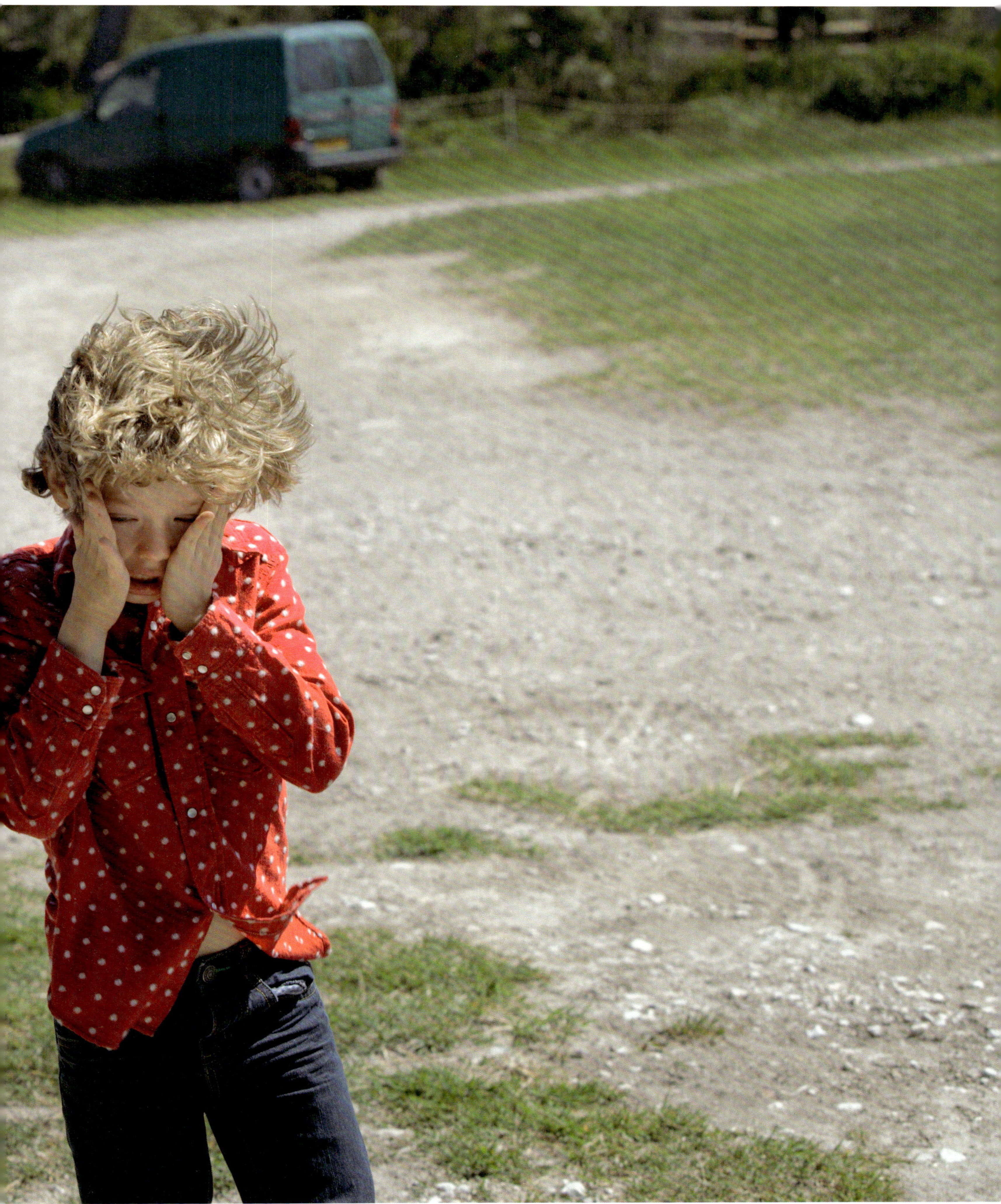

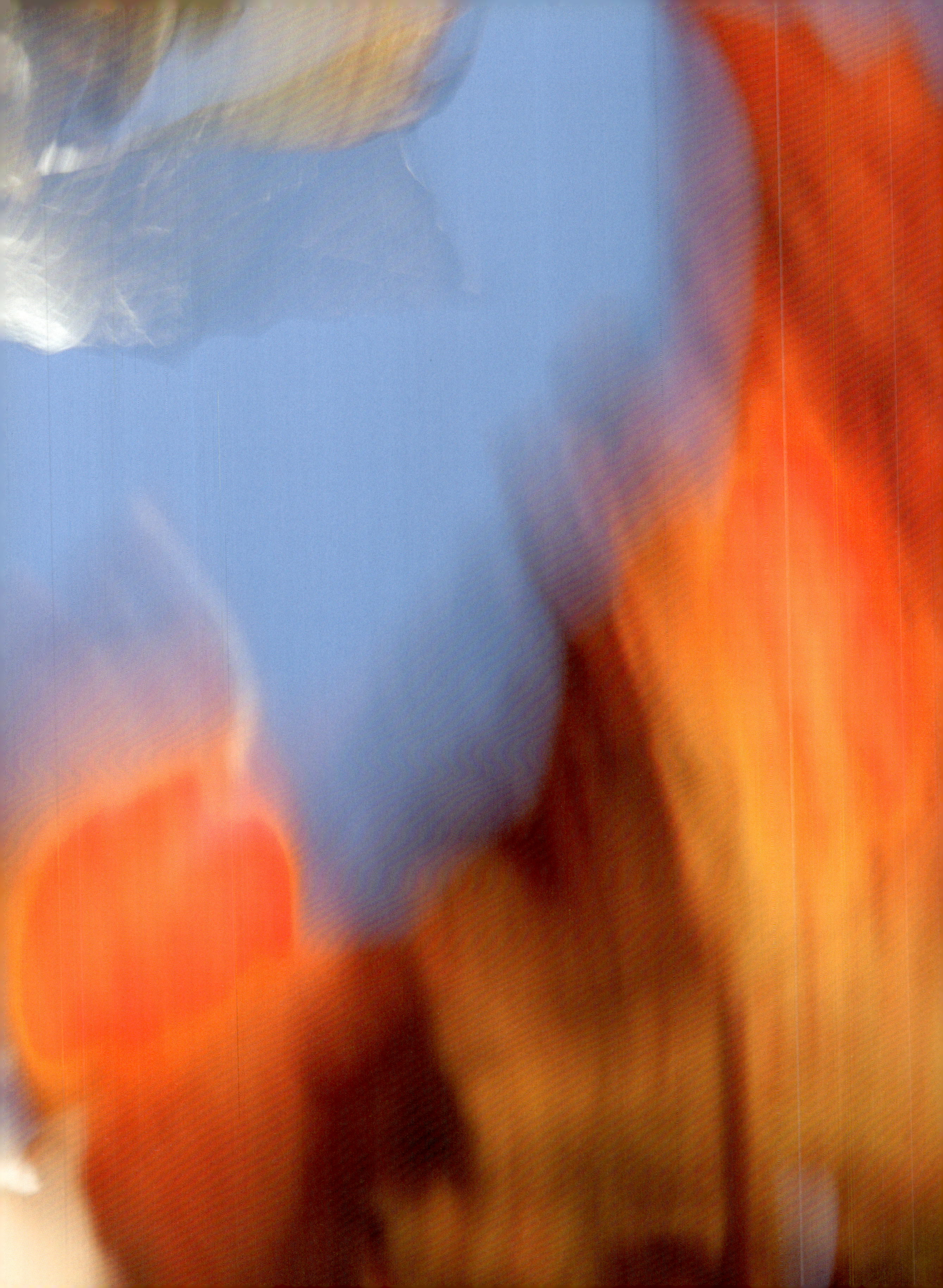

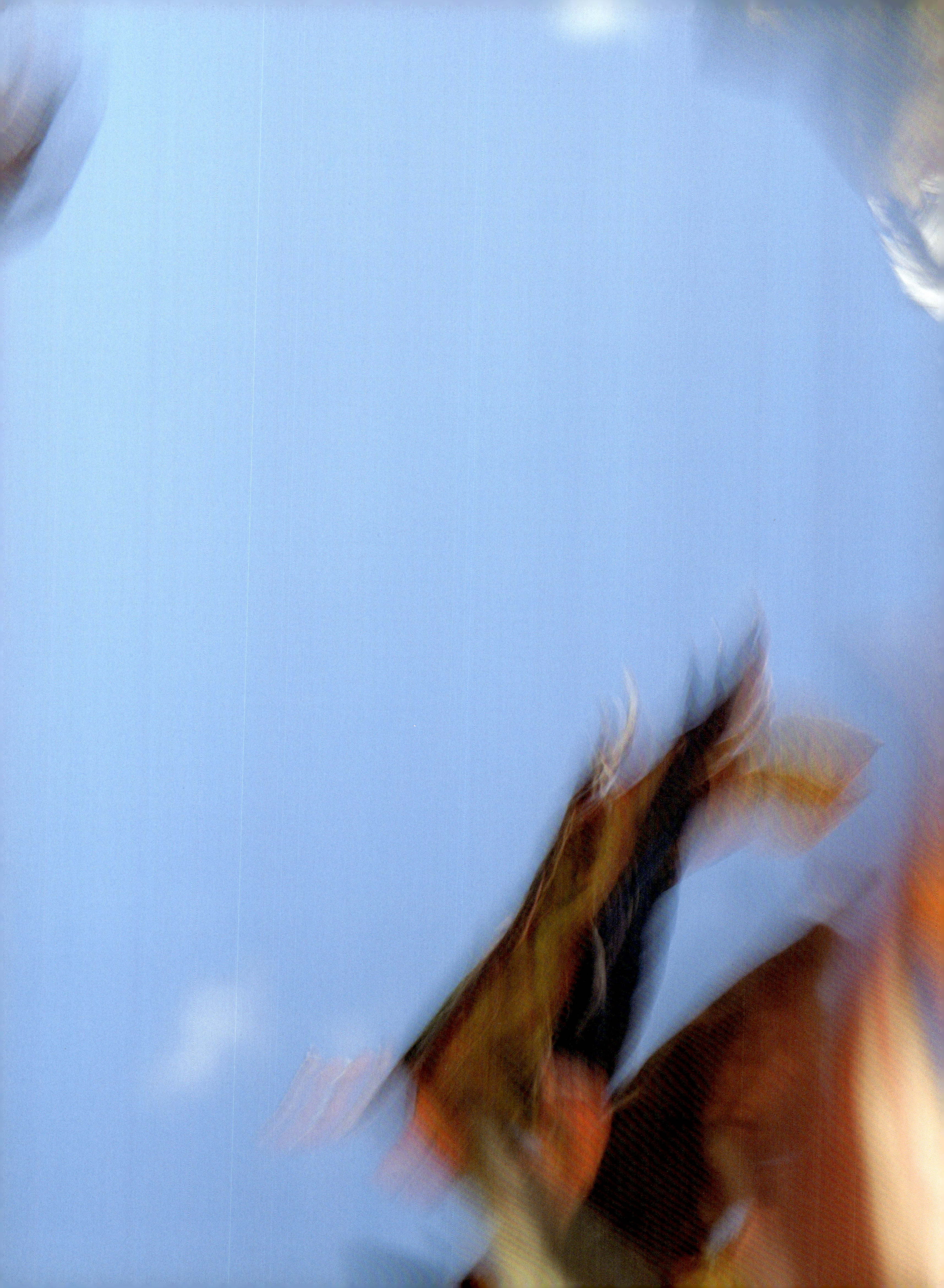

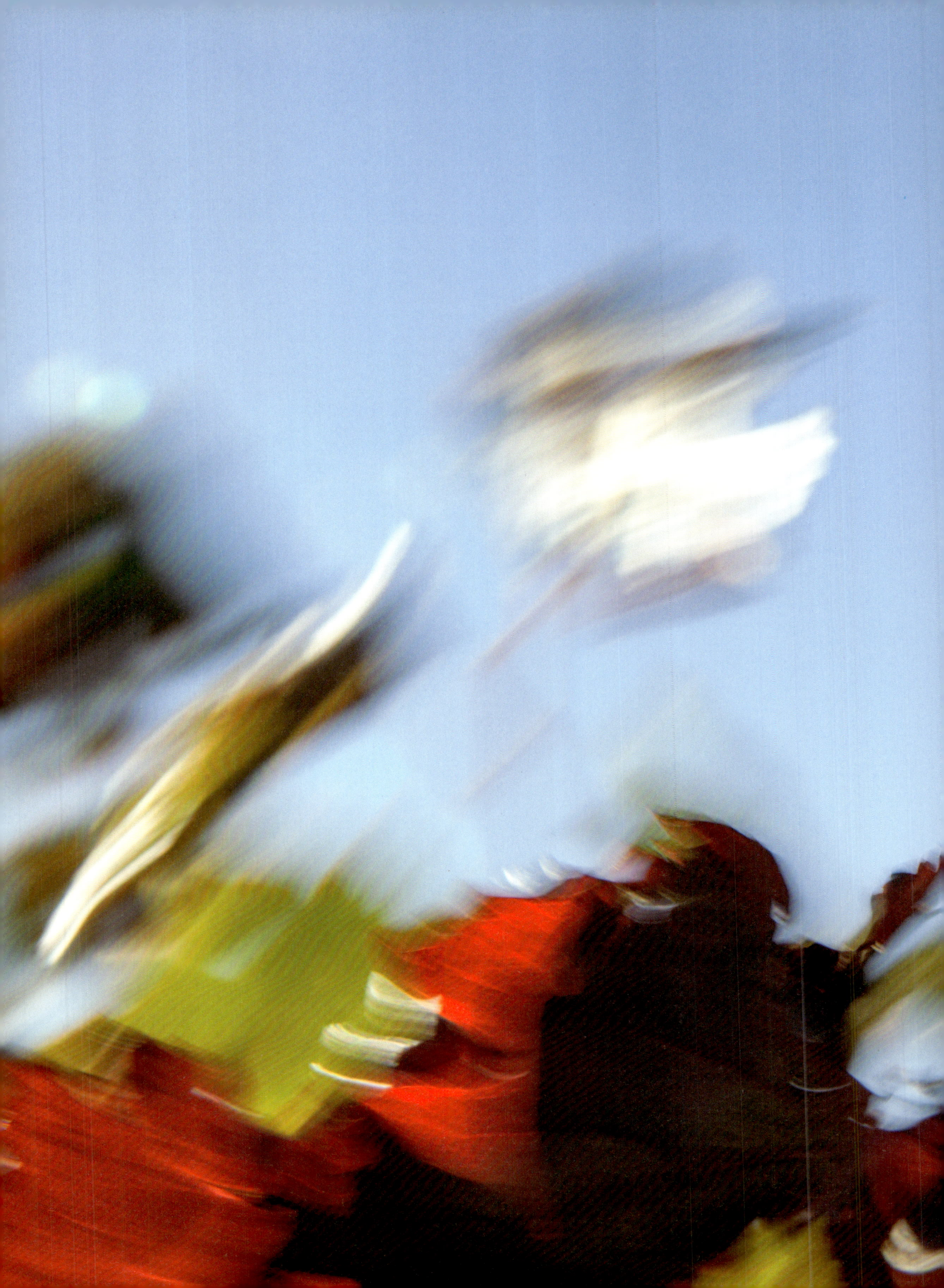

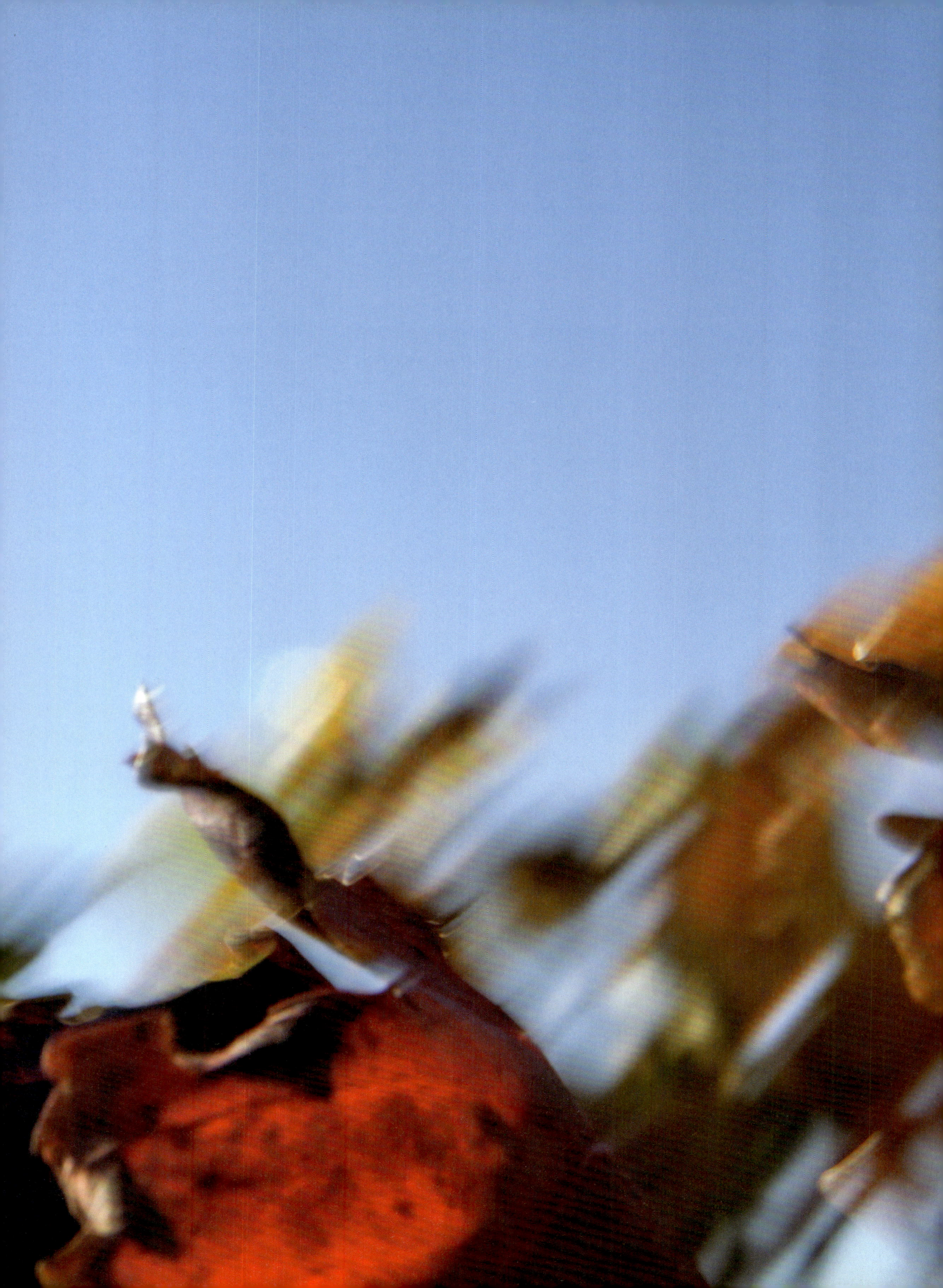

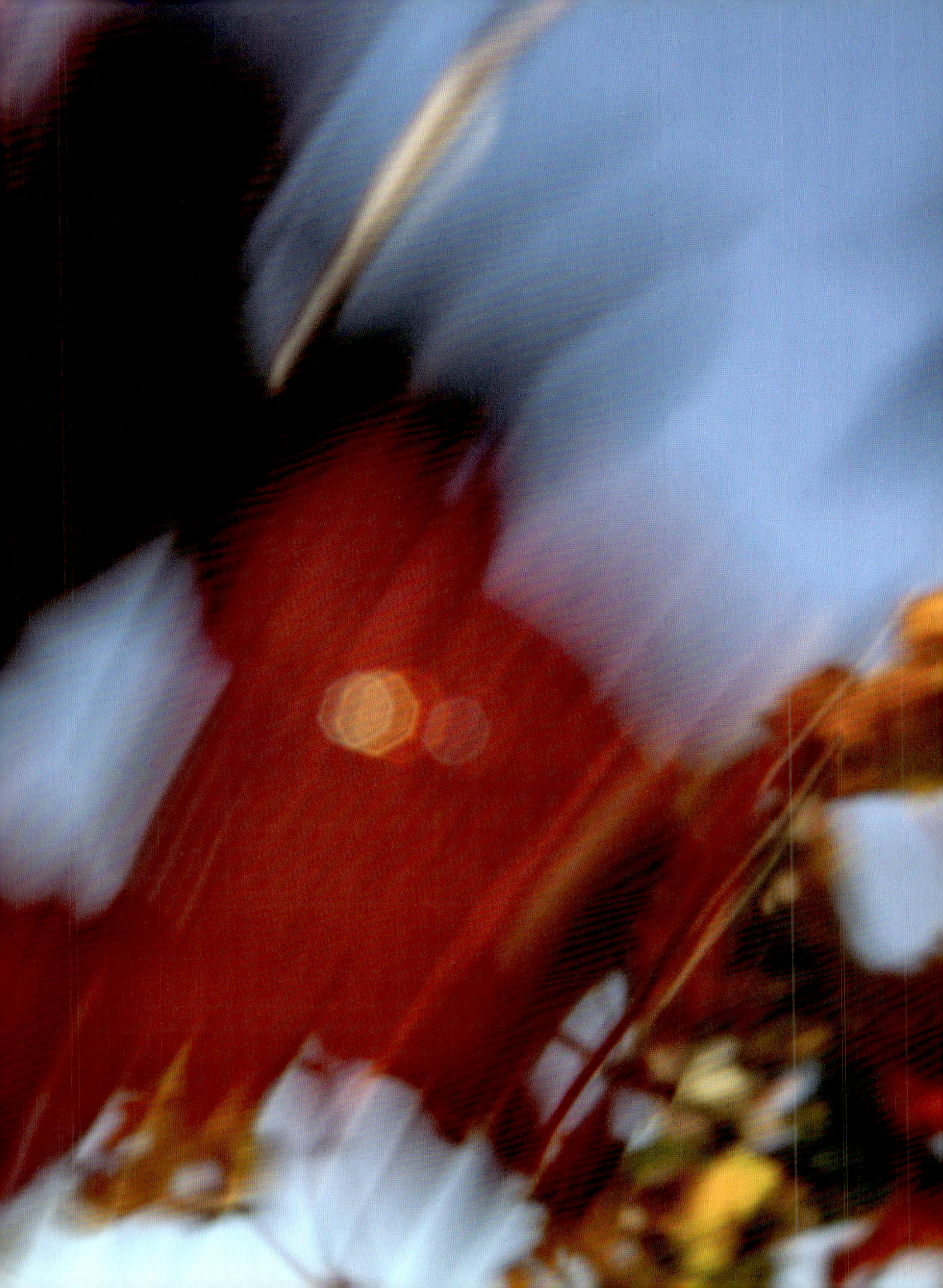

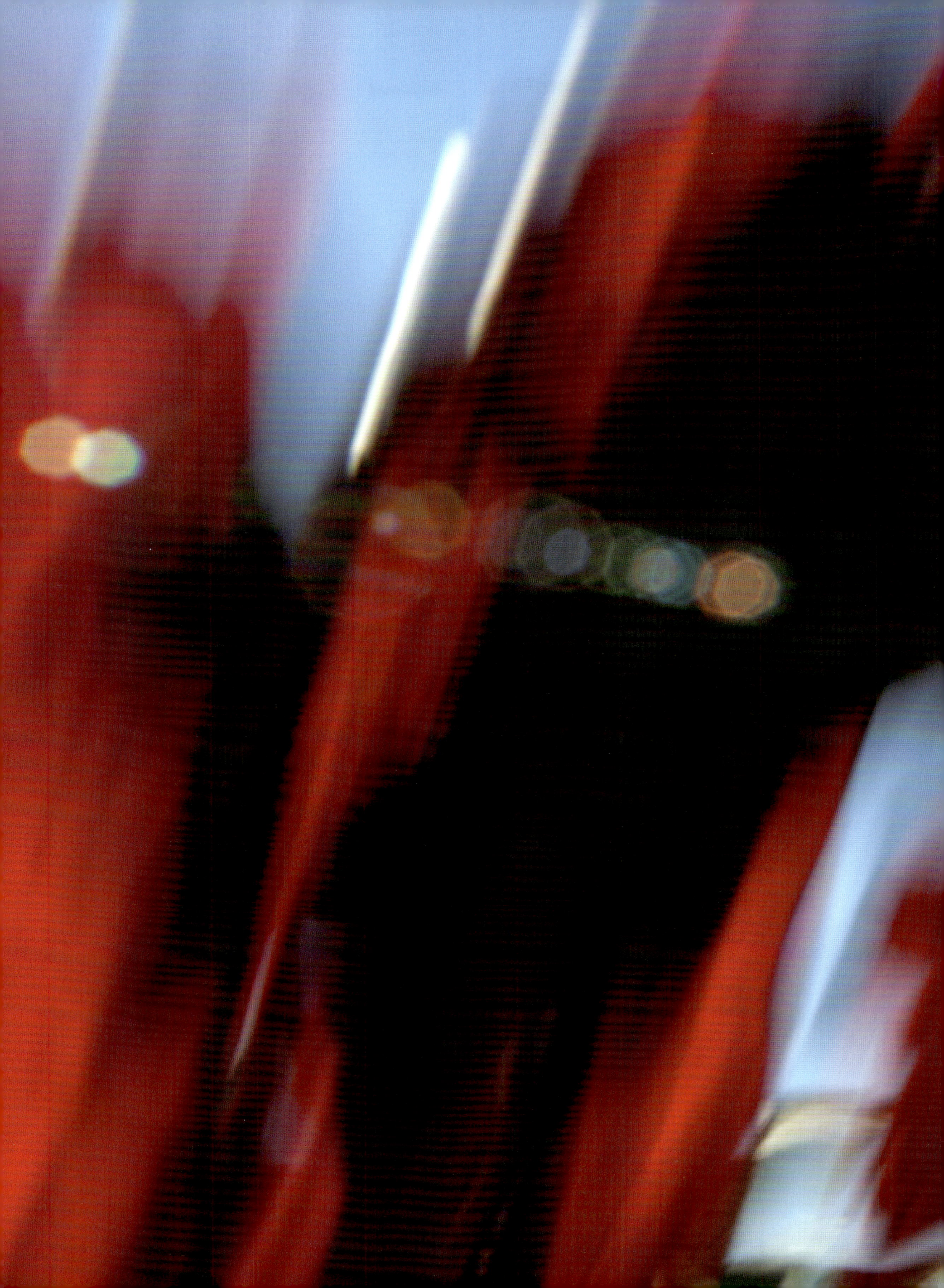

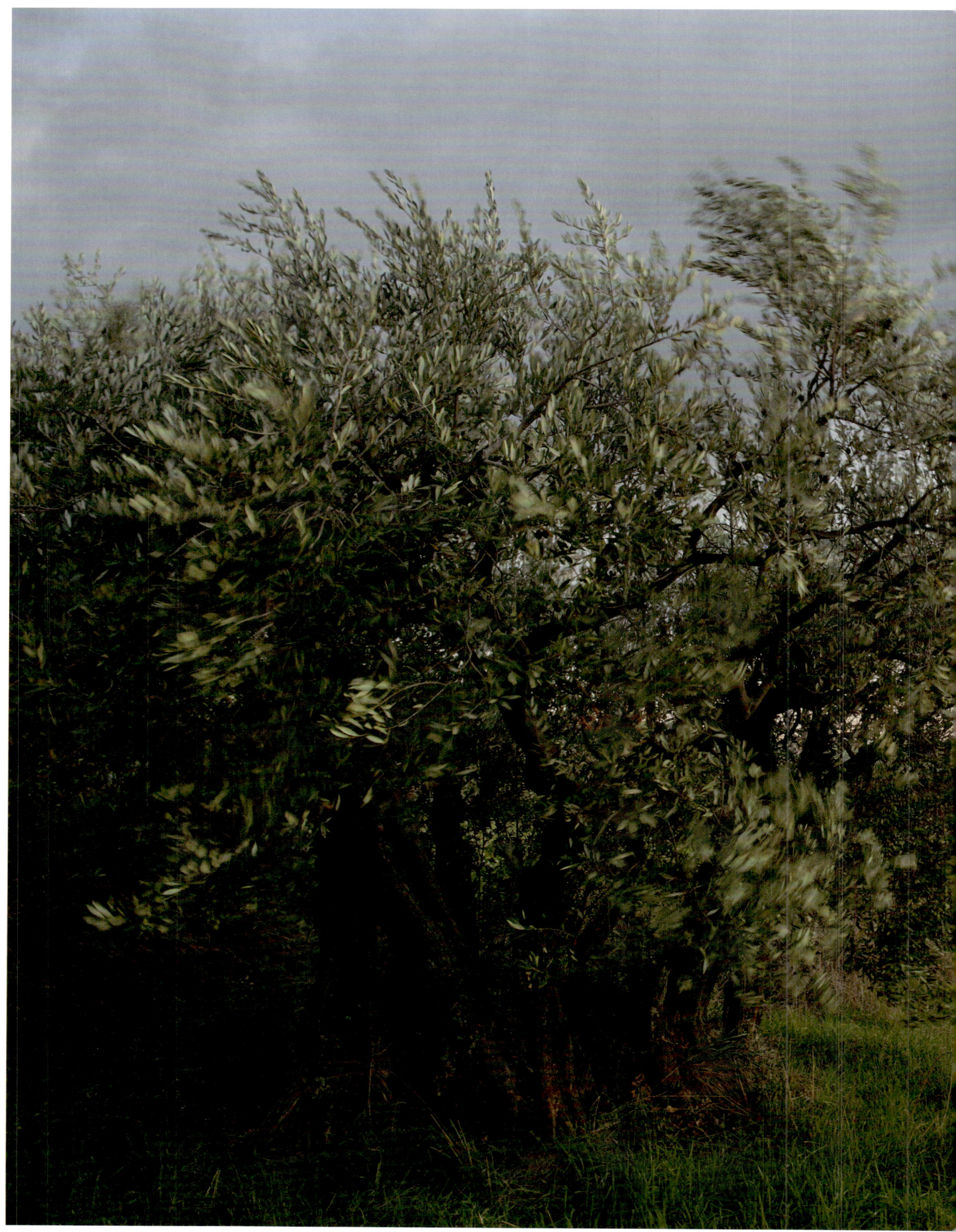

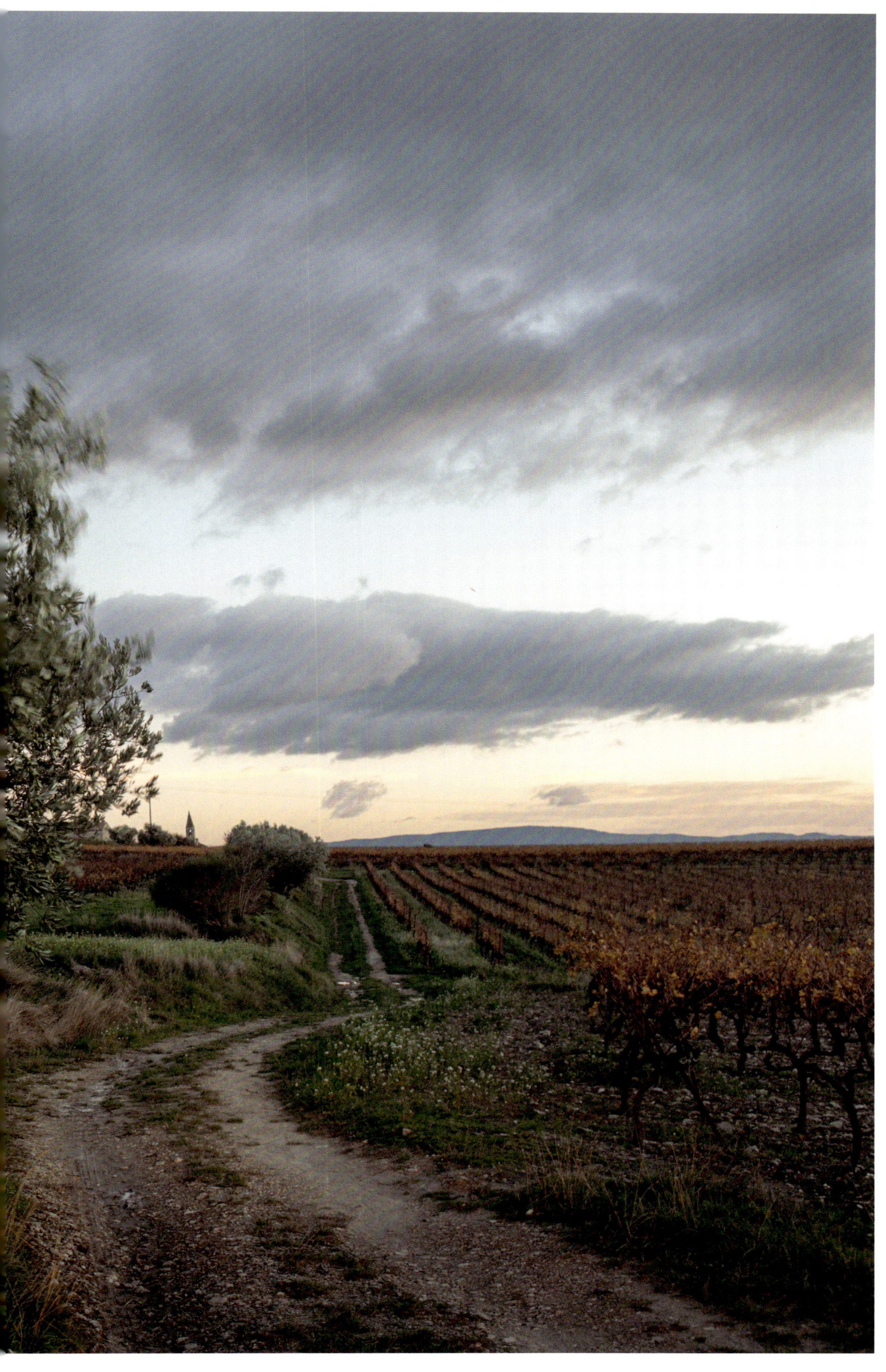

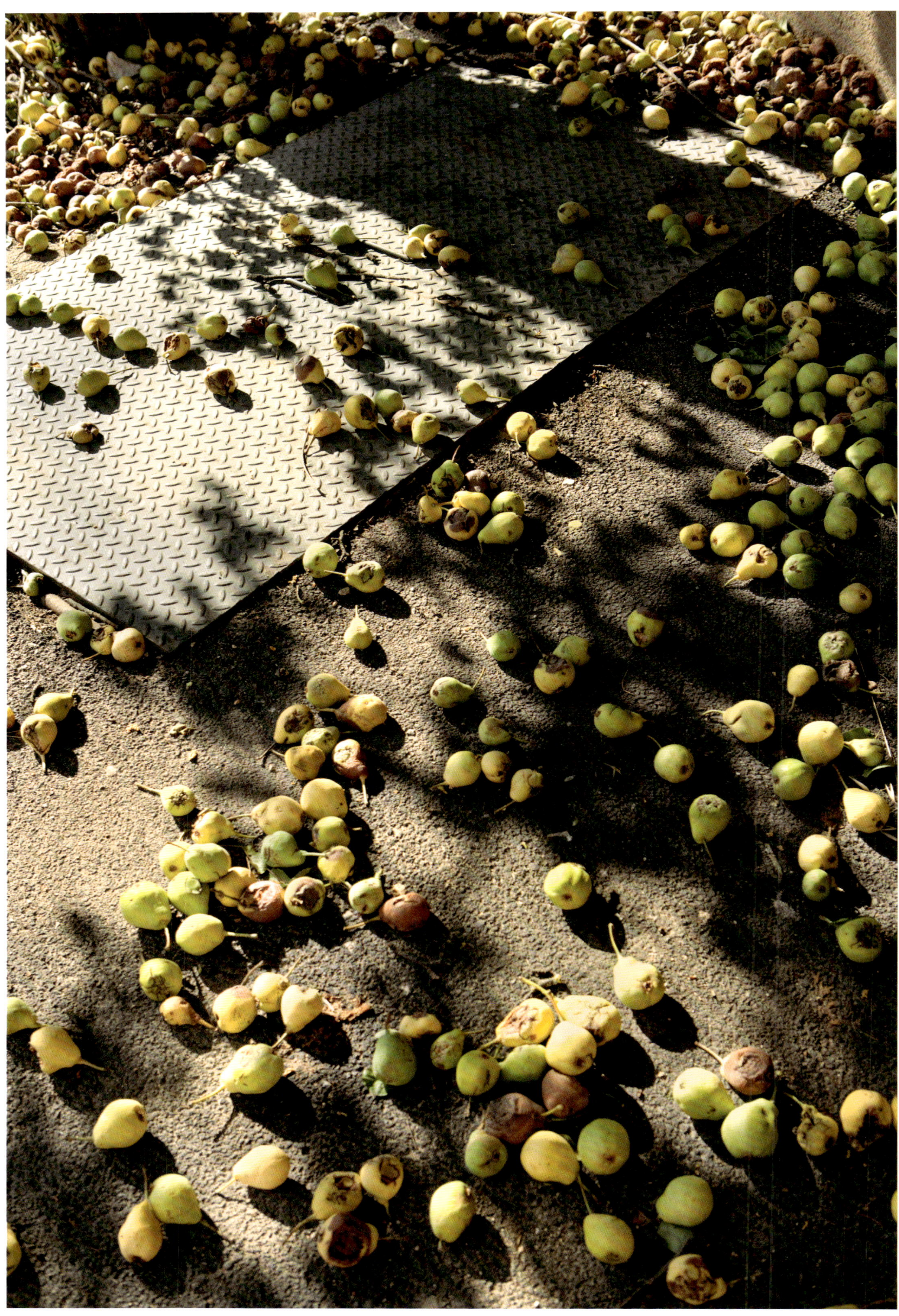

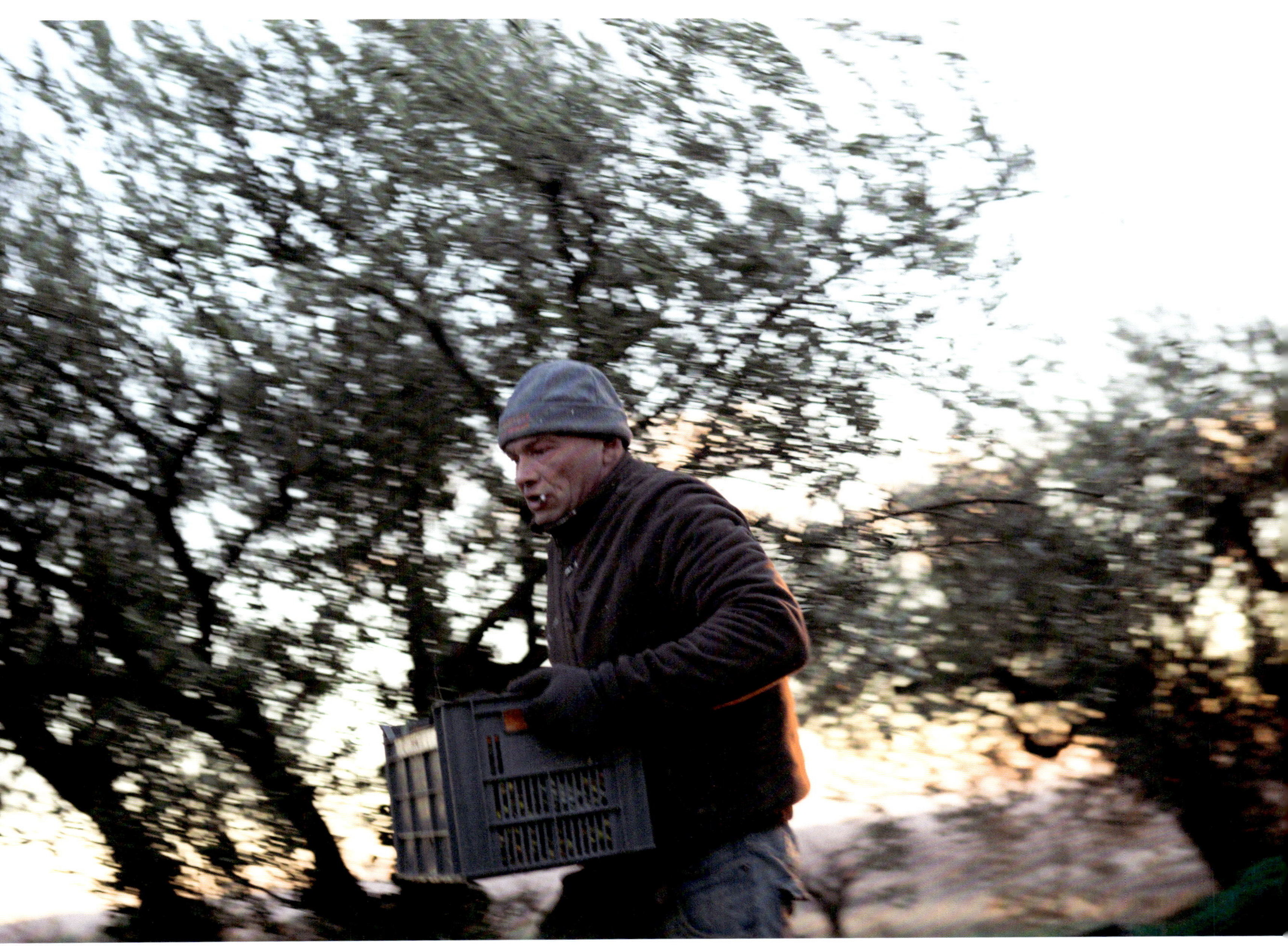

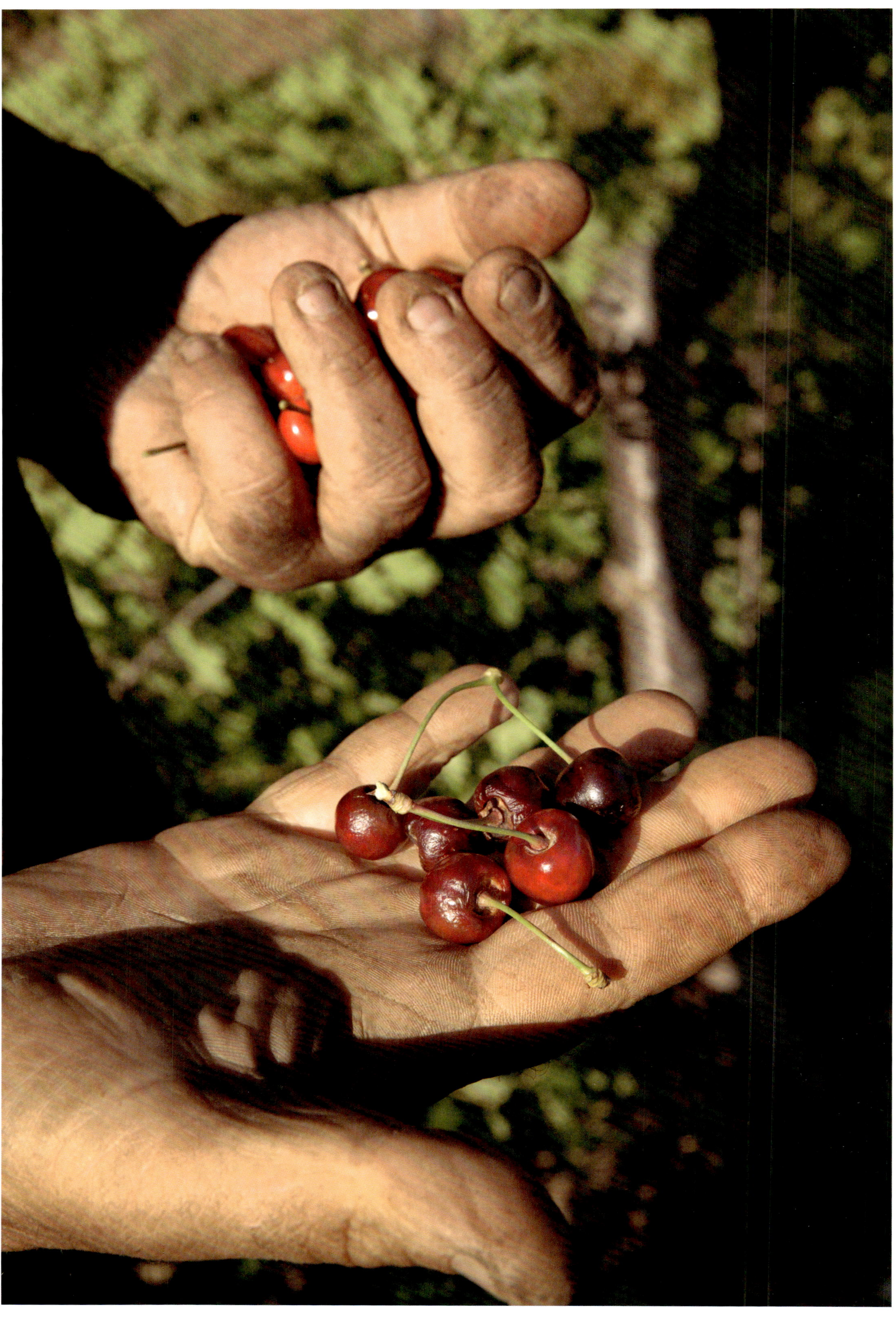

The sky becomes very red.
That means mistral the next day.
This is always touching to me;
it's nature that guides me.

—Pierre Vadon, farmer,
Mas Saint Germain, Camargue

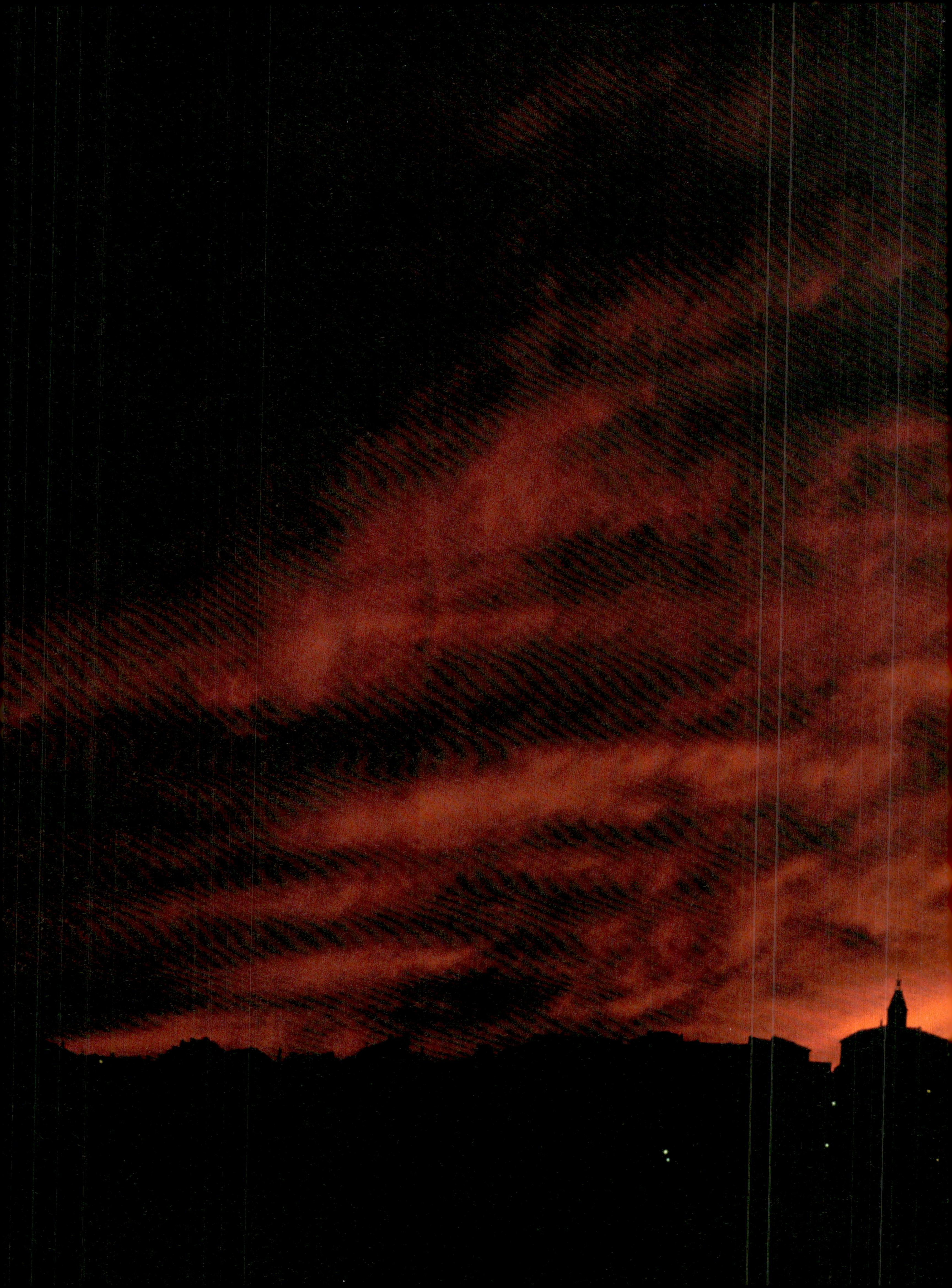

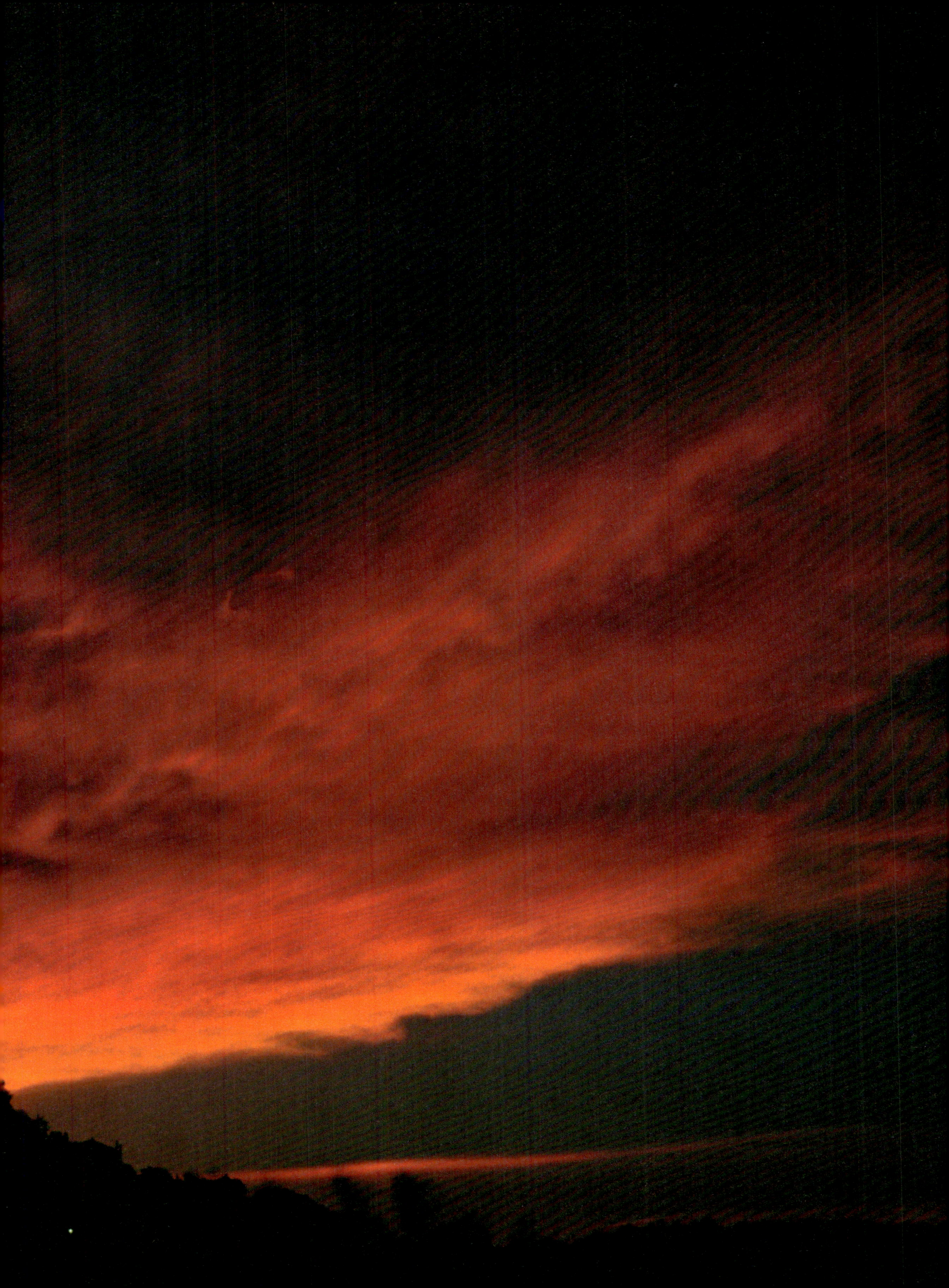

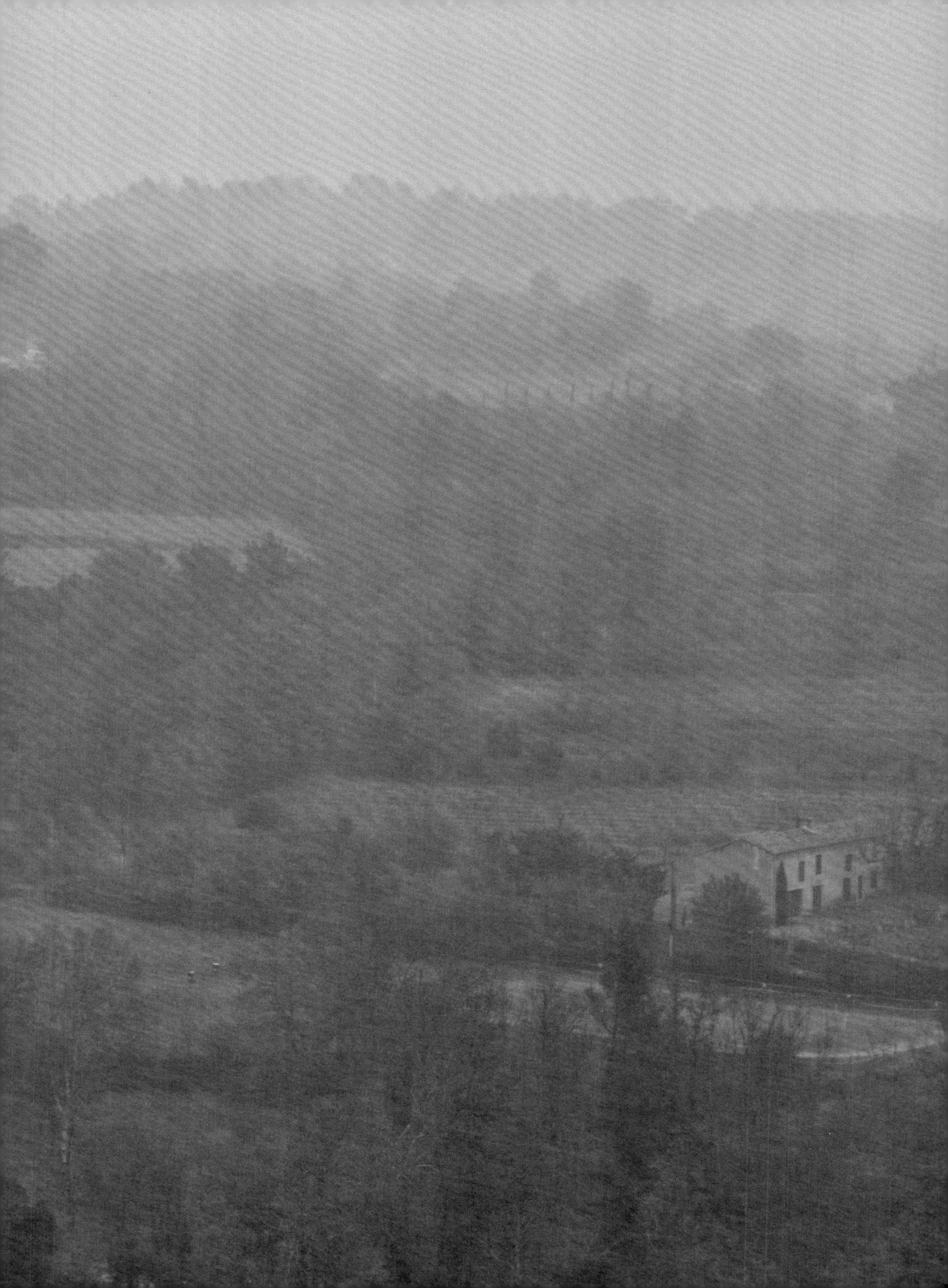

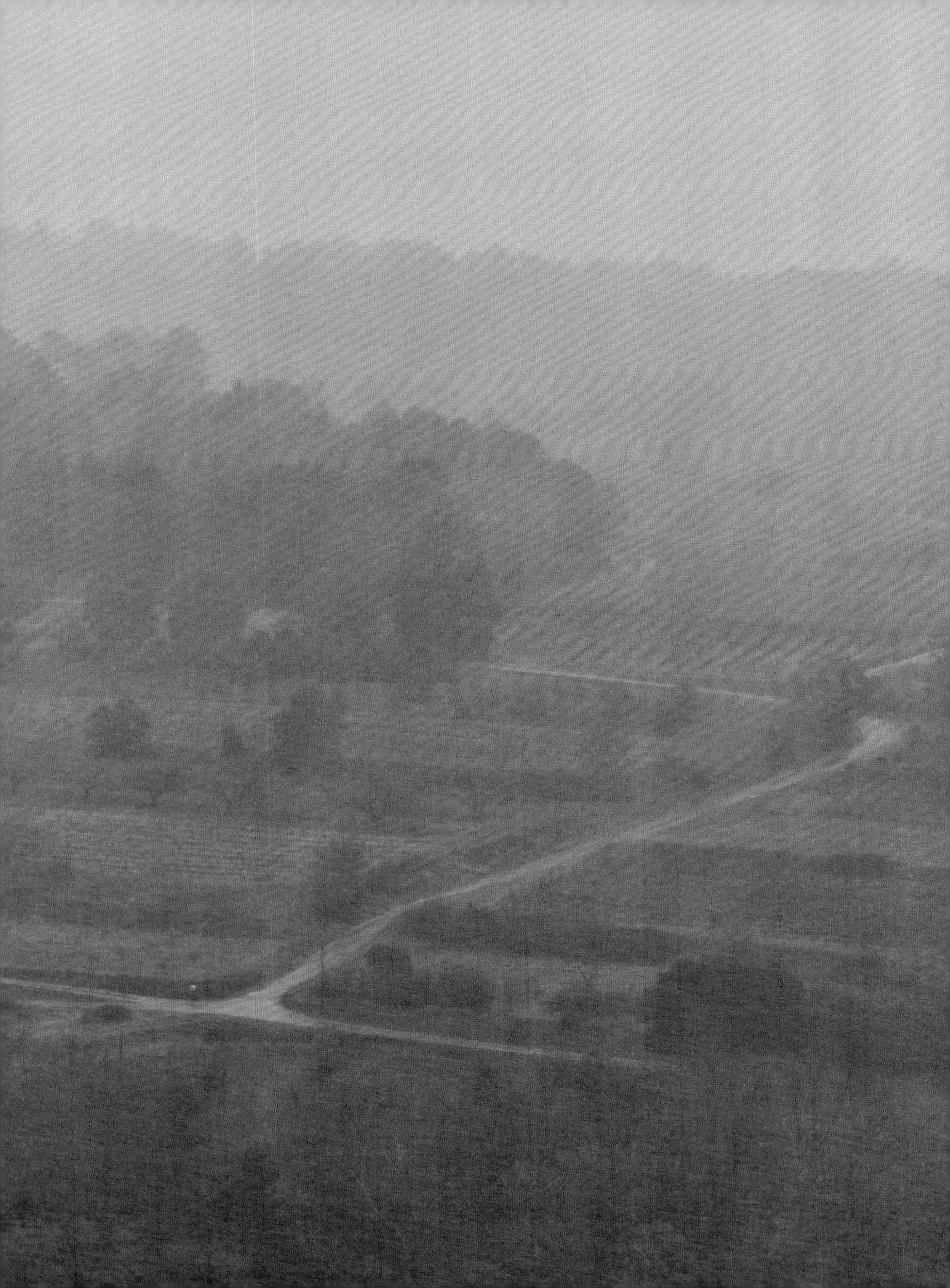

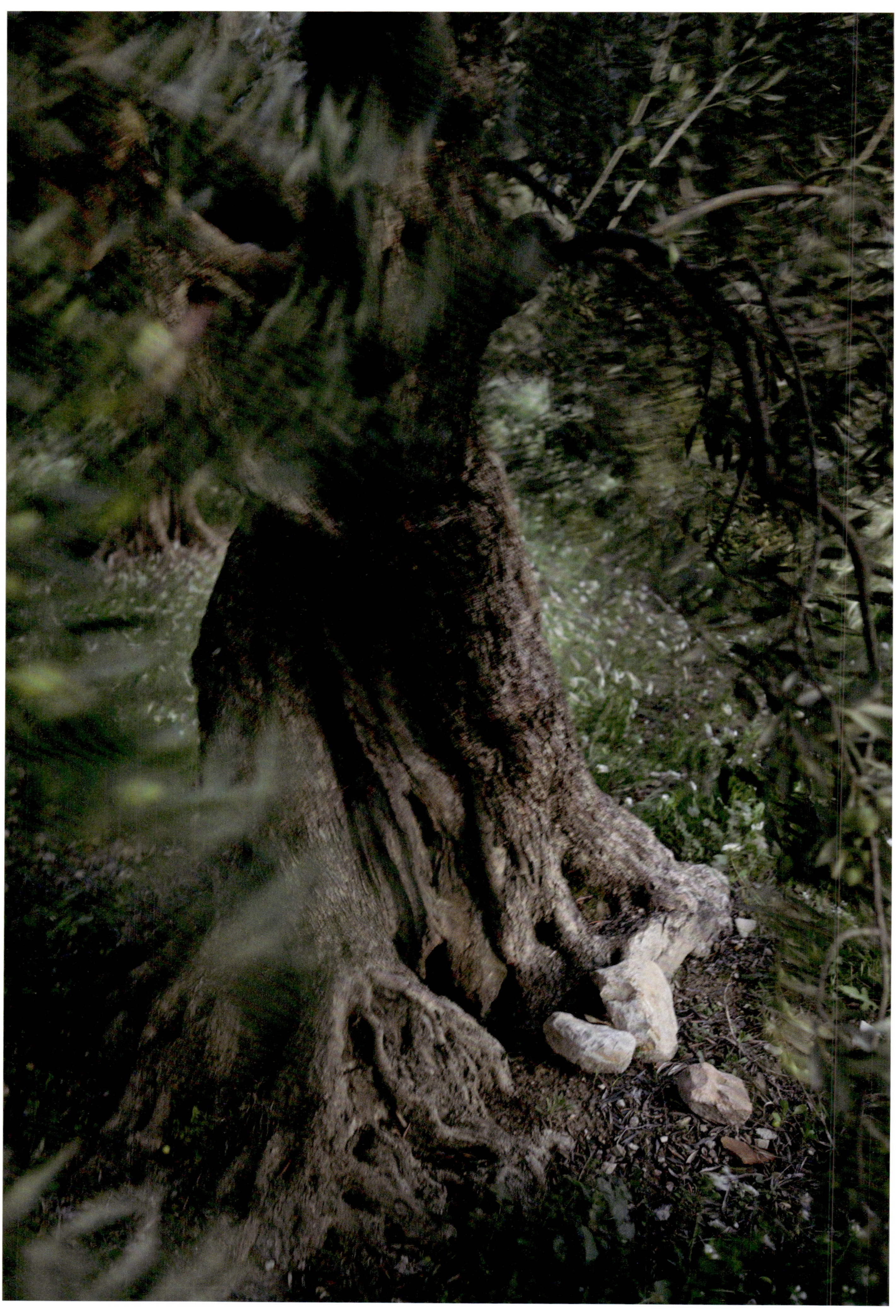

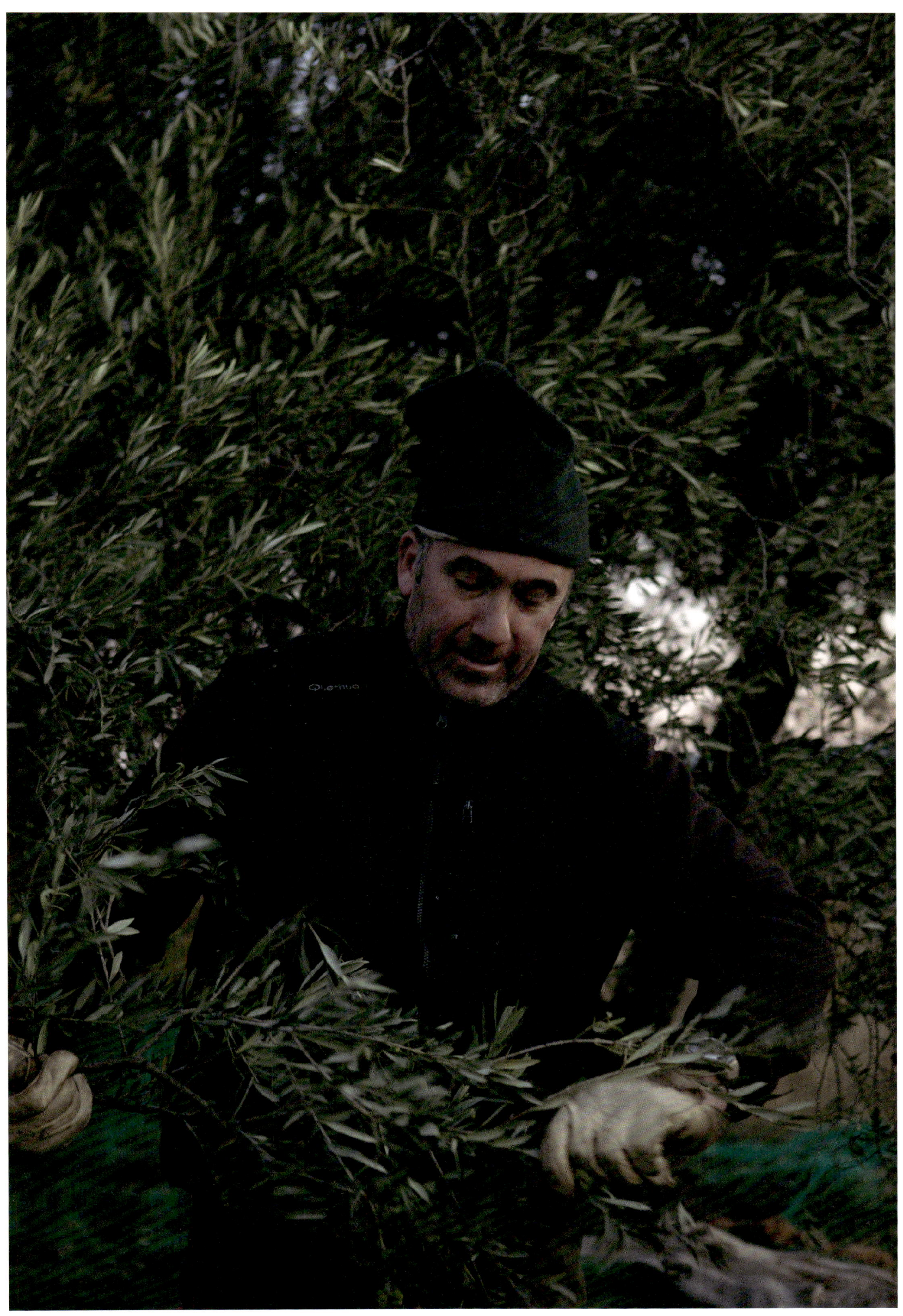

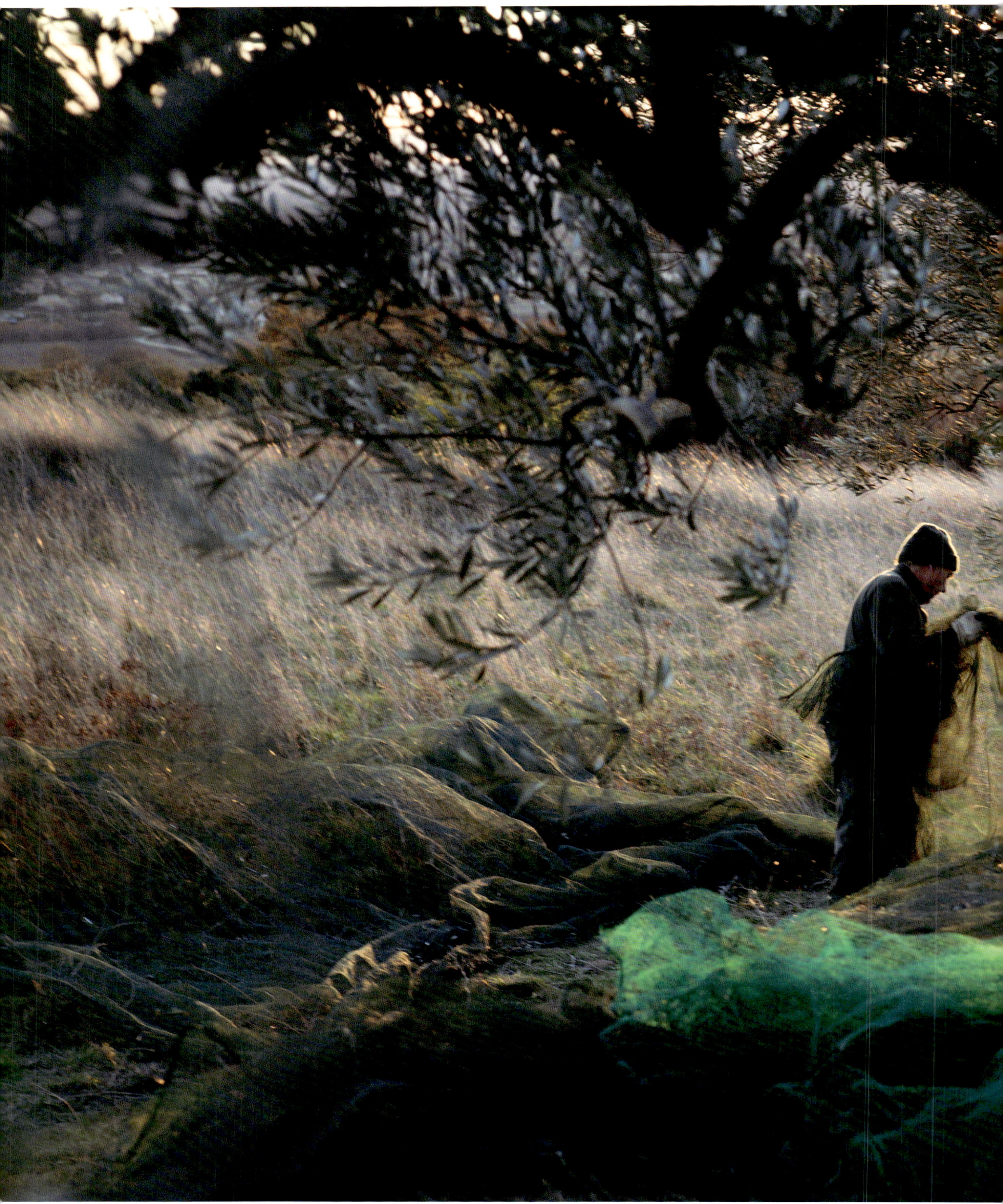

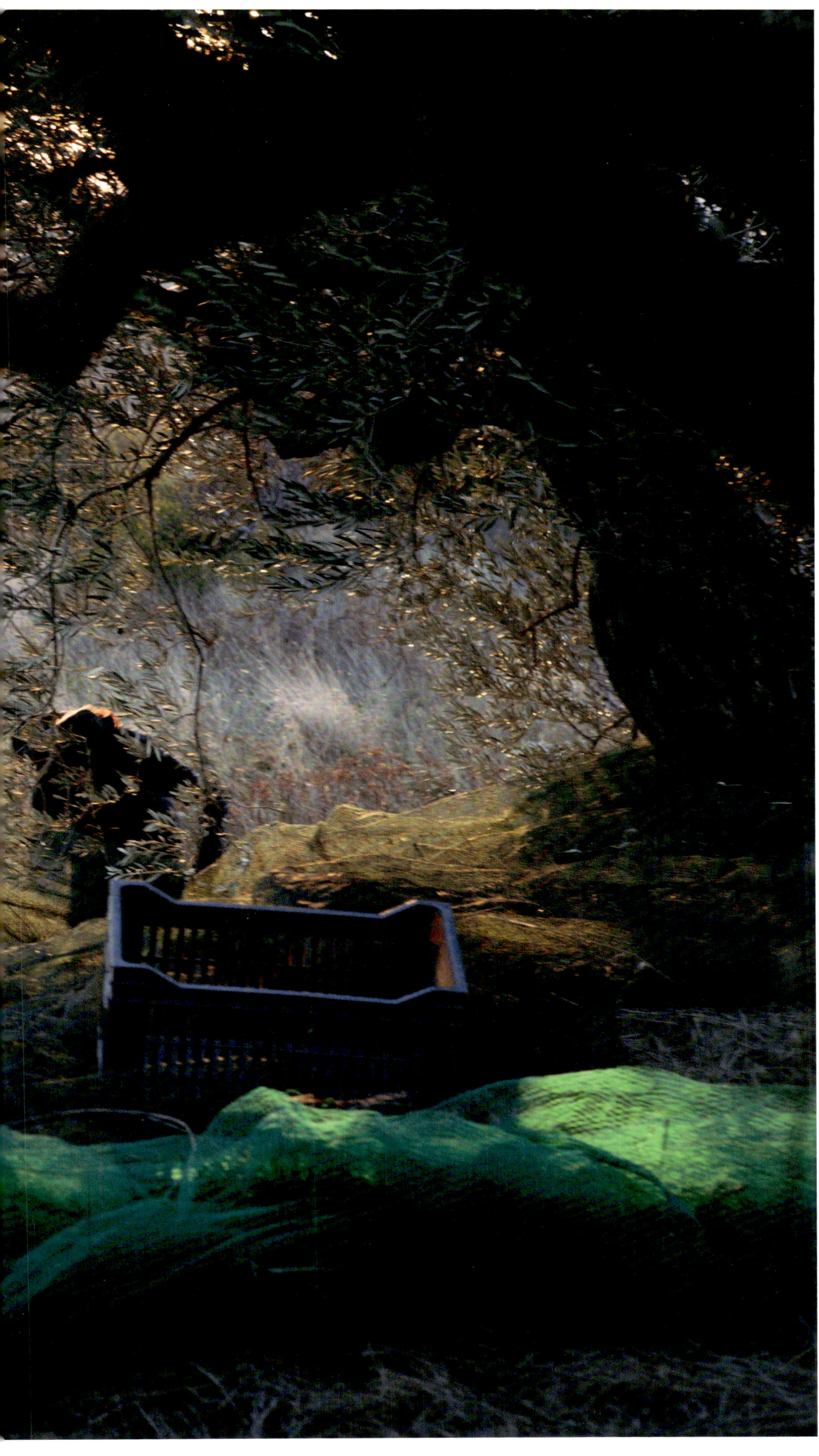

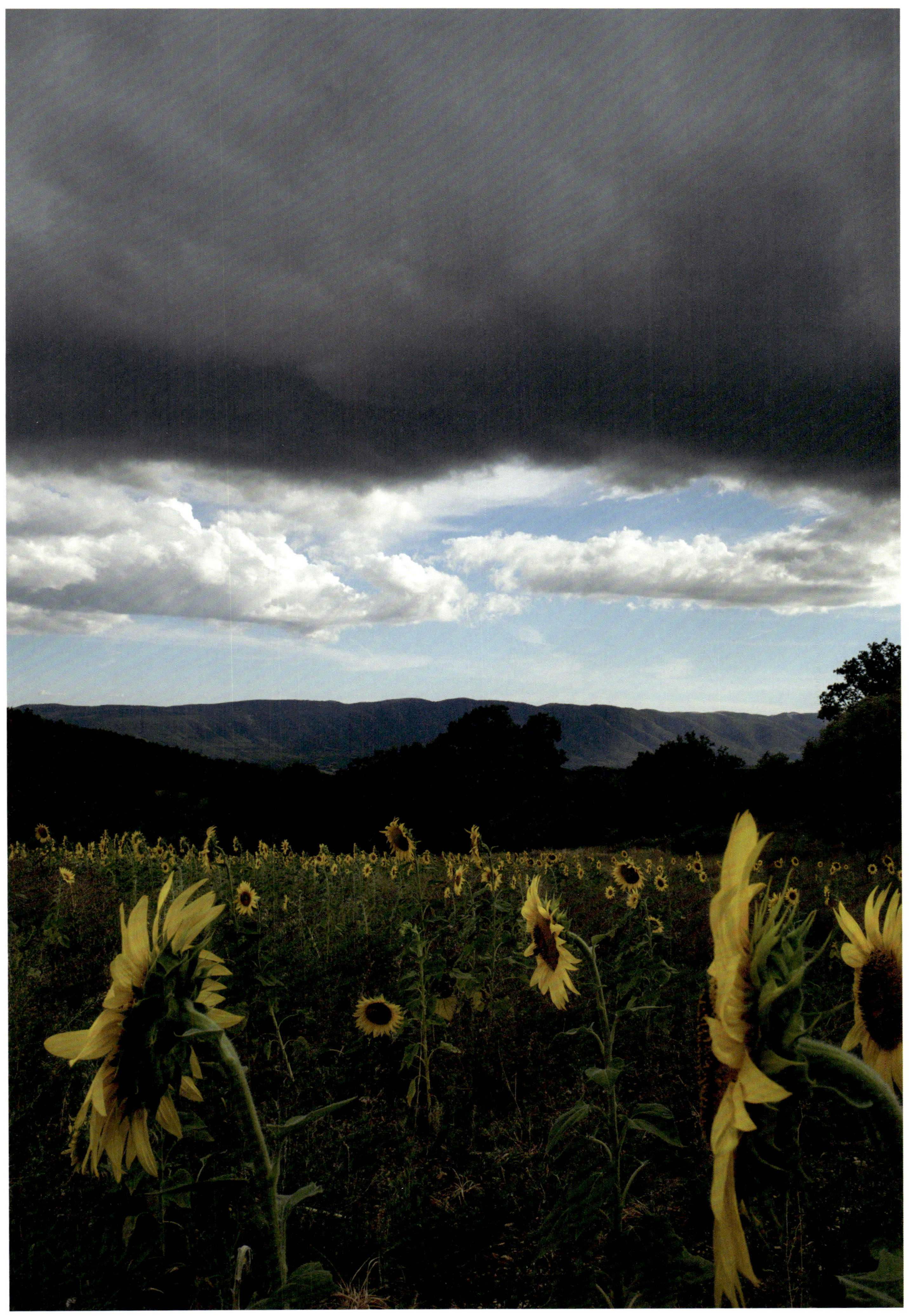

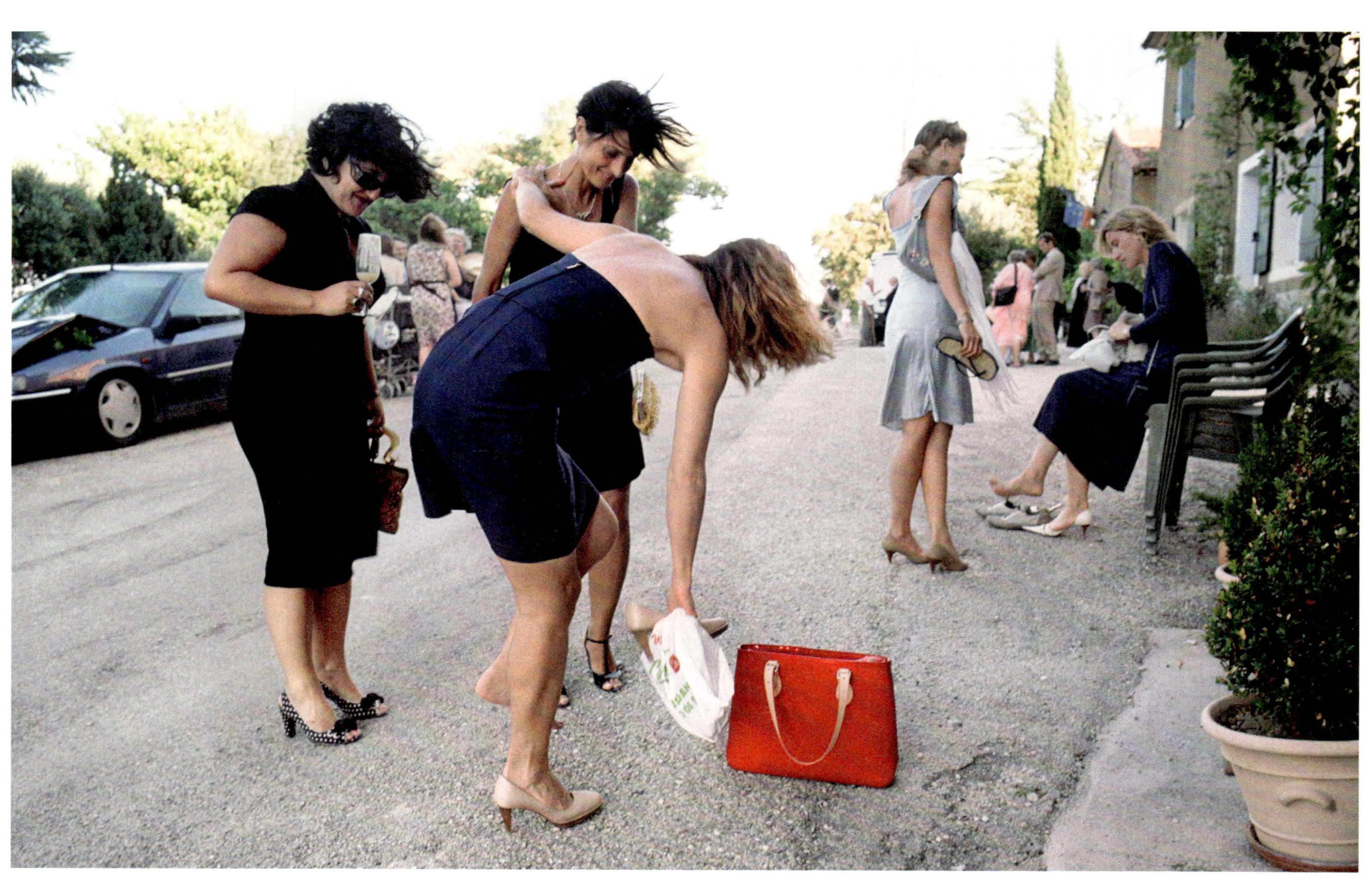

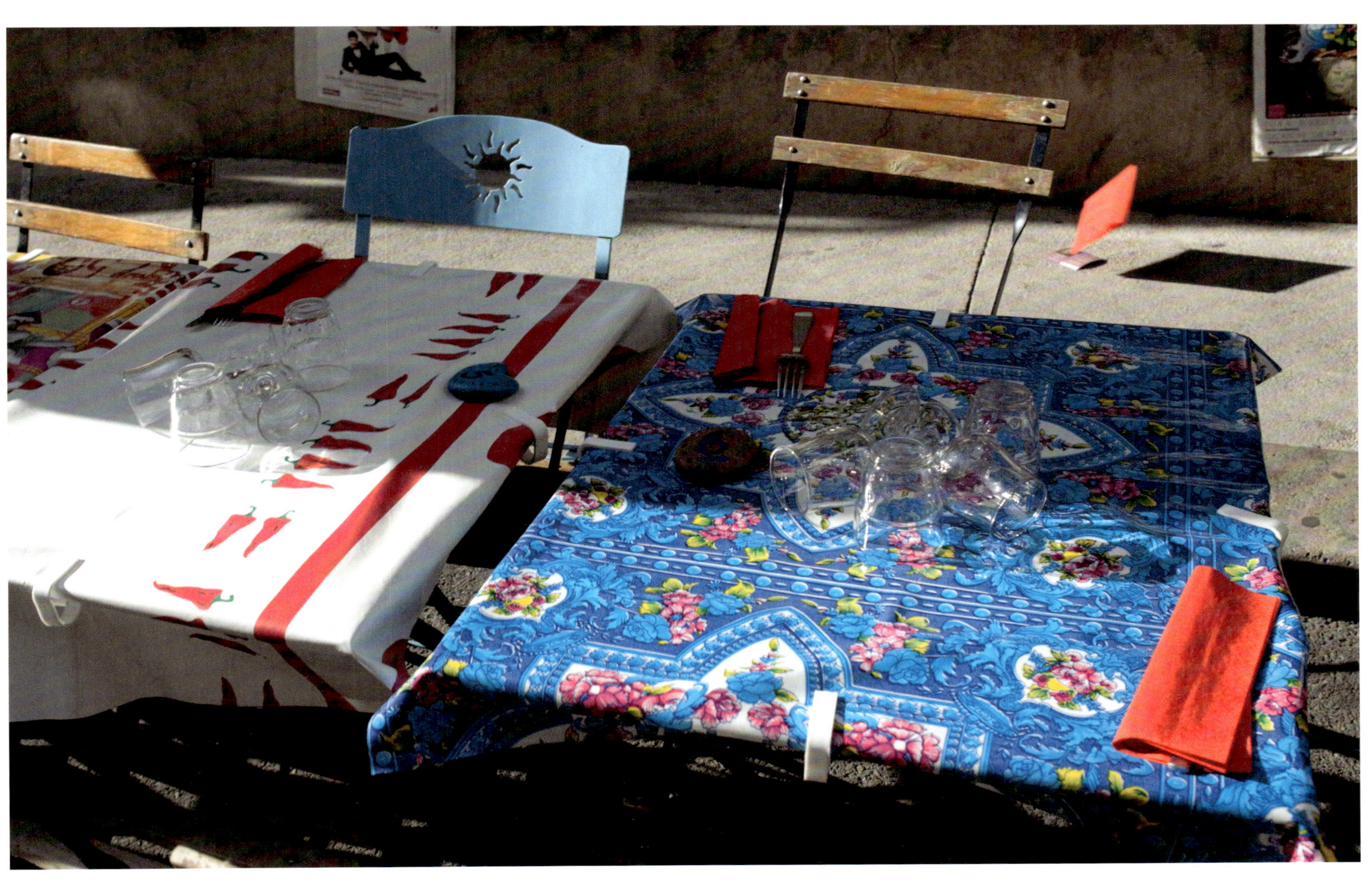

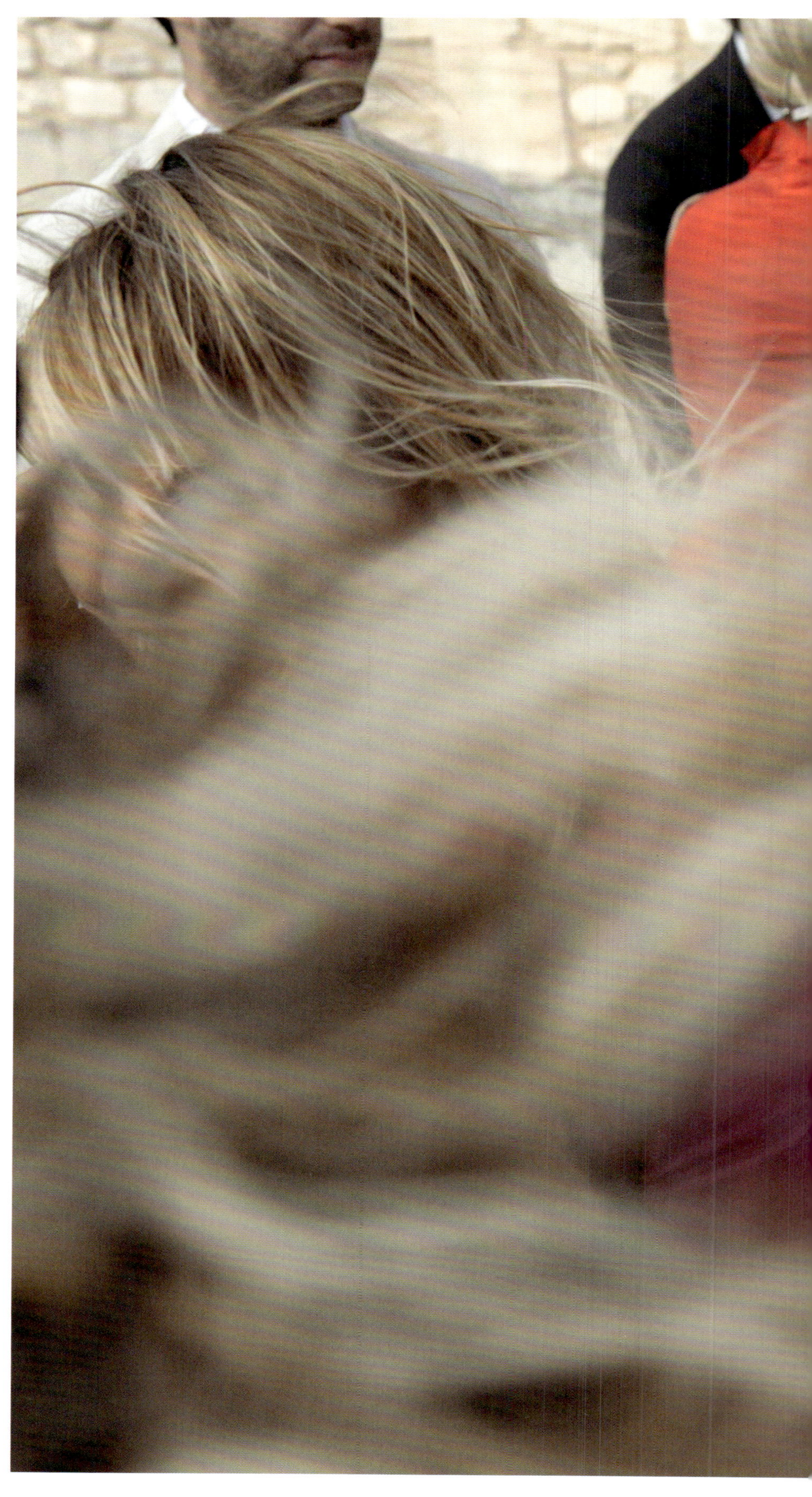

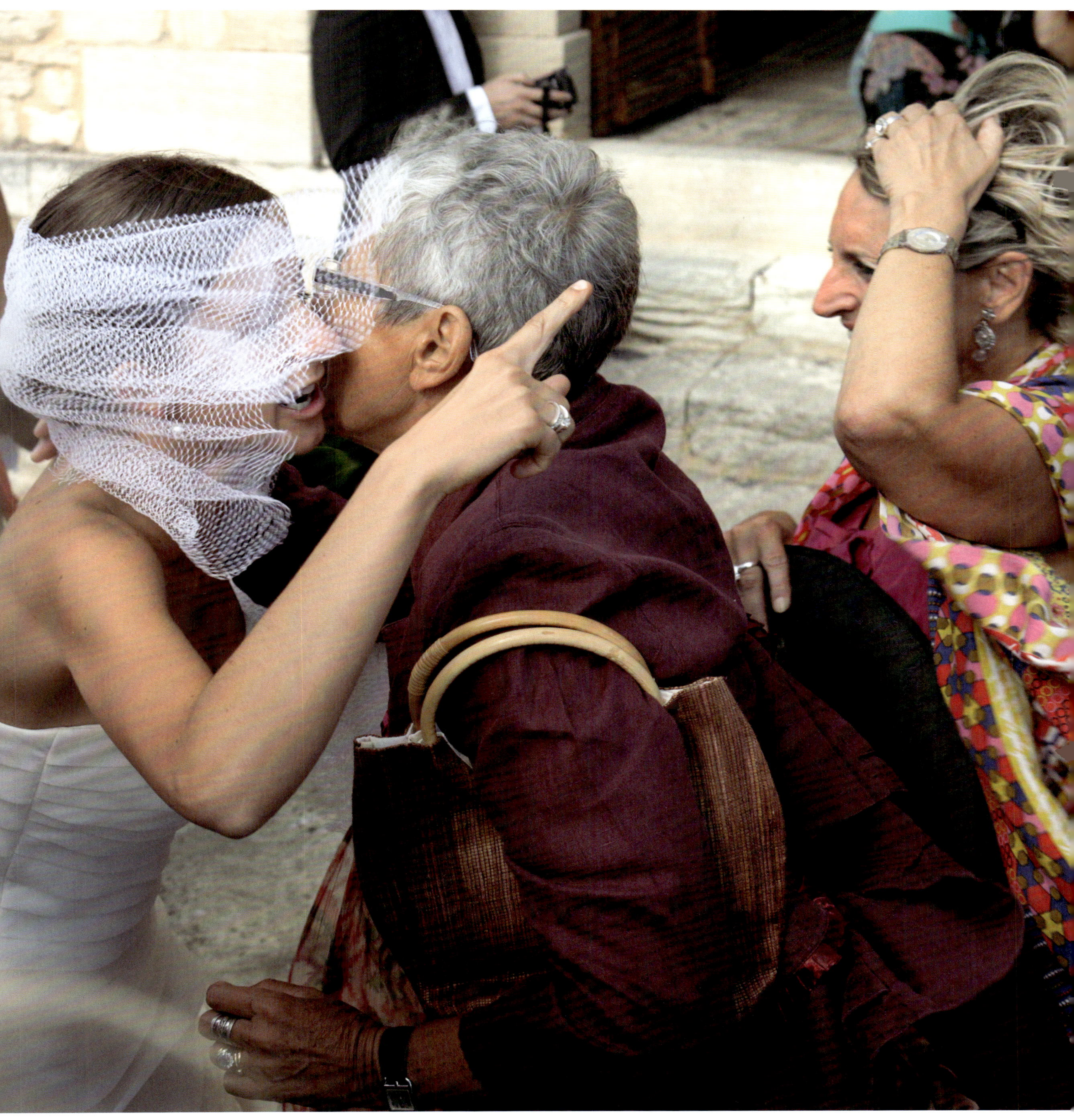

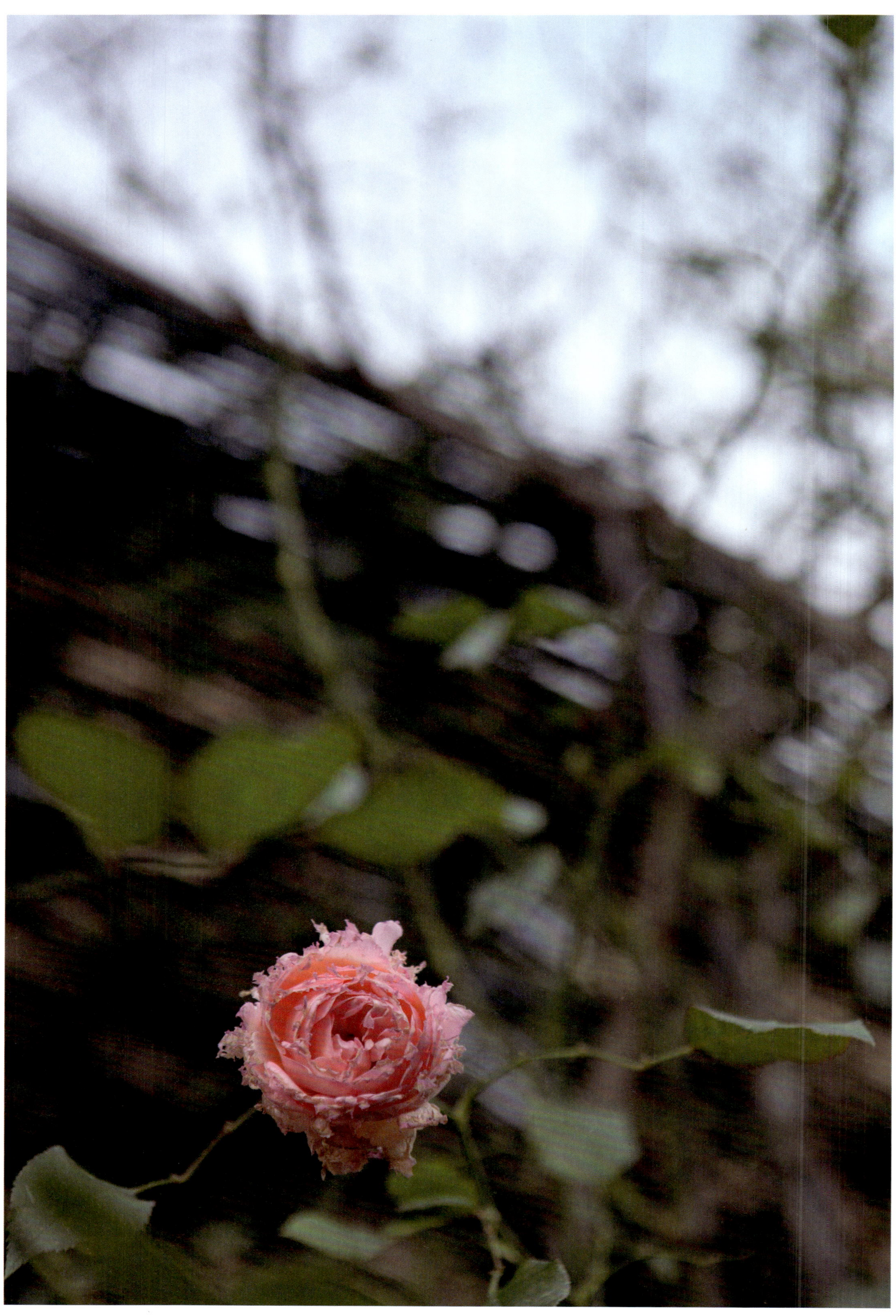

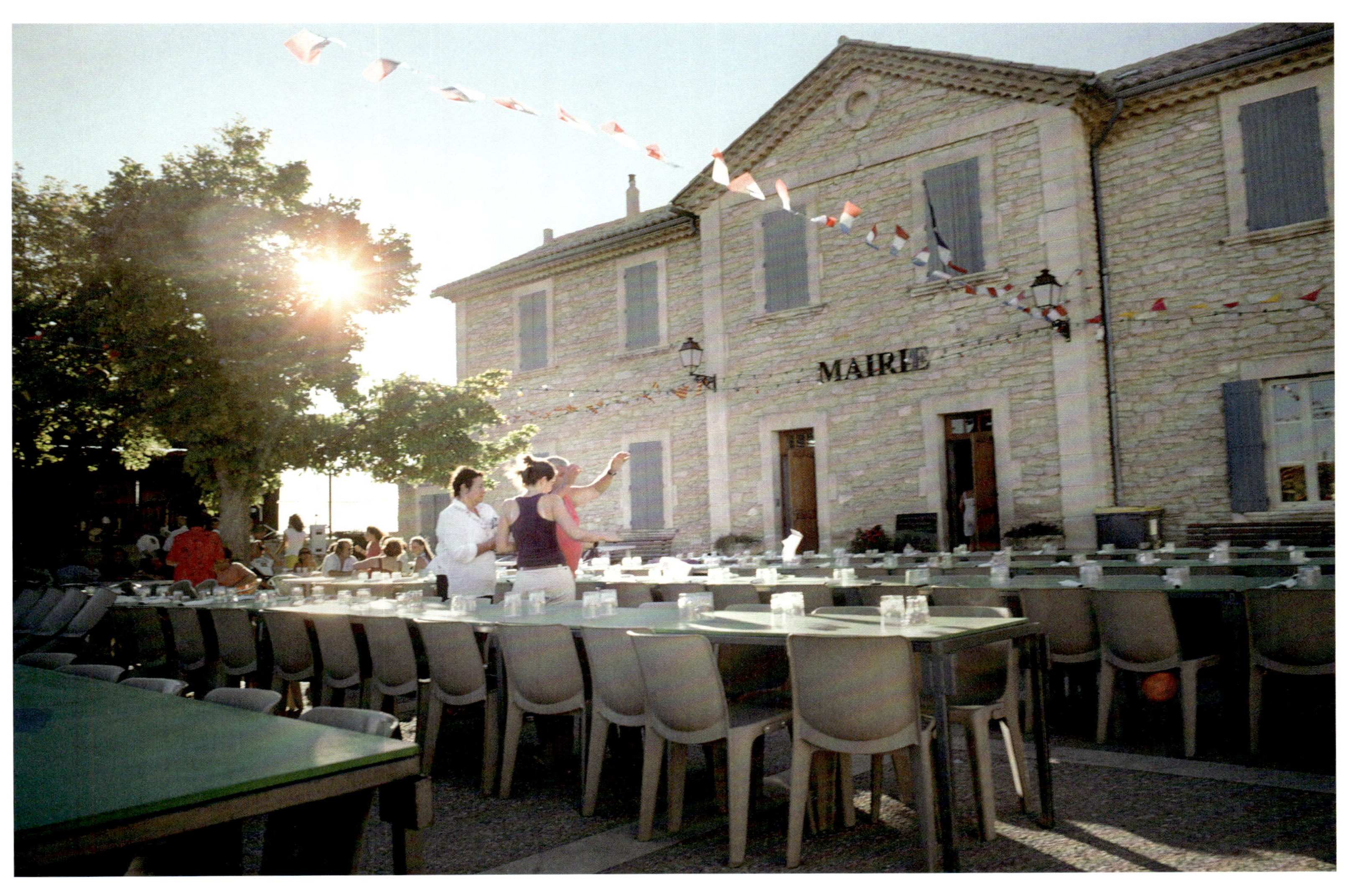
MAIRIE

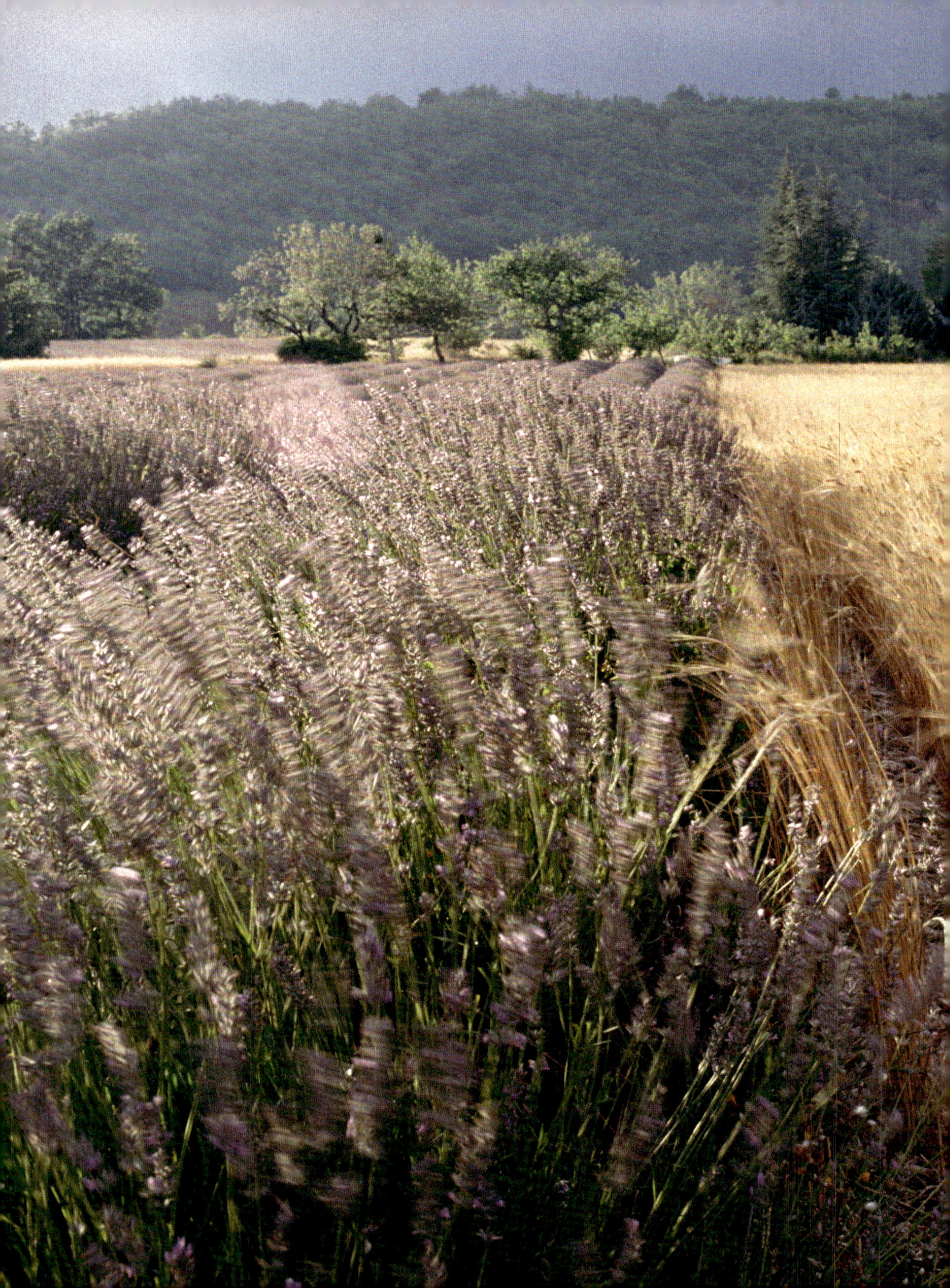

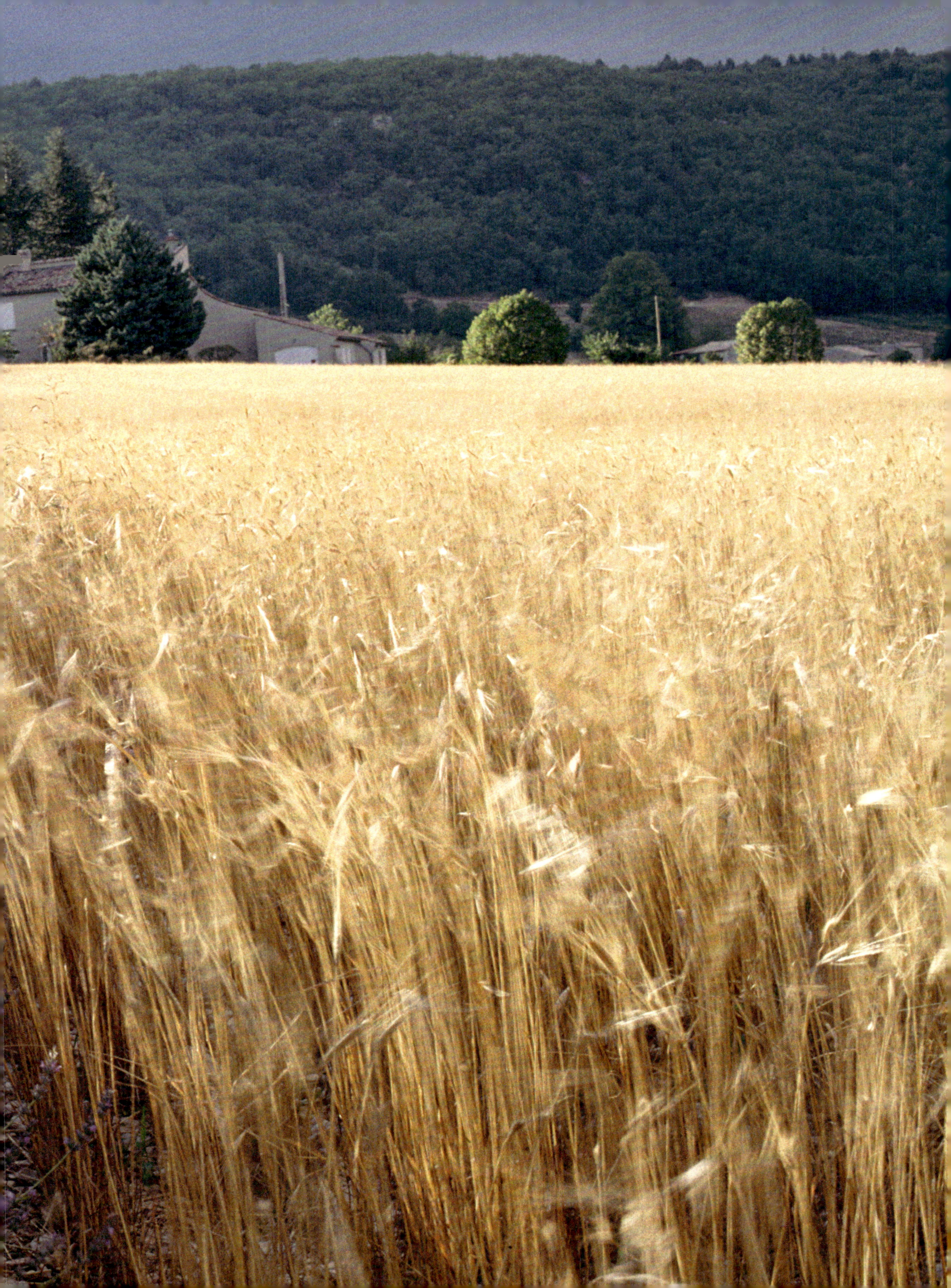

Wildly rushing, clouds outleaping,
Care-destroying, Heaven sweeping,
Mistral wind, thou art my friend!
Surely 'twas one womb did bear us,
Surely 'twas one fate did pair us,
Fellows for a common end.

—Friedrich Nietzsche,
"A Dancing Song to the Mistral Wind,"
The Joyful Wisdom

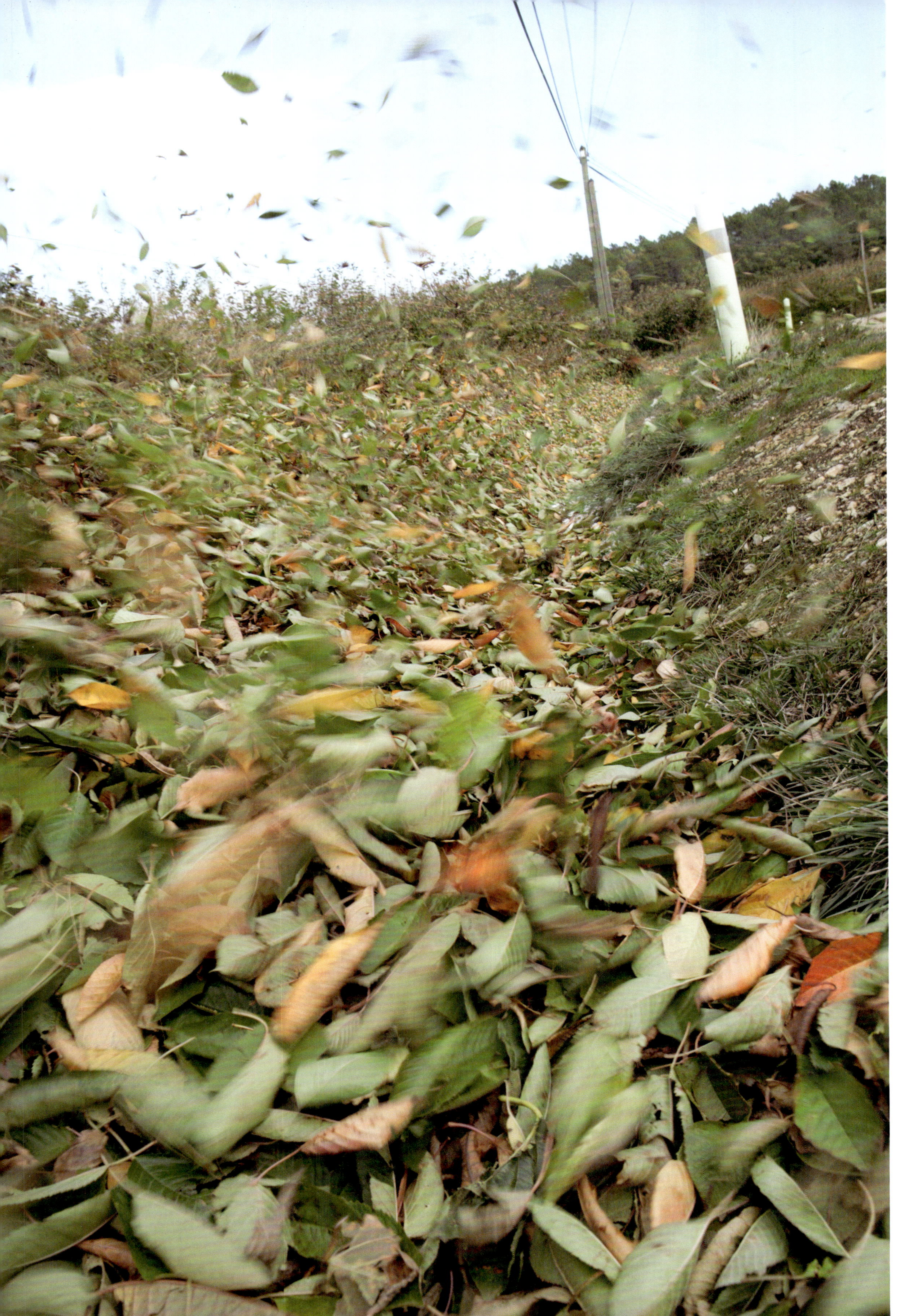

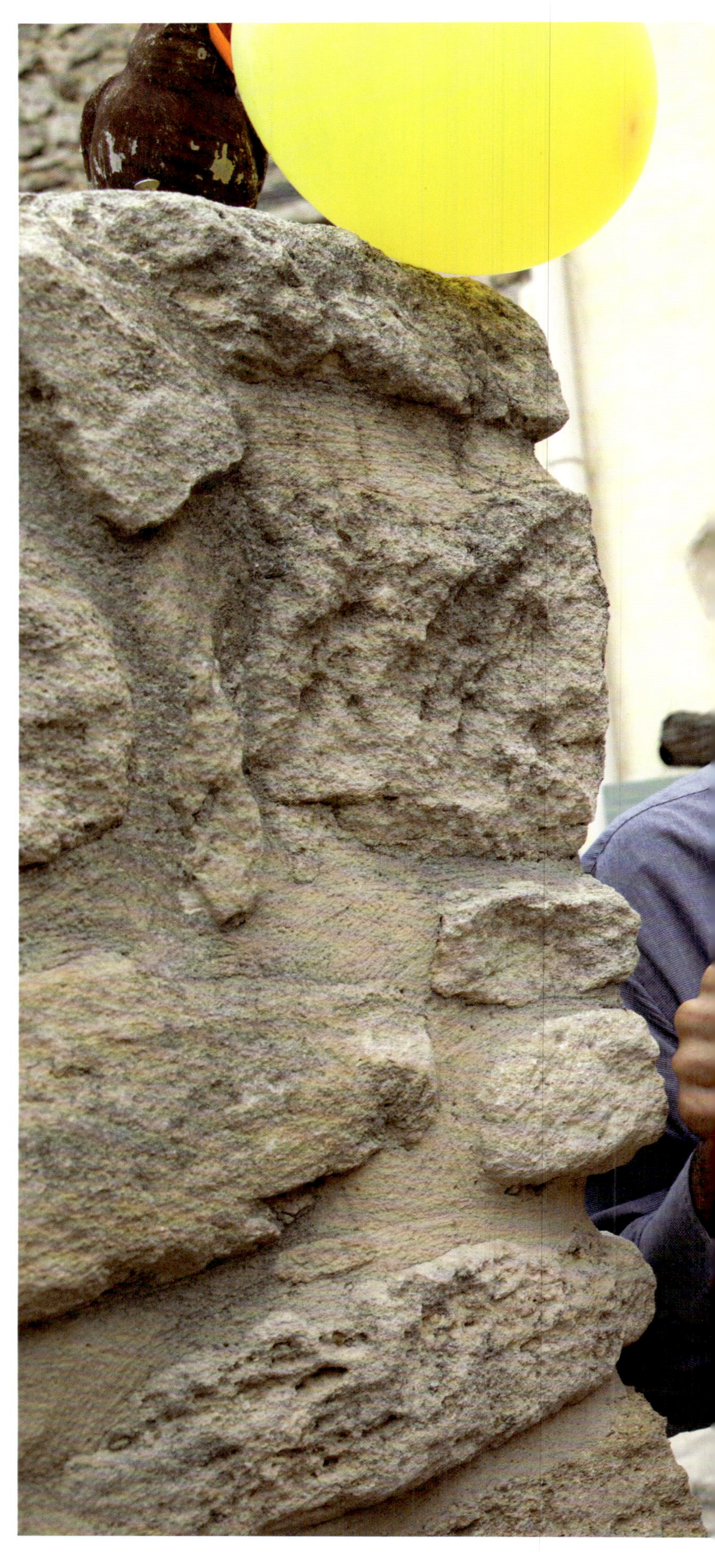

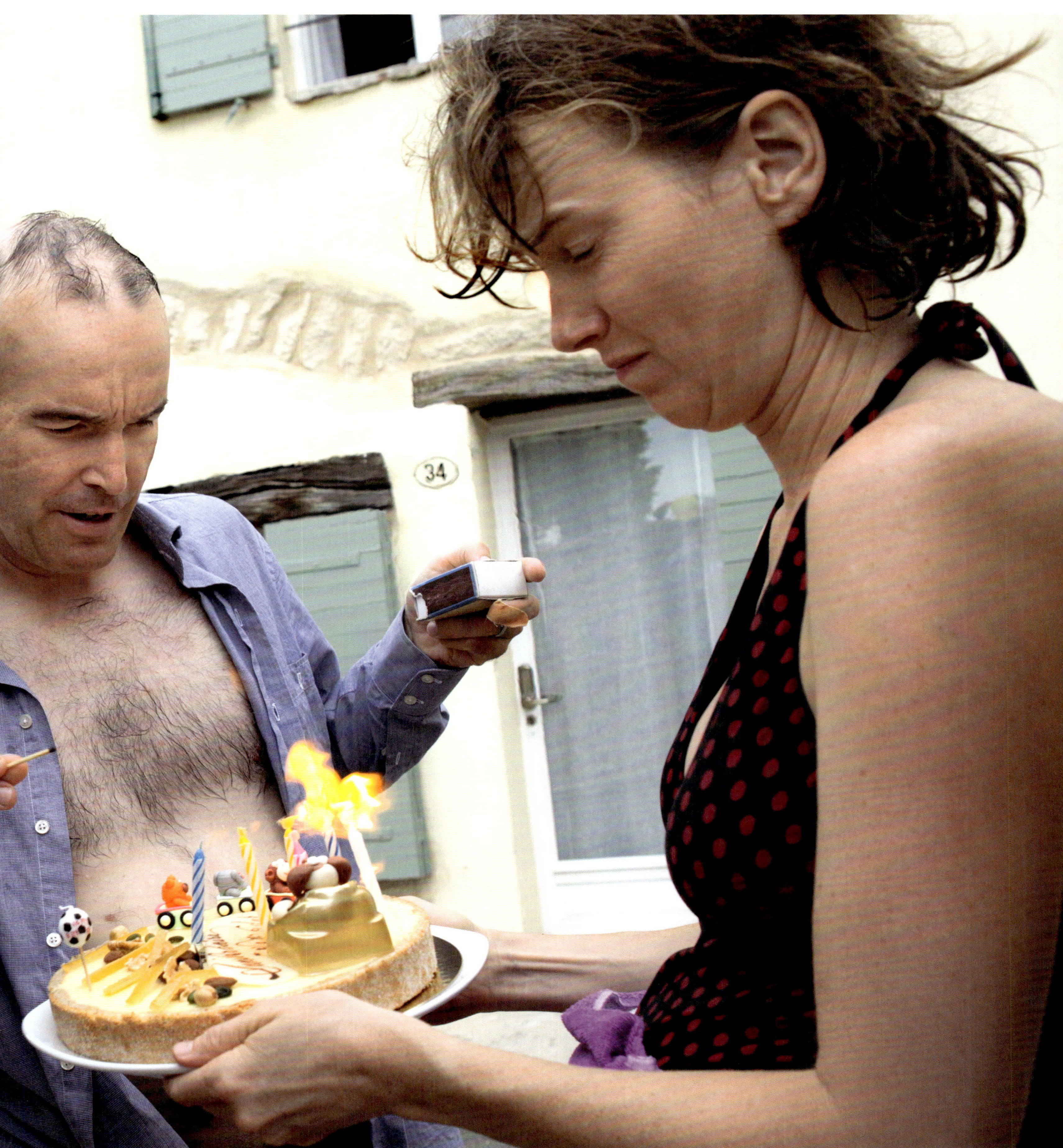
34

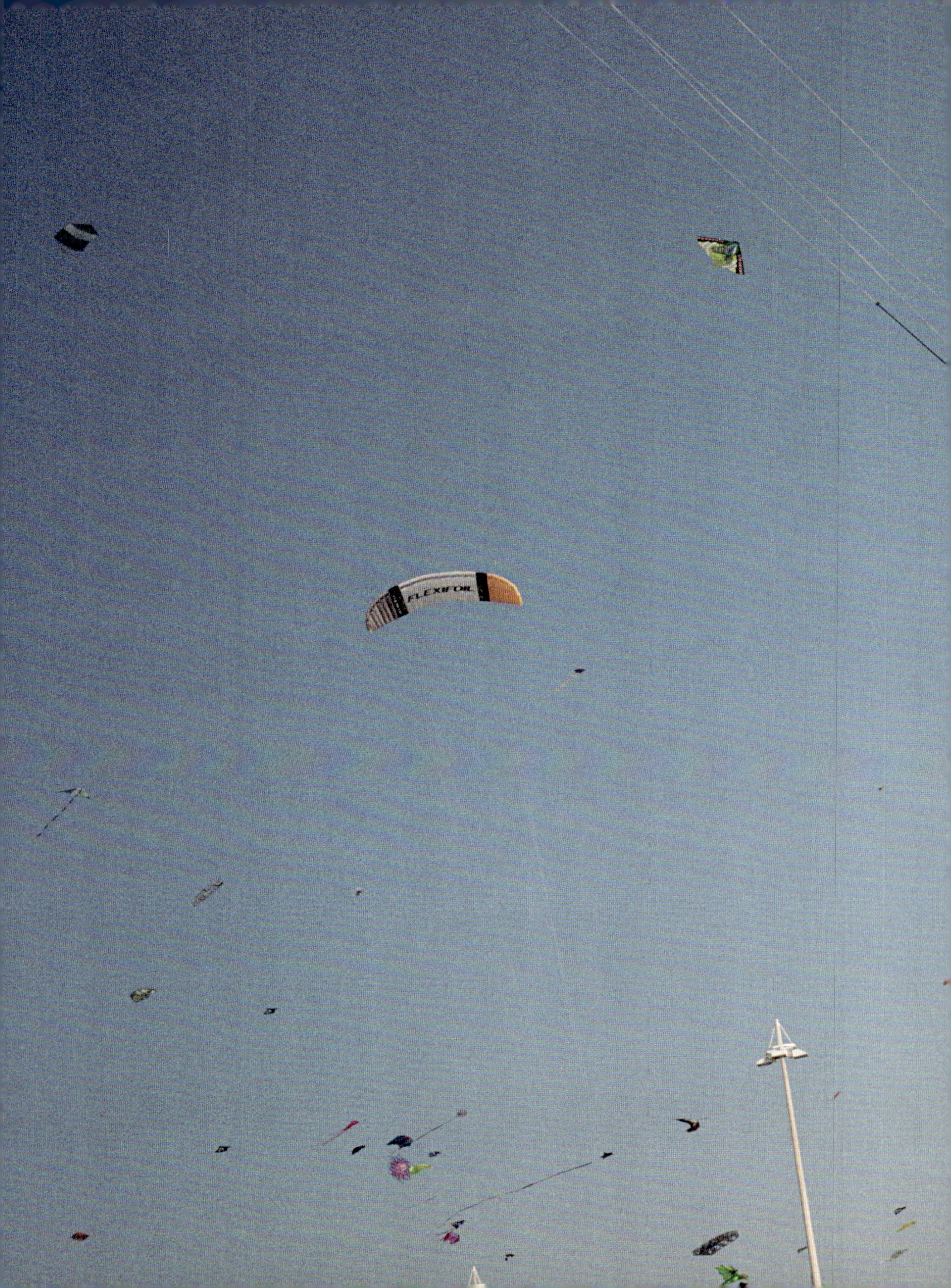
FLEXIFOIL

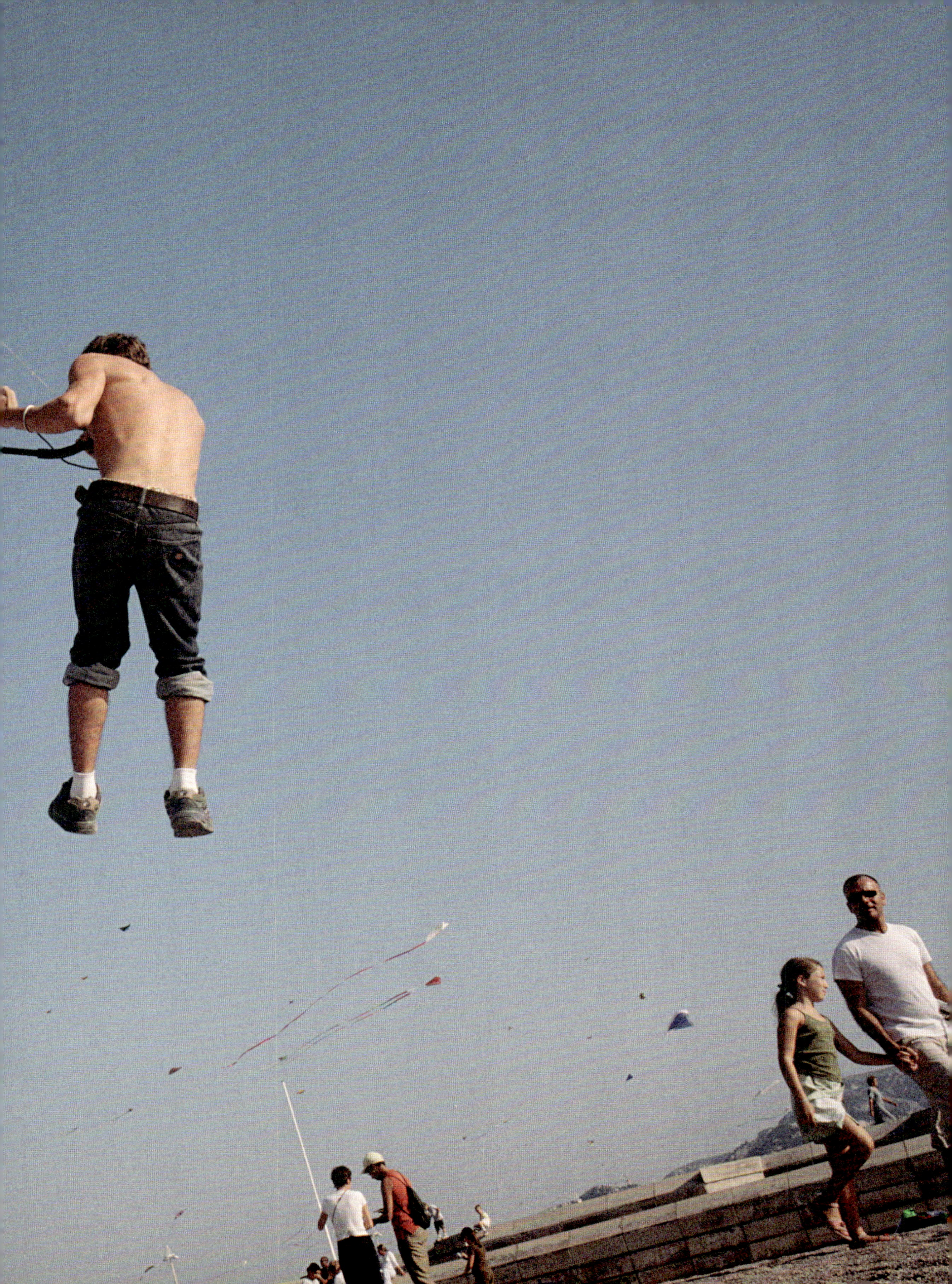

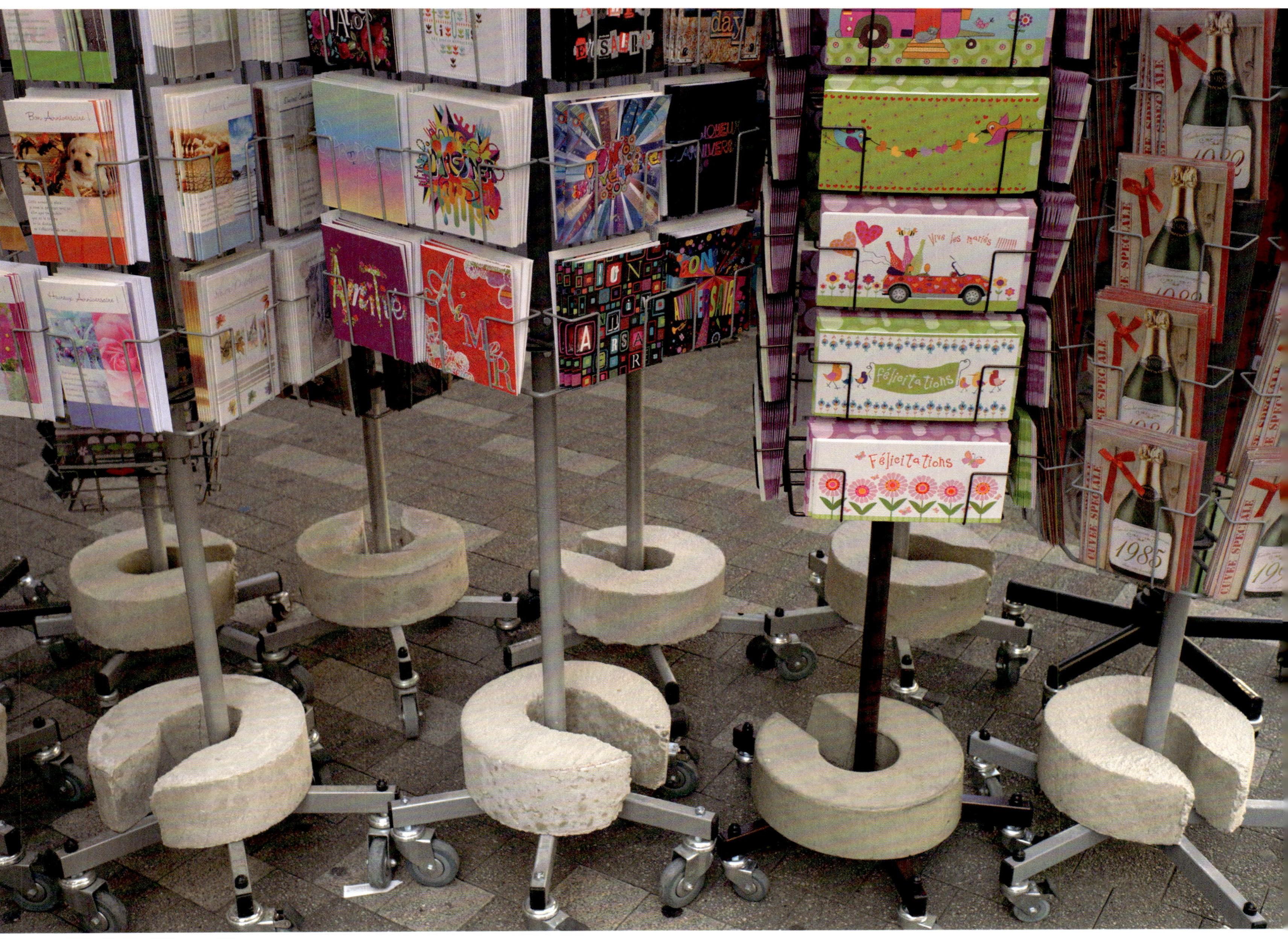
Vive les mariés
félicitations
Félicitations
1985

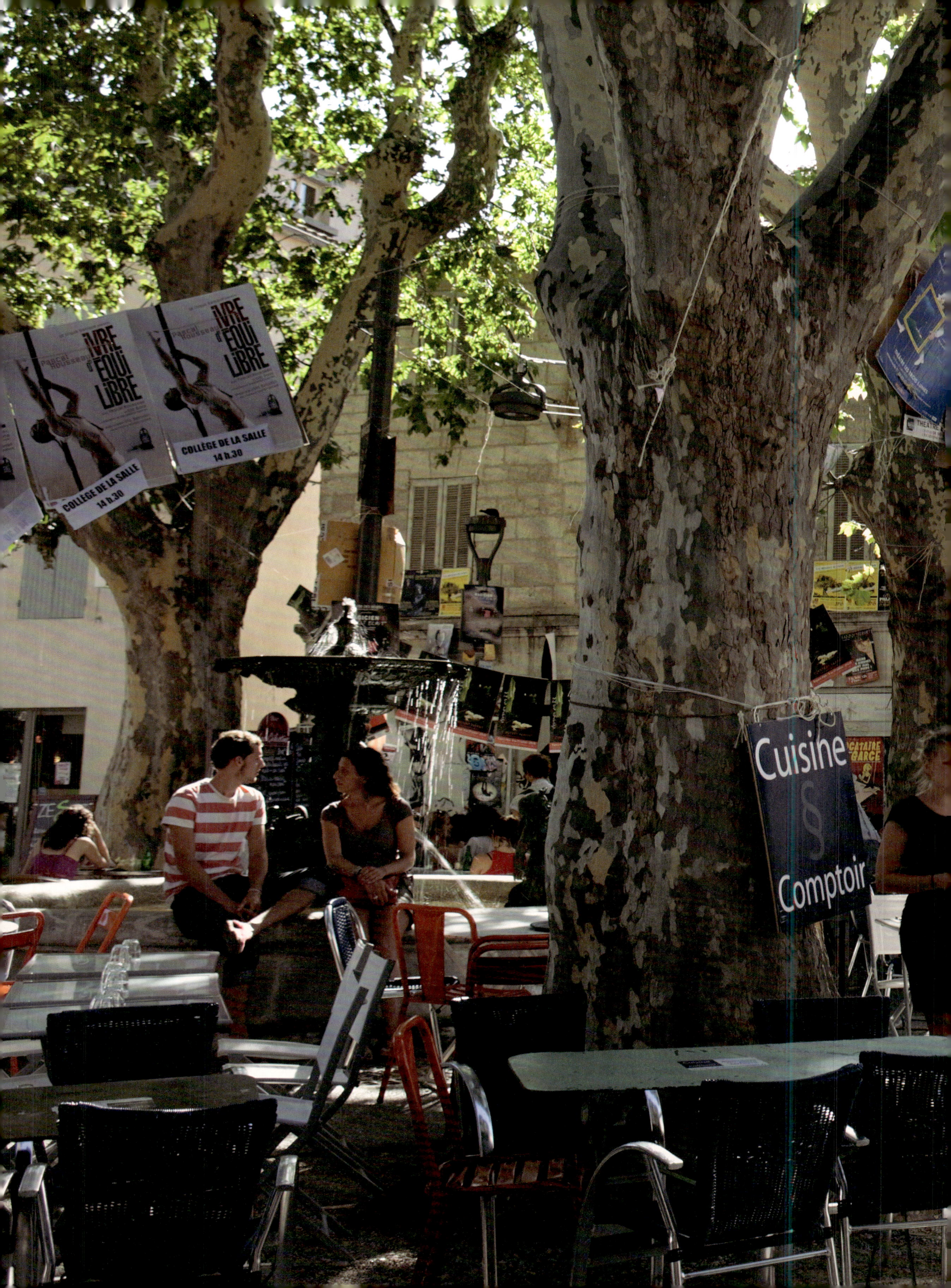

IVRE D'EQUILIBRE
COLLÈGE DE LA SALLE
14 h.30
IVRE D'EQUILIBRE
COLLÈGE DE LA SALLE
14 h.30
Cuisine
§
Comptoir

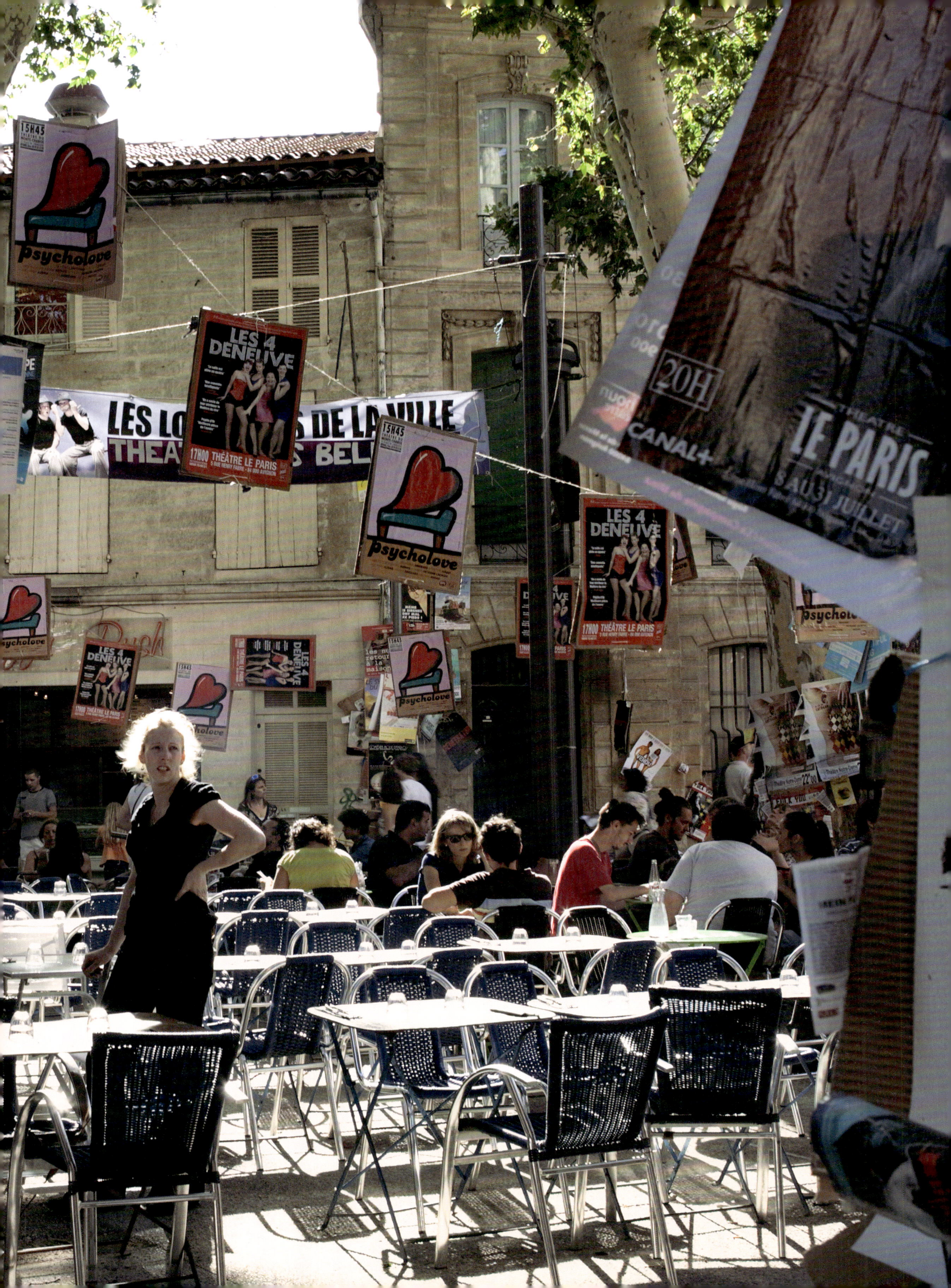

15H45
psycholove
LES 4 DENEUVE
17H00 THÉÂTRE LE PARIS
DE LA VILLE
20H
CANAL+
THÉÂTRE
LE PARIS
JUILLET

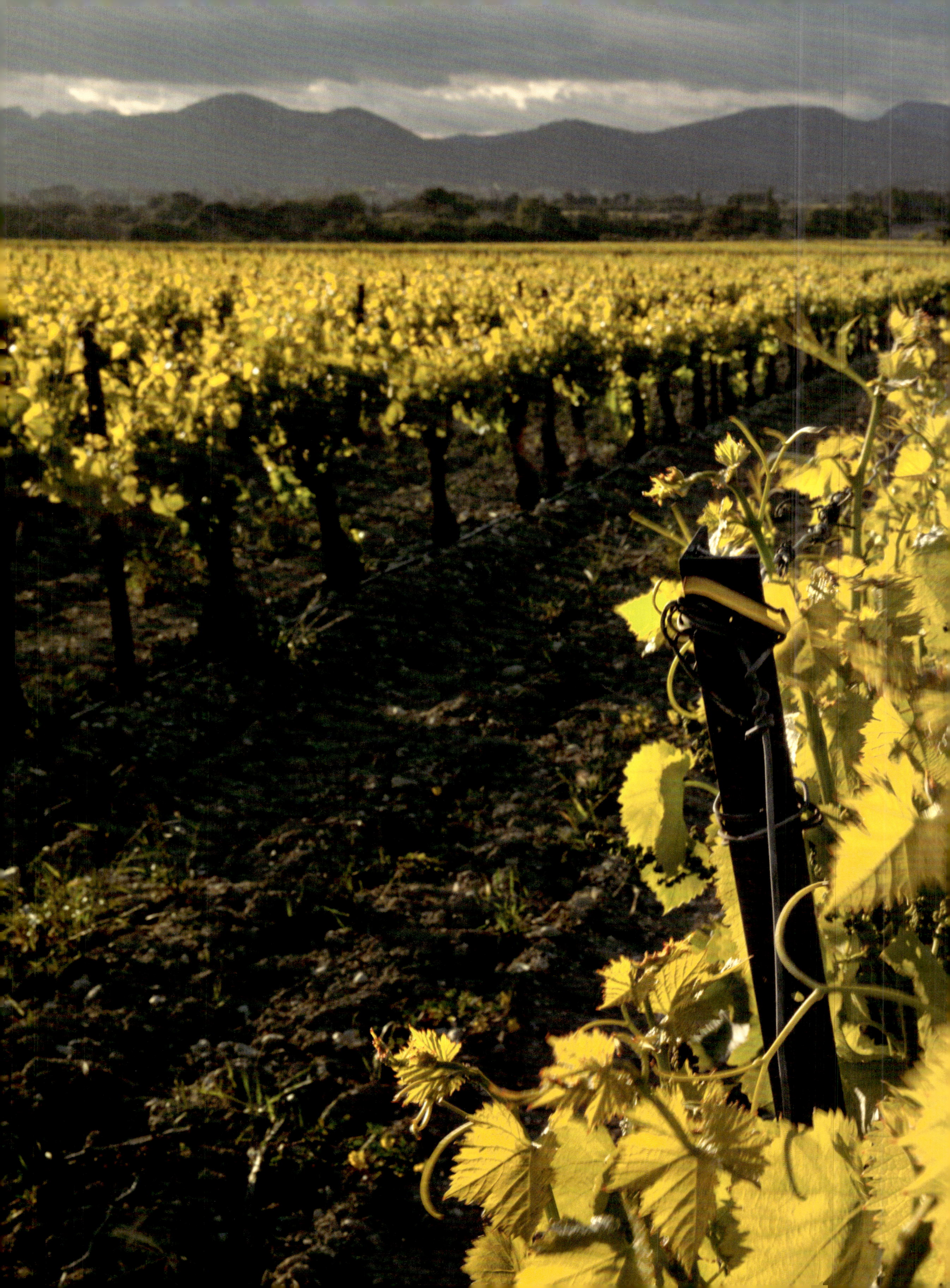

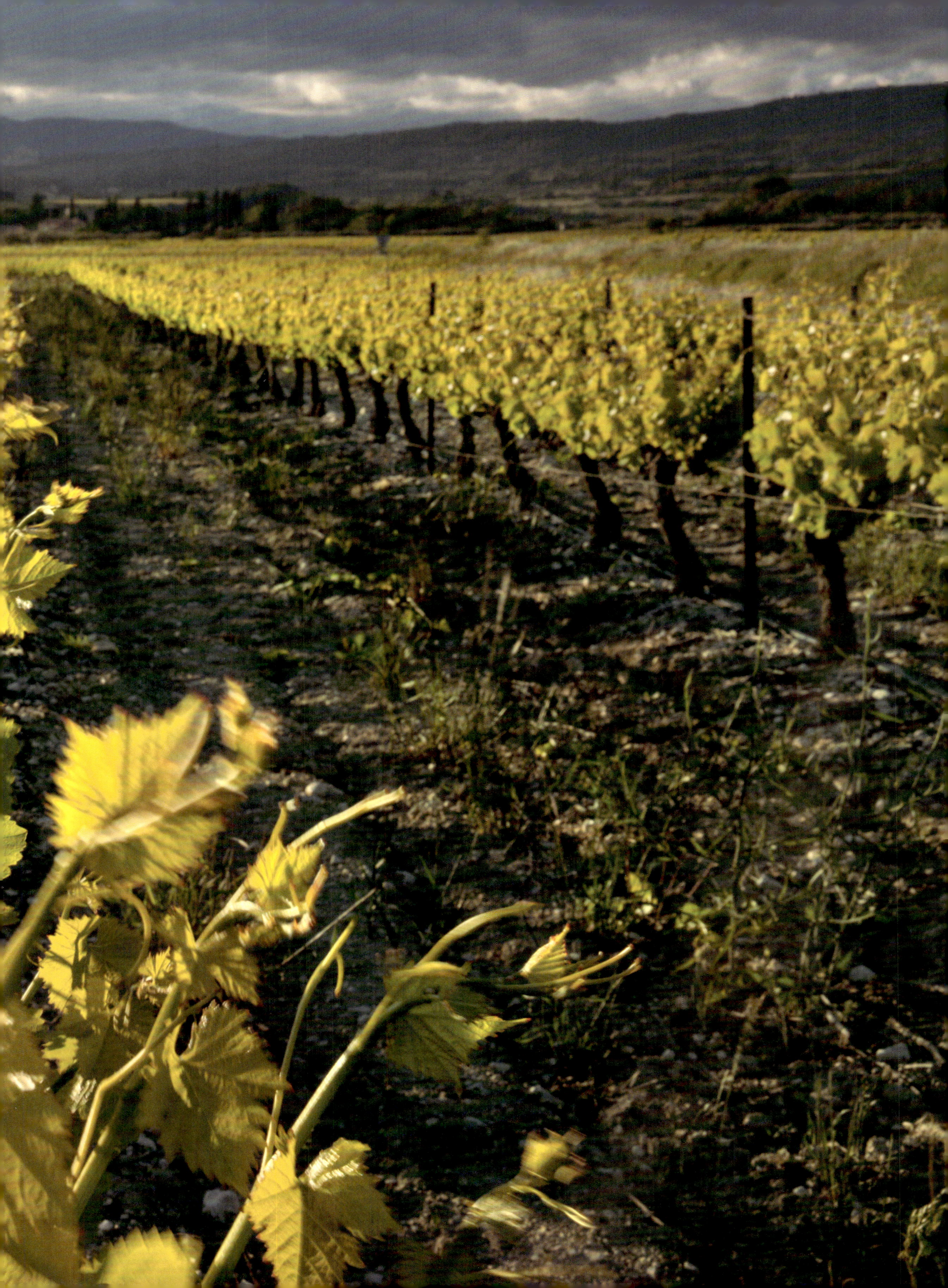

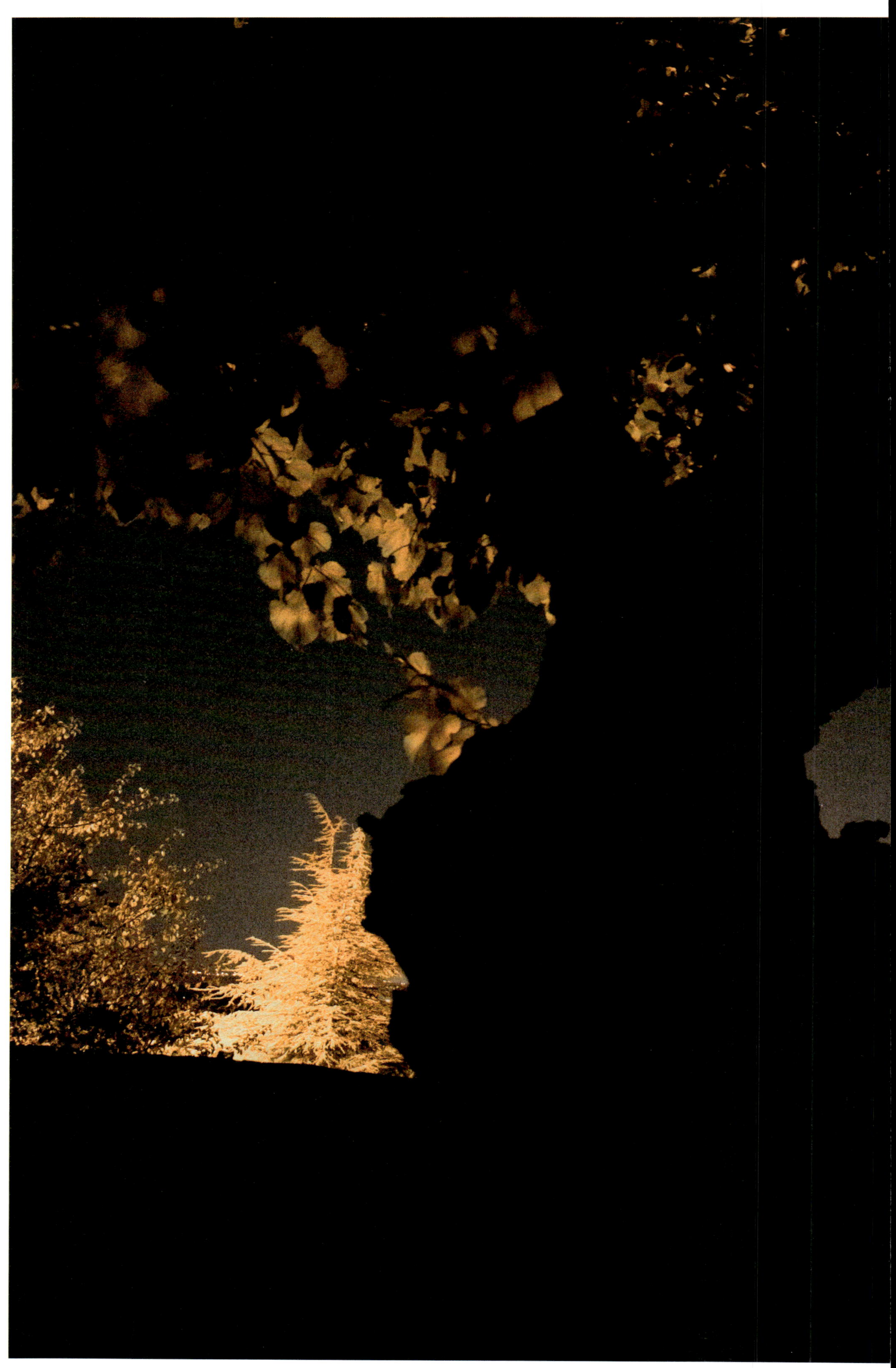

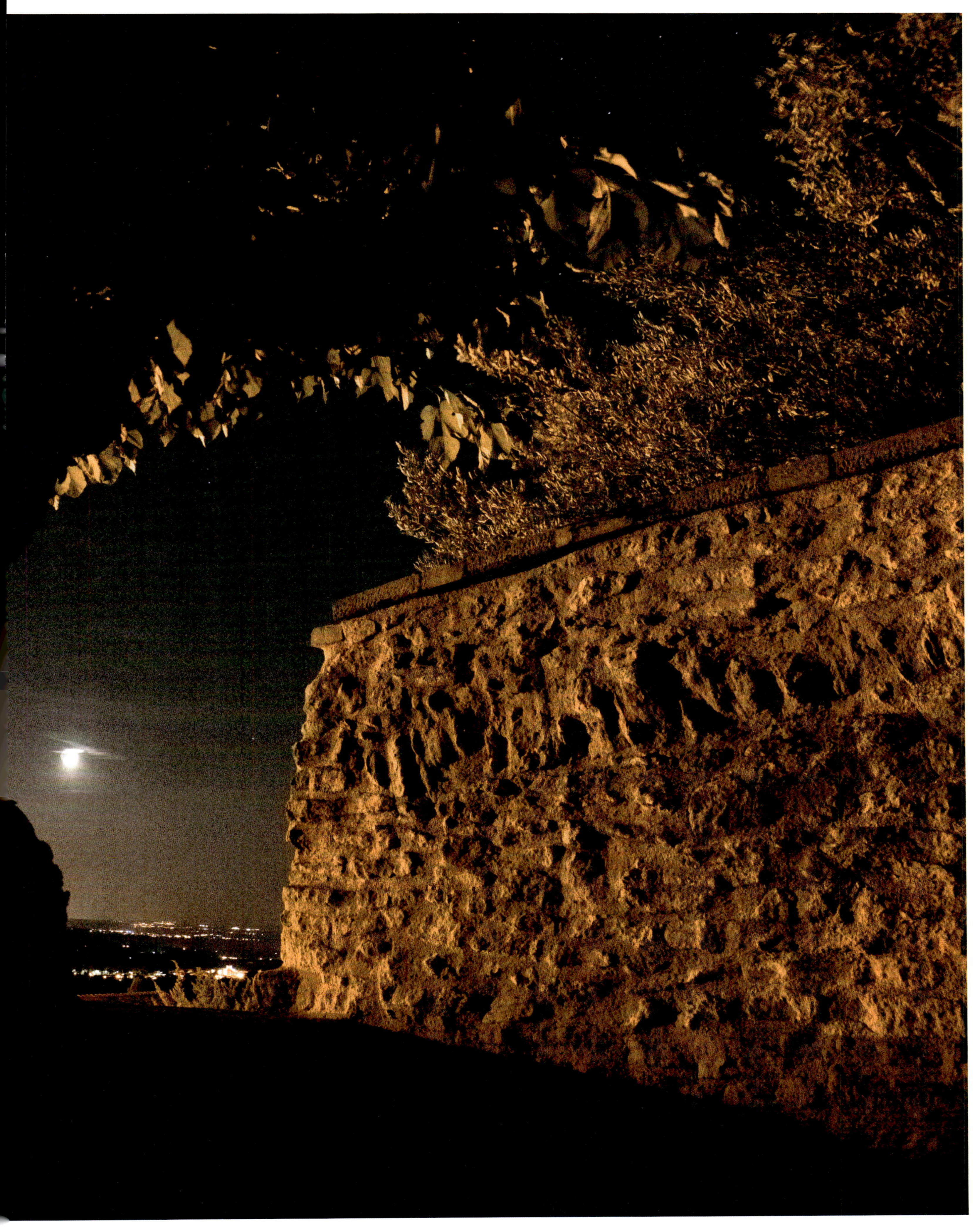

You can taste wine better

when there's a mistral blowing.

—Madame Barrot,
Domaine La Barroche, Châteauneuf-du-Pape

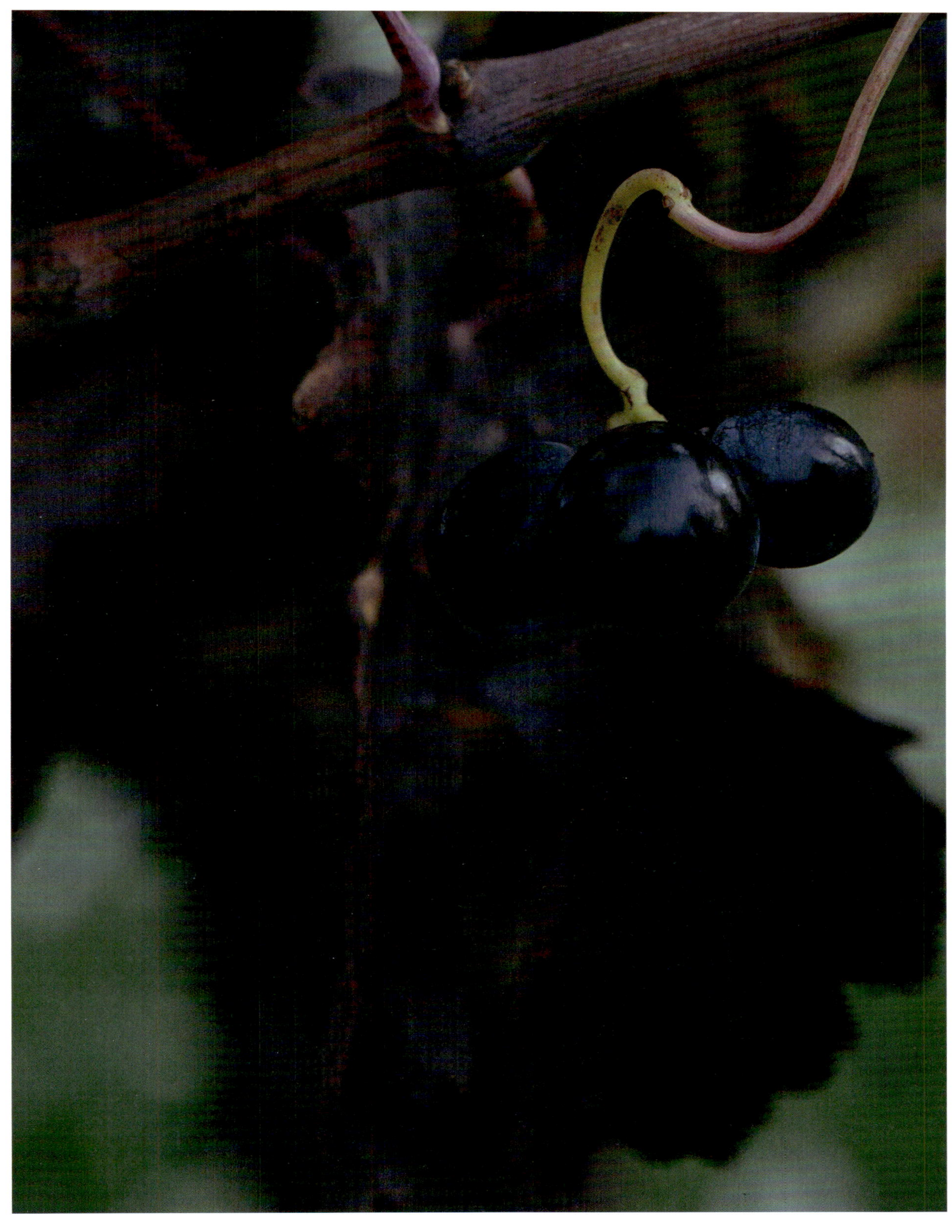

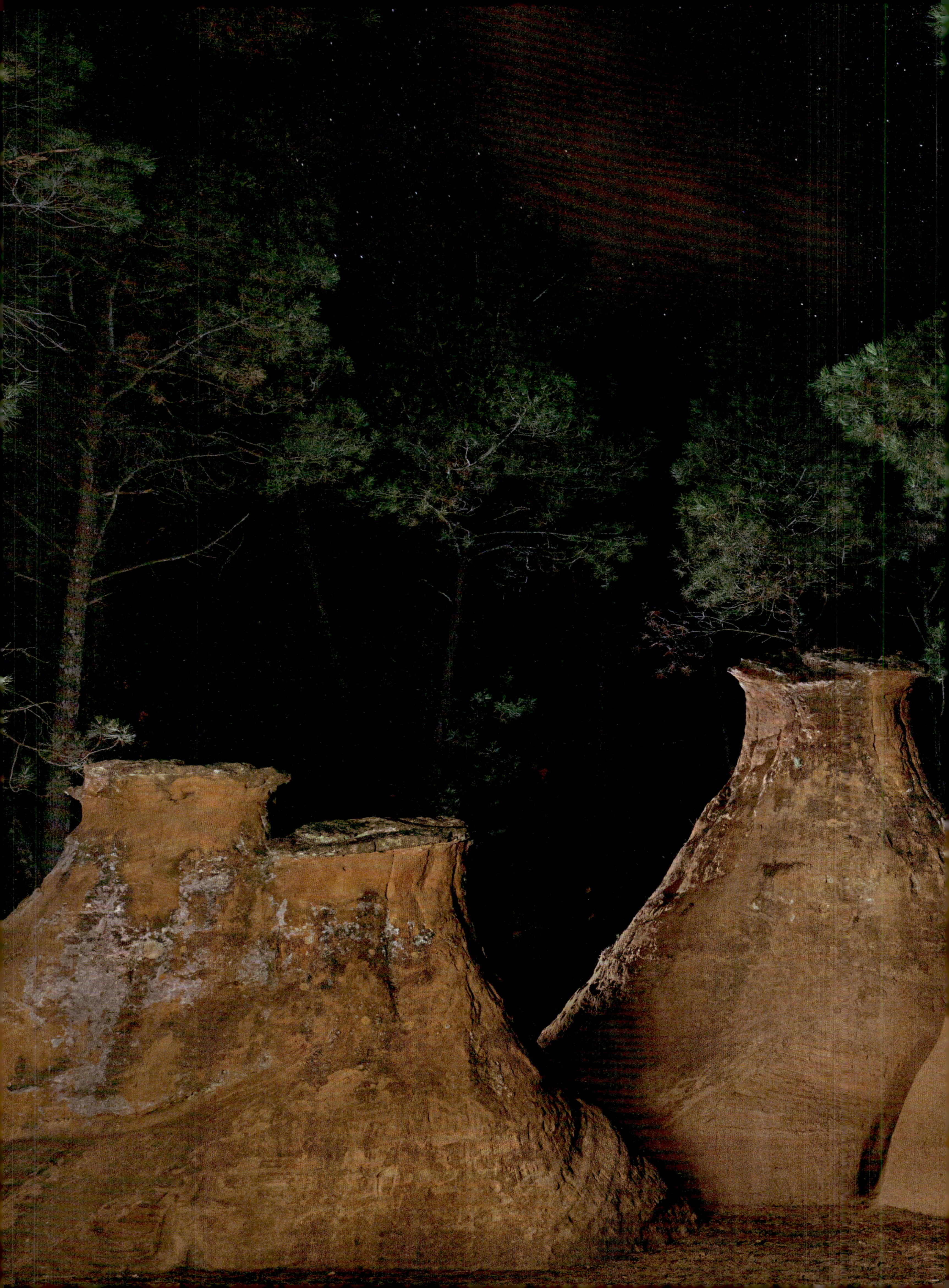

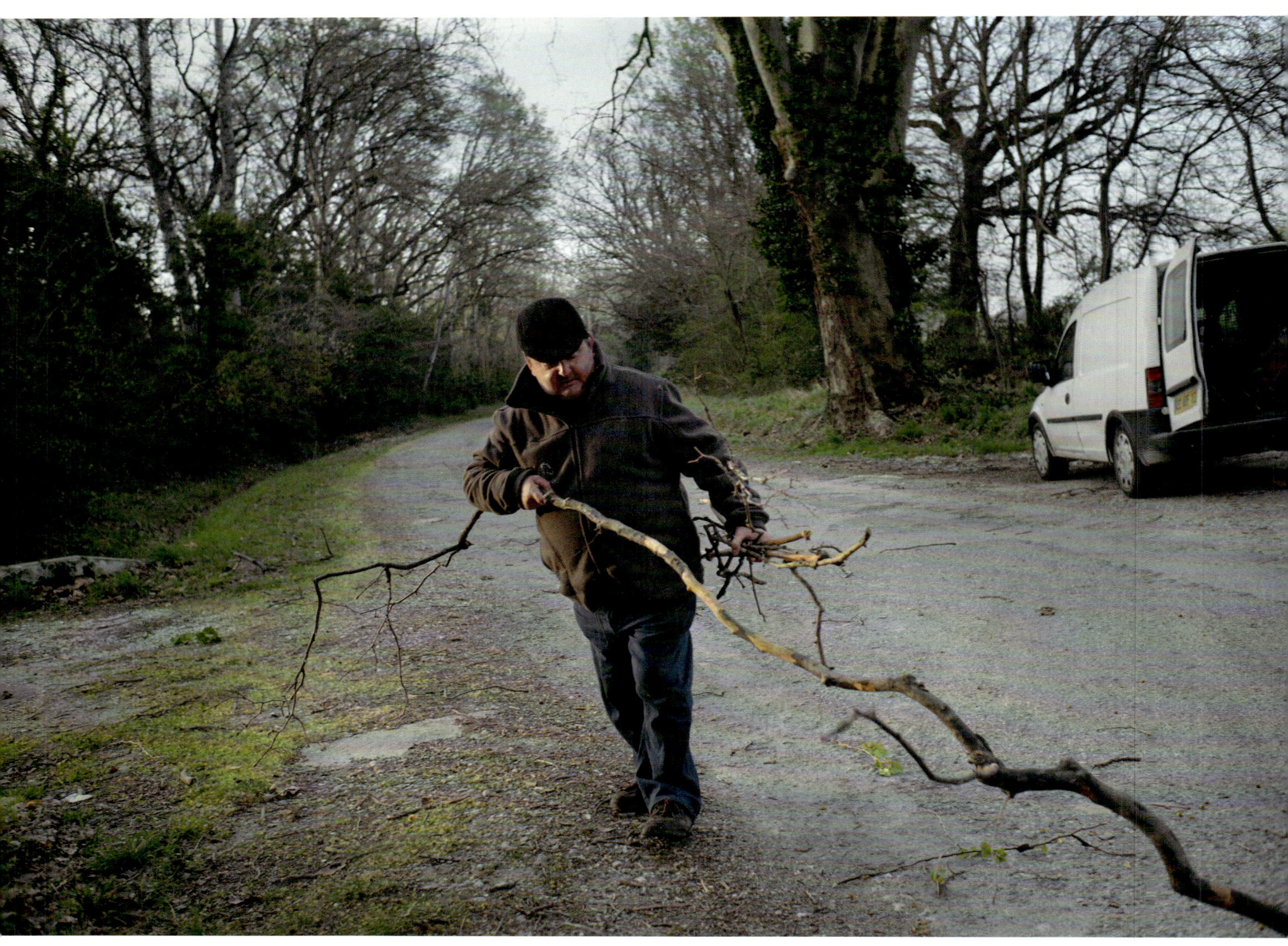

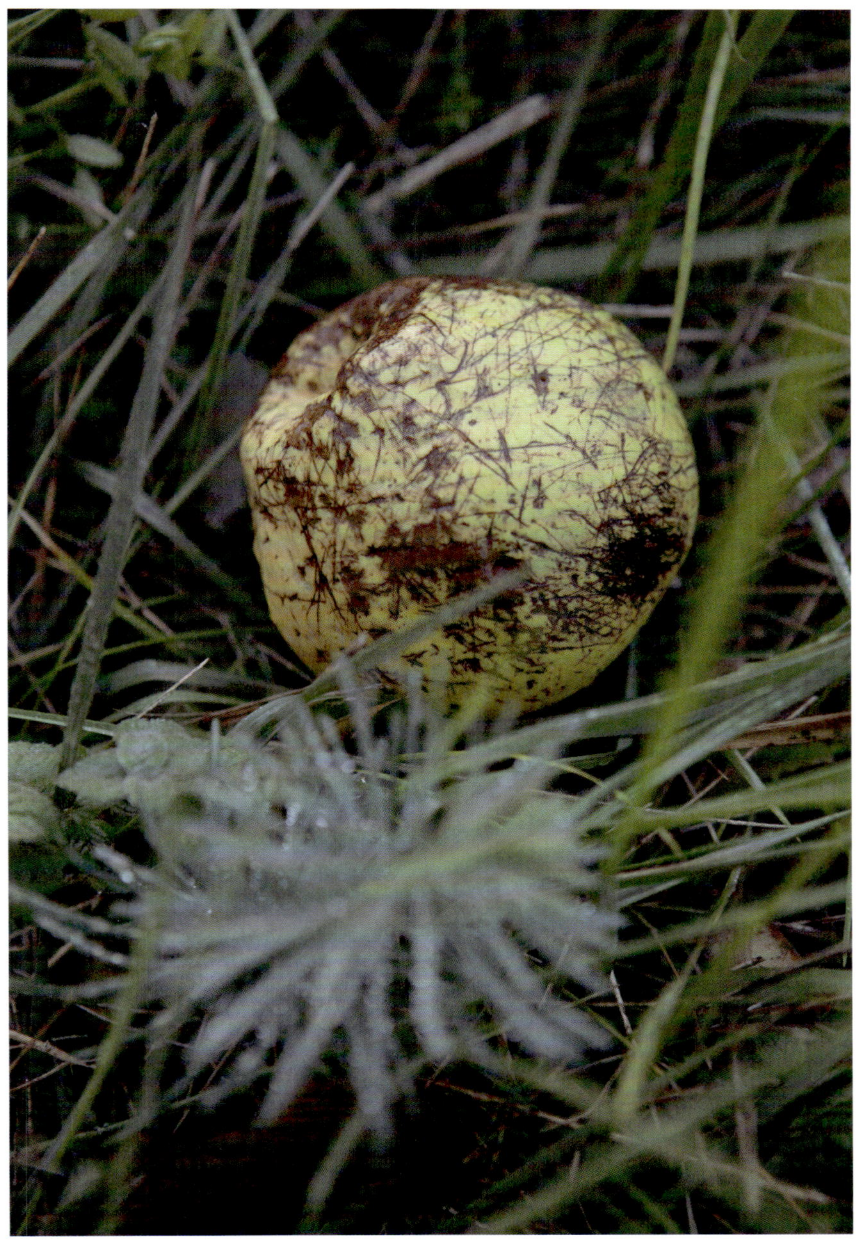

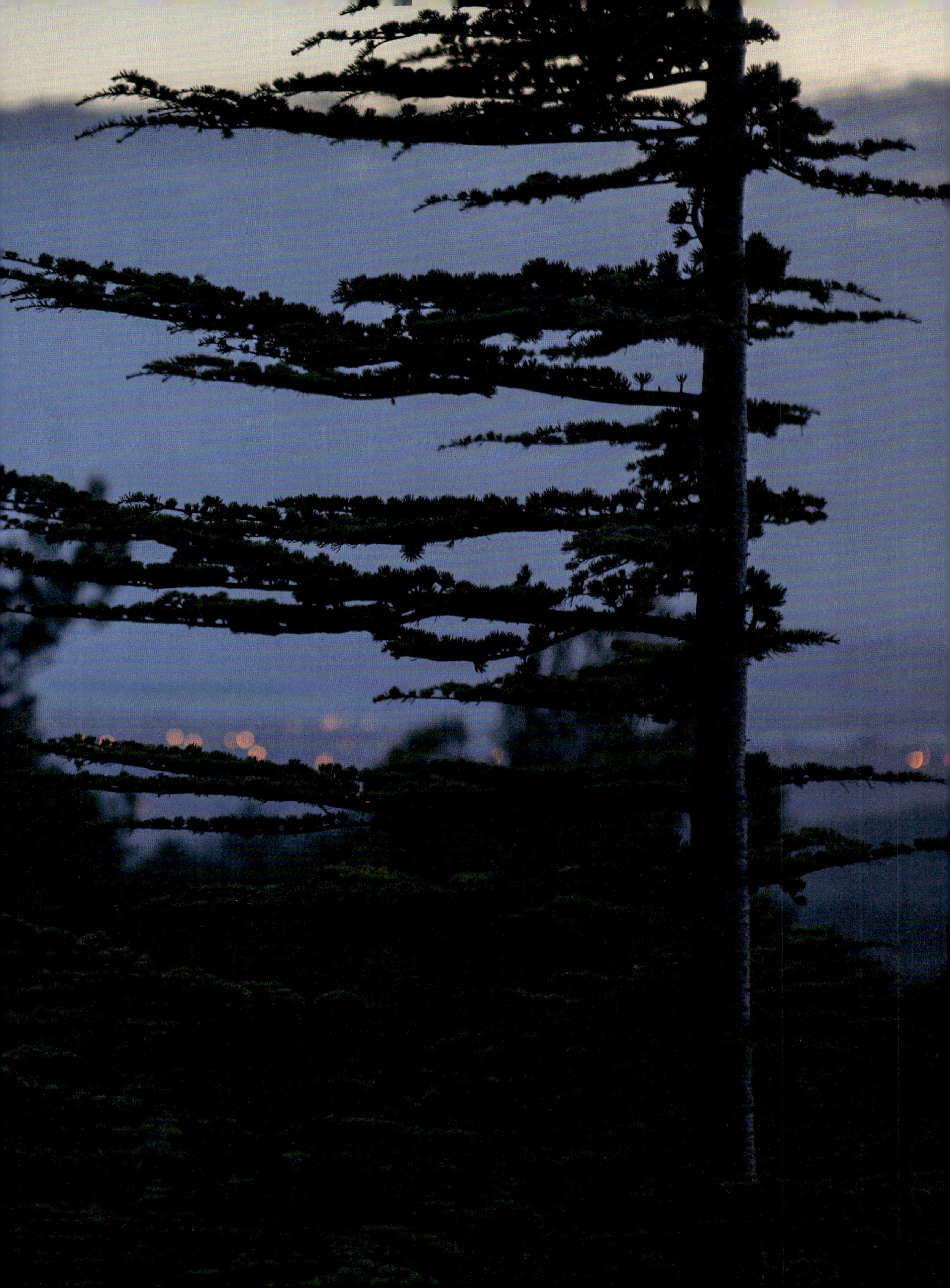

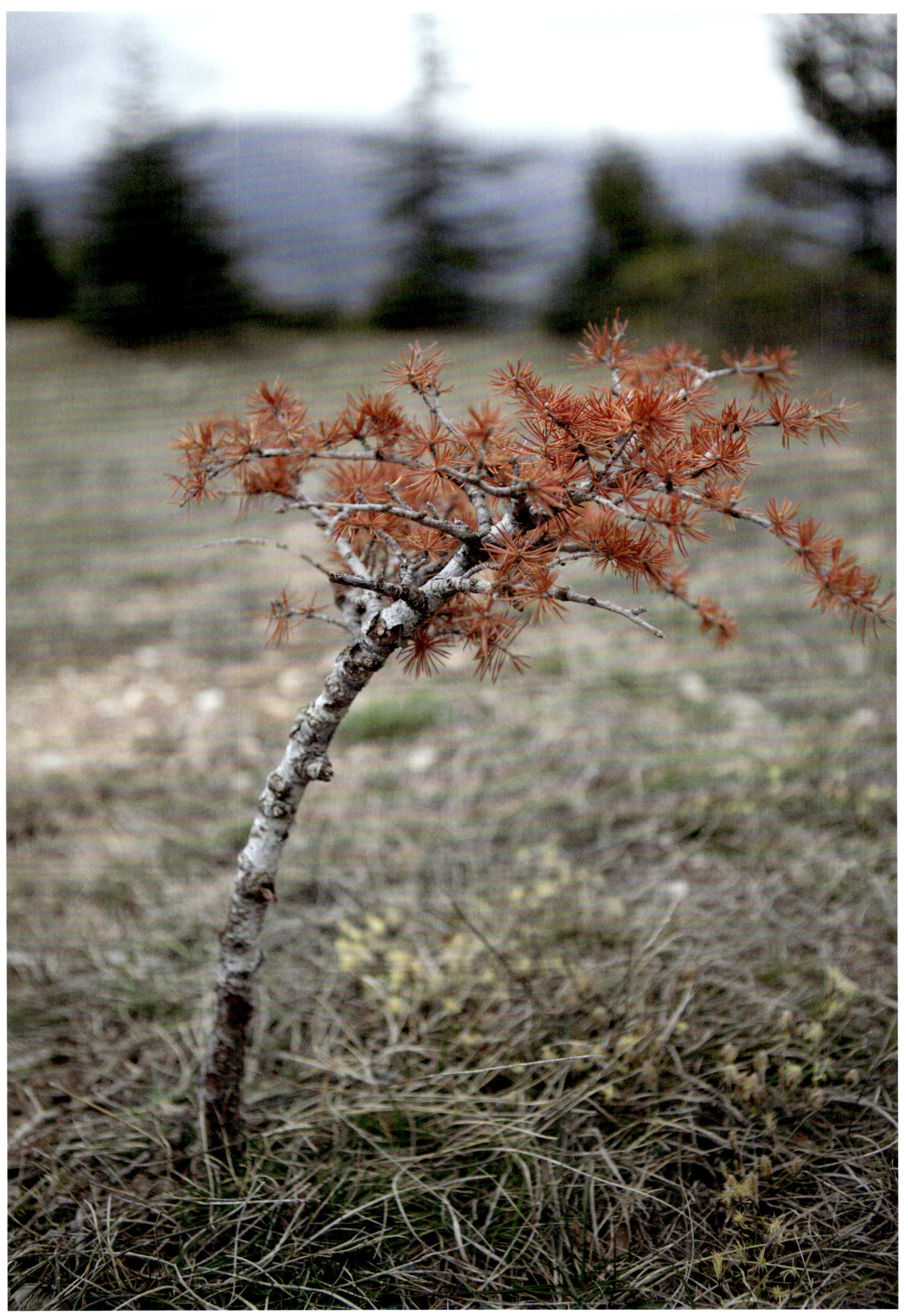

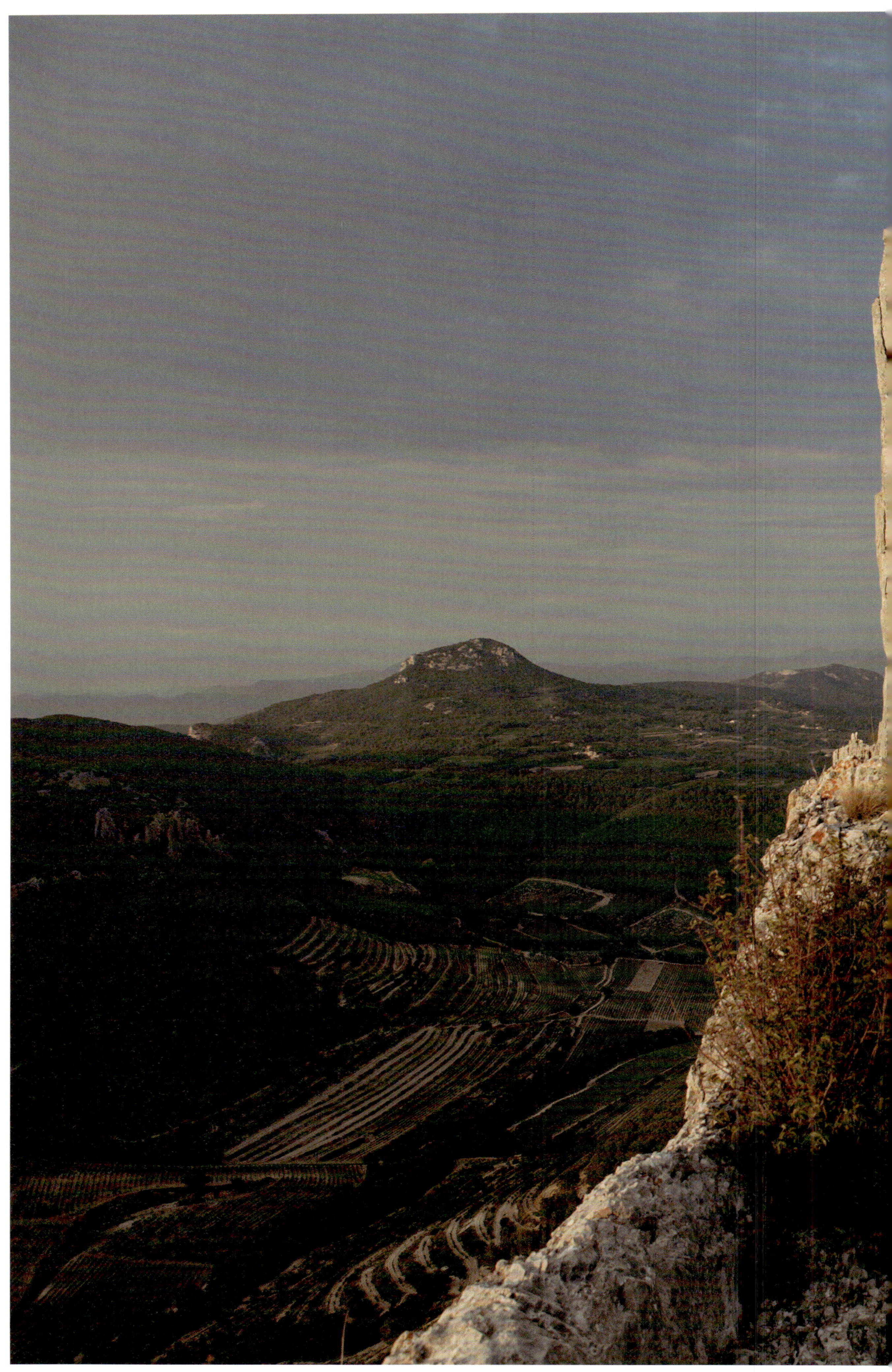

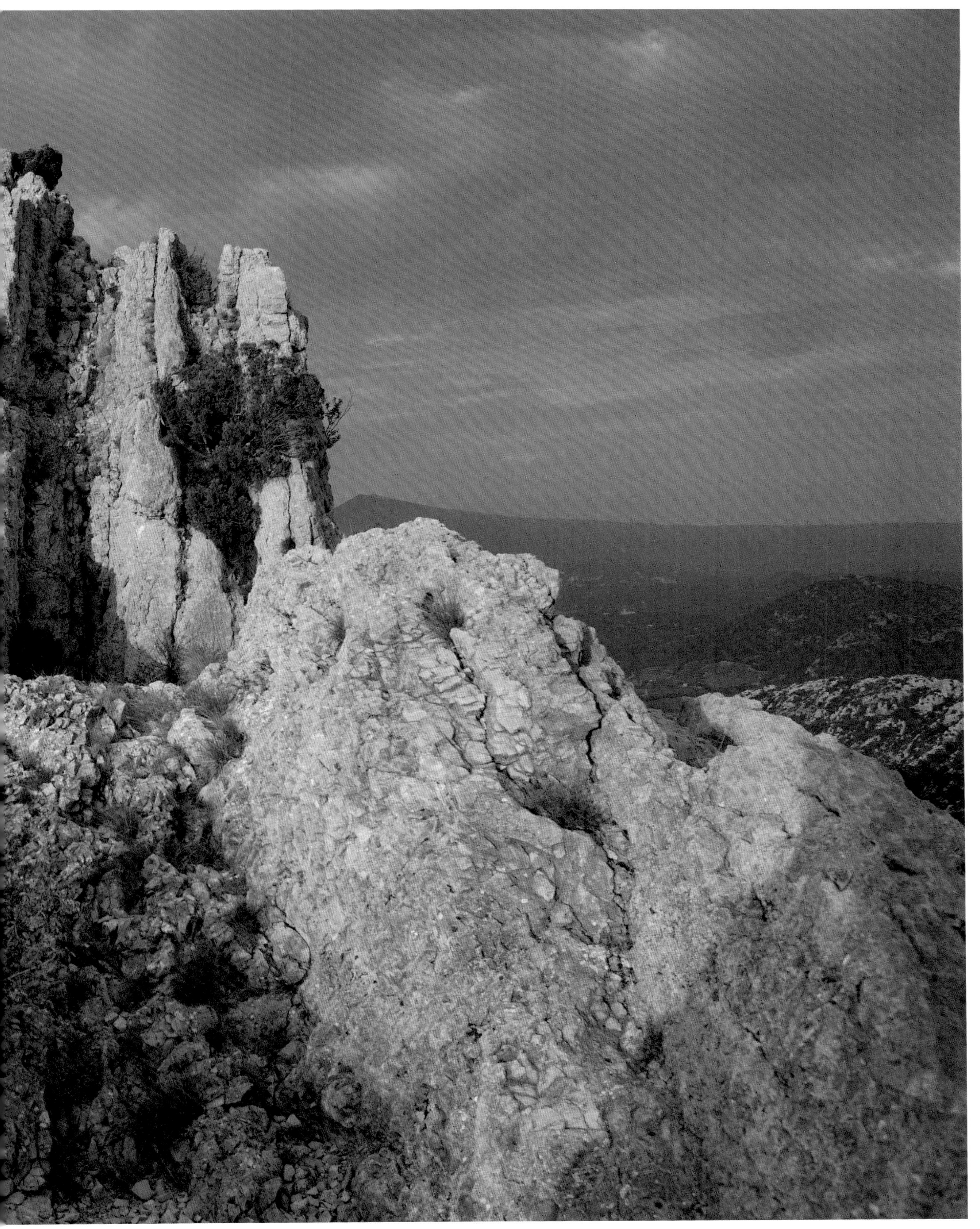

13. Saint Martin; Moissac-Bellevue, Var. A farmhouse in southeastern Provence. Two stories, immensely thick stone walls, red-tile roof, dark green shutters and doors, several acres of surrounding fields flanked by a national forest on one side and a dirt road on the other: the middle of nowhere. One of the stones above the front door was engraved with the words *L'An VI*—year six—which you took to mean the sixth year of the revolution, suggesting that the house was built in 1794 or 1795. Age 26 to 27. You and your girlfriend spent nine months as caretakers of that remote southern property, living there from early September 1973 to the end of May 1974, and although you have already written about some of the things that happened to you in that house (*The Red Notebook*, Story No. 2), there was much that you did not talk about in those five pages. When you think about the time you spent in that part of the world now, what comes back to you first is the air, the scents of thyme and lavender that rose up around you whenever you walked through the fields that bordered the house, the redolent air, the muscular air when the wind was blowing, the languorous air when the sun lowered itself into the valley and lizards and salamanders crawled out from the crevices in the stones to drowse in the heat, and then the dryness and roughness of the country, the gray, molten rocks, the chalky white soil, the red earth along certain paths and stretches of road, the scarab beetles in the forest pushing their mountainous spheres of dung, the magpies swooping over the fields and neighboring vineyards, the flocks of sheep that passed through the meadow just beyond the house, the sudden apparitions of sheep, hundreds of sheep bunched together and moving forward with the clattering sounds of their bells, the violence of the mistrals, the wind-storms that would last for seventy-two unbroken hours, shaking every window, every shutter, every door and loosened tile of the house, the yellow broom that covered the hillsides in spring, the flowering almond trees, the rosemary bushes, the scrubby, stunted live oaks with gnarled trunks and shimmering leaves, the frigid winter that forced you to close off the second floor of the house and live in the three downstairs rooms . . .

—Paul Auster, *Winter Journal*

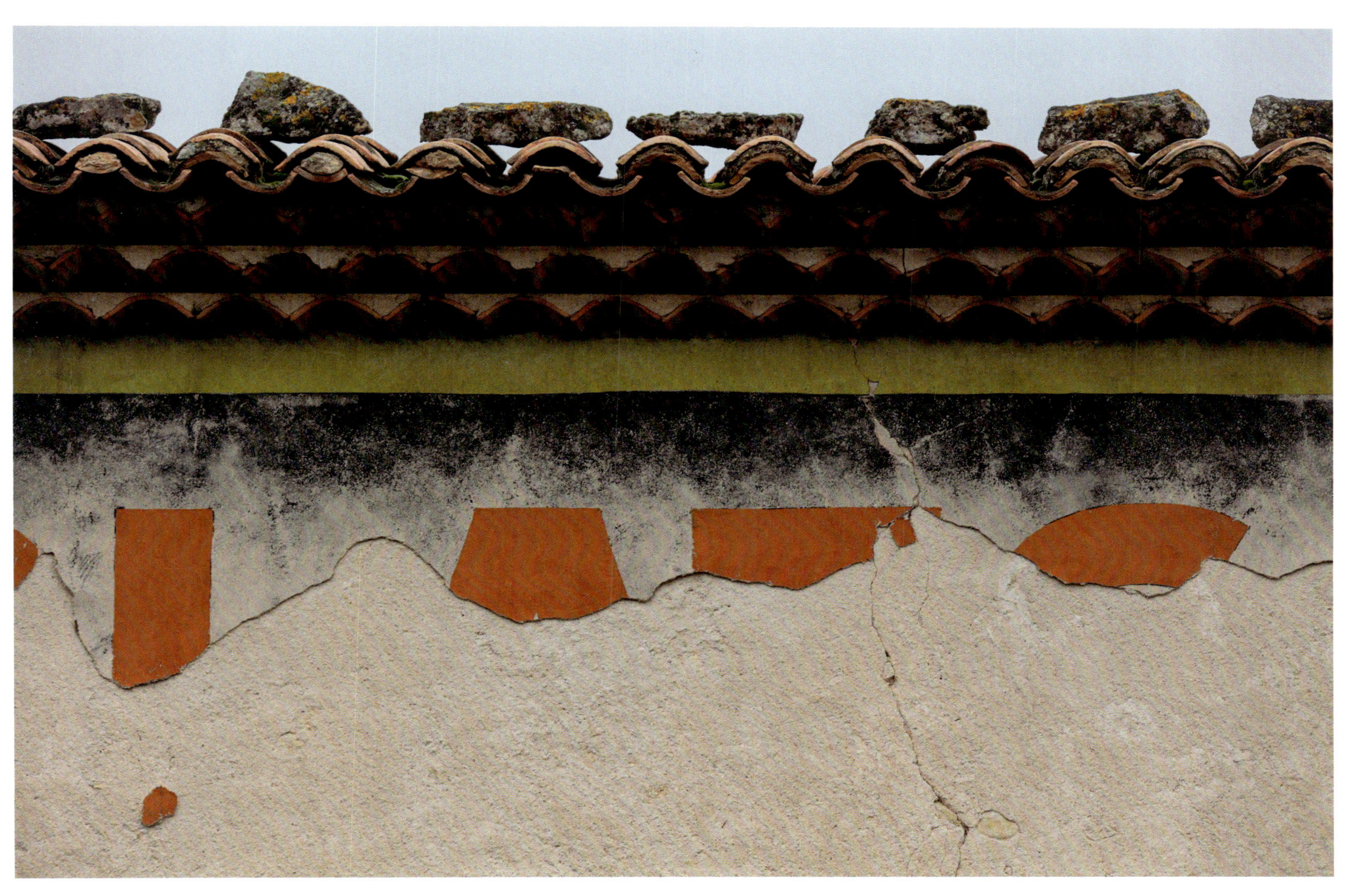

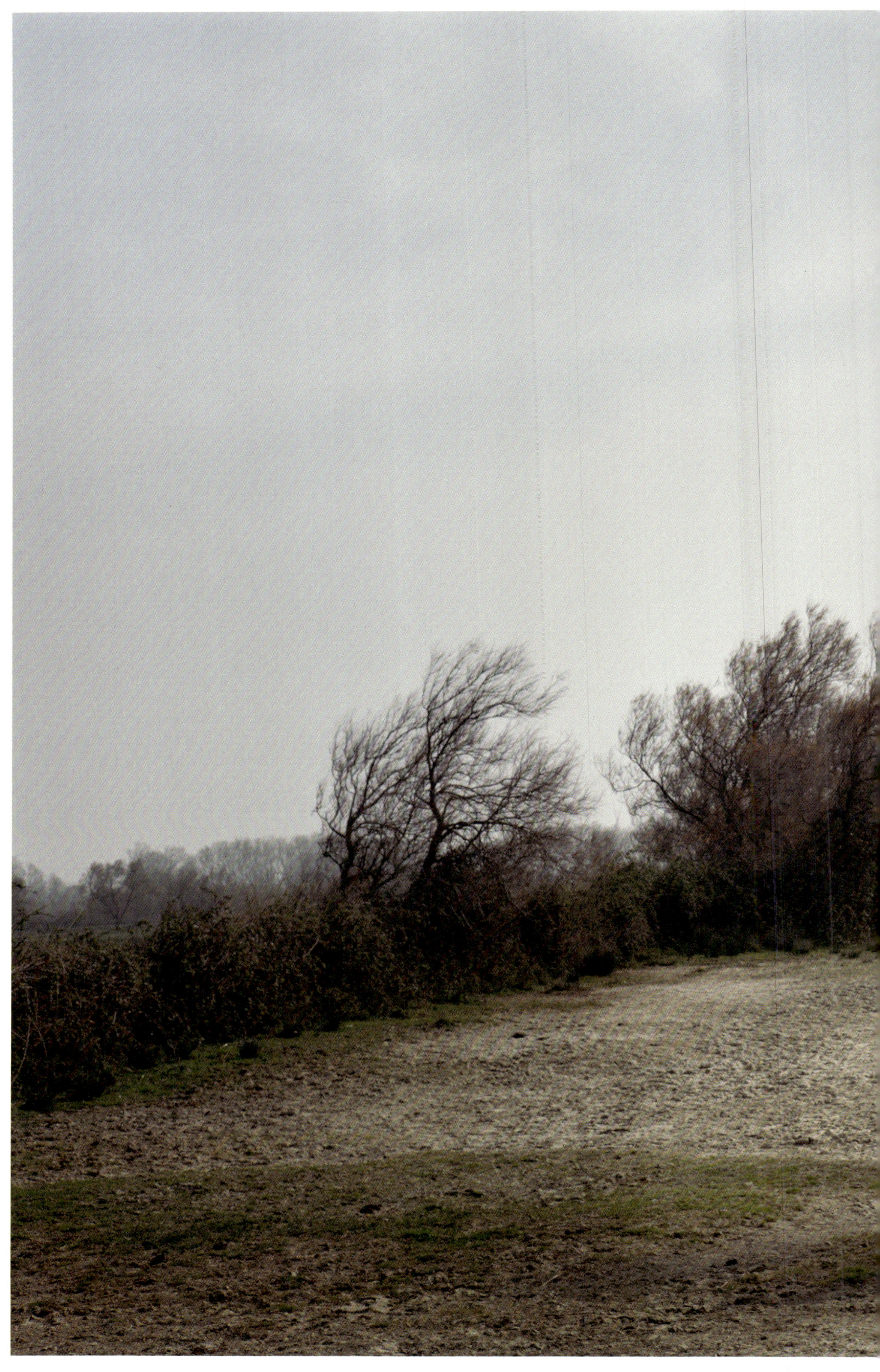

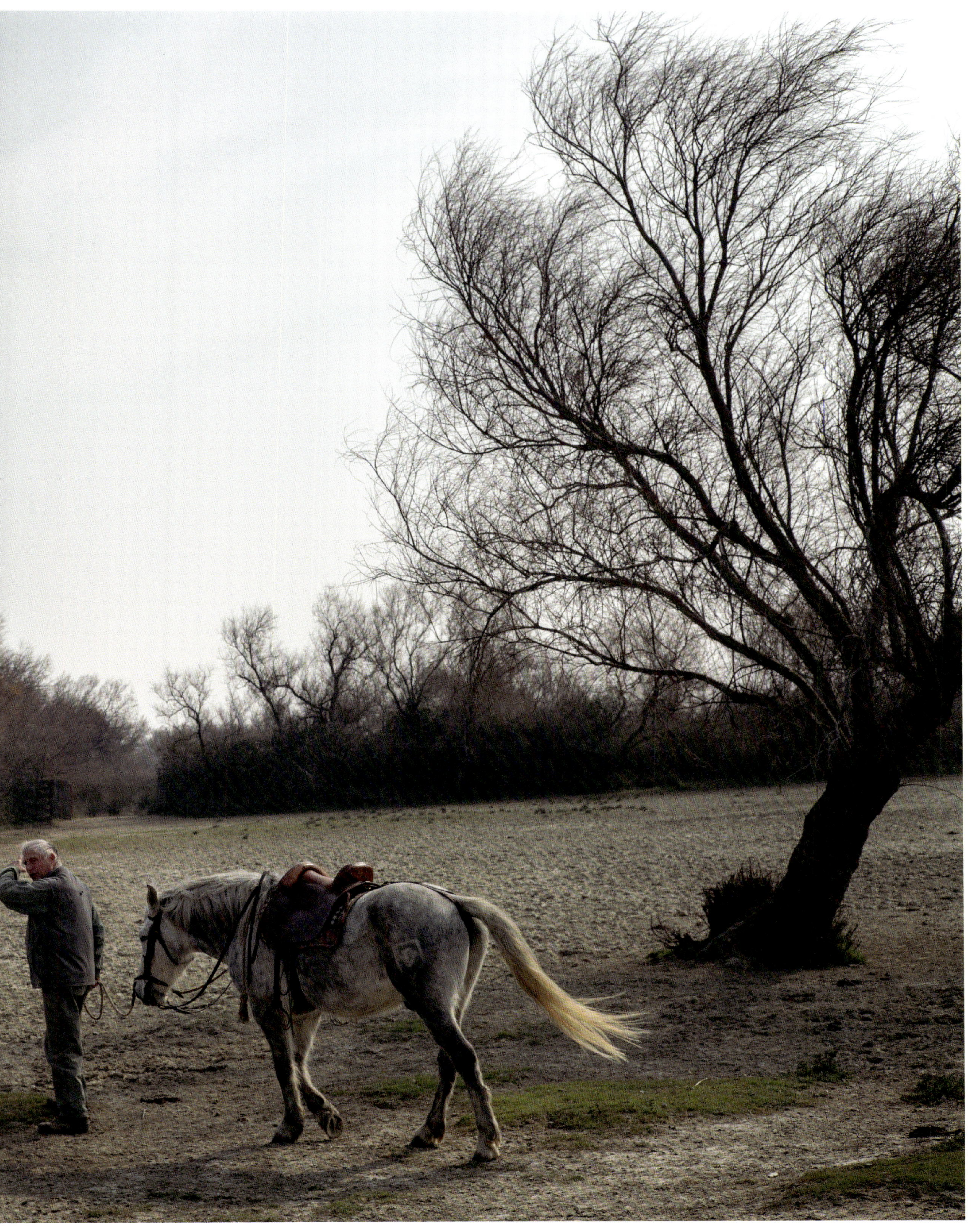

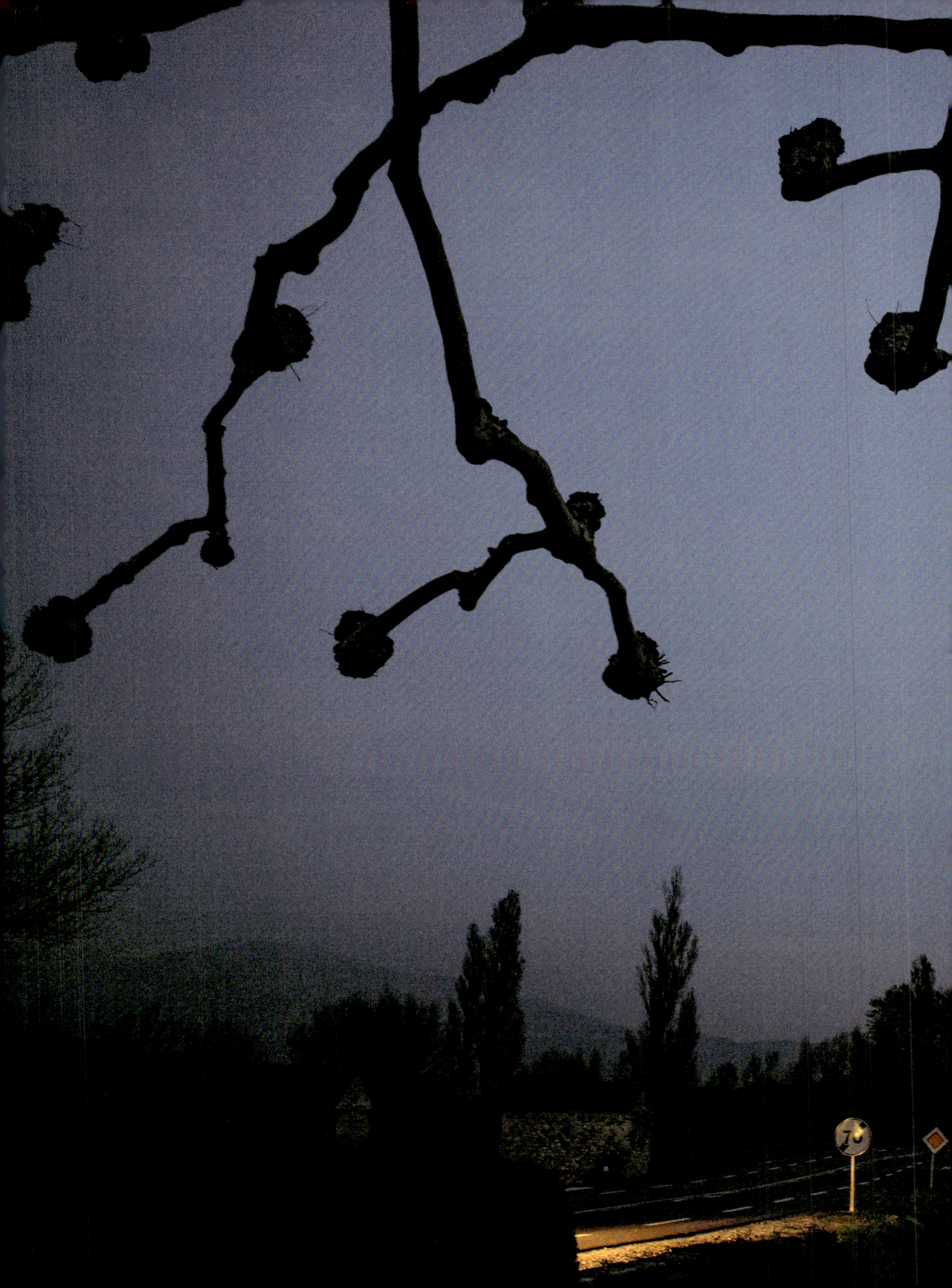

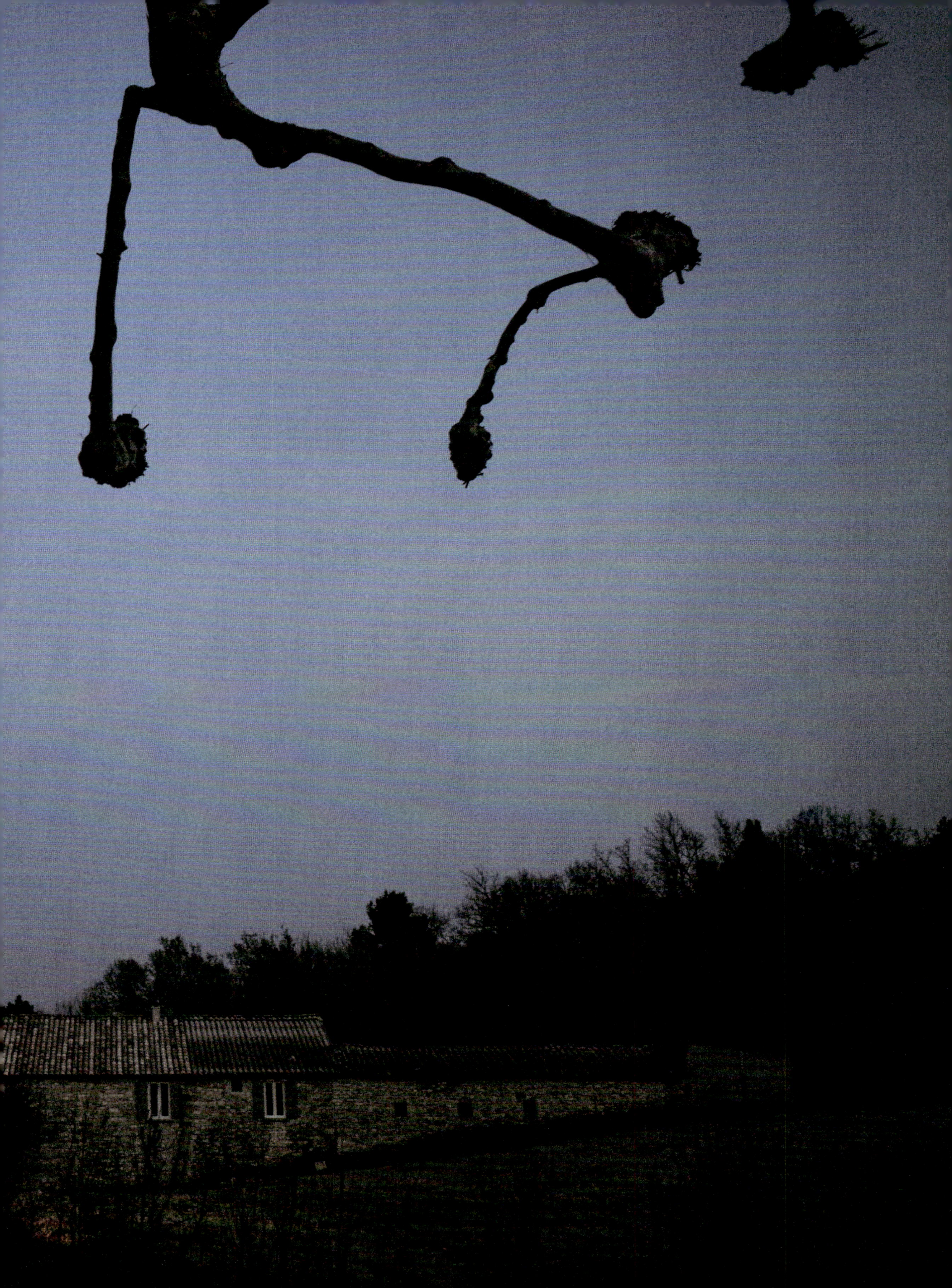

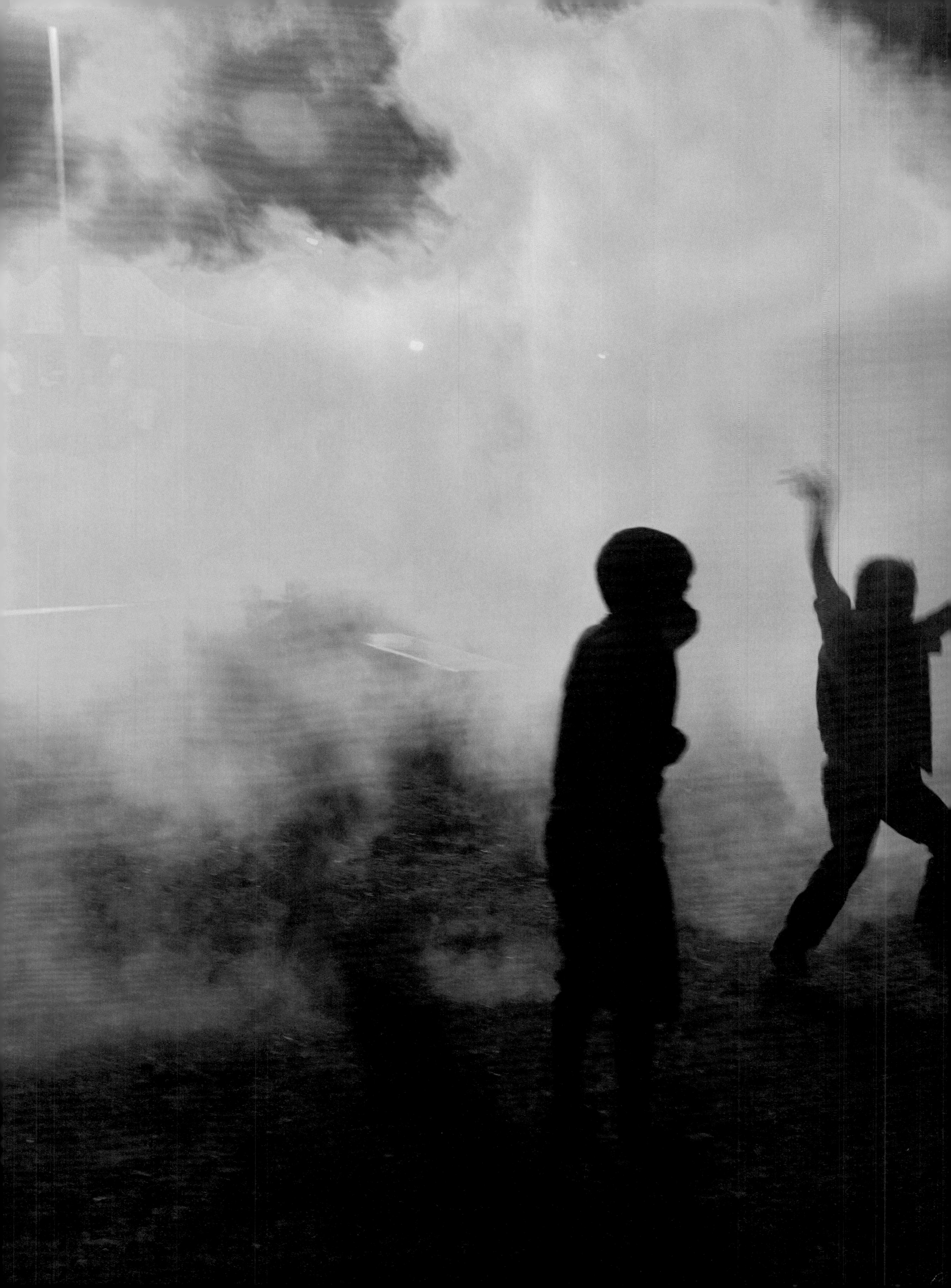

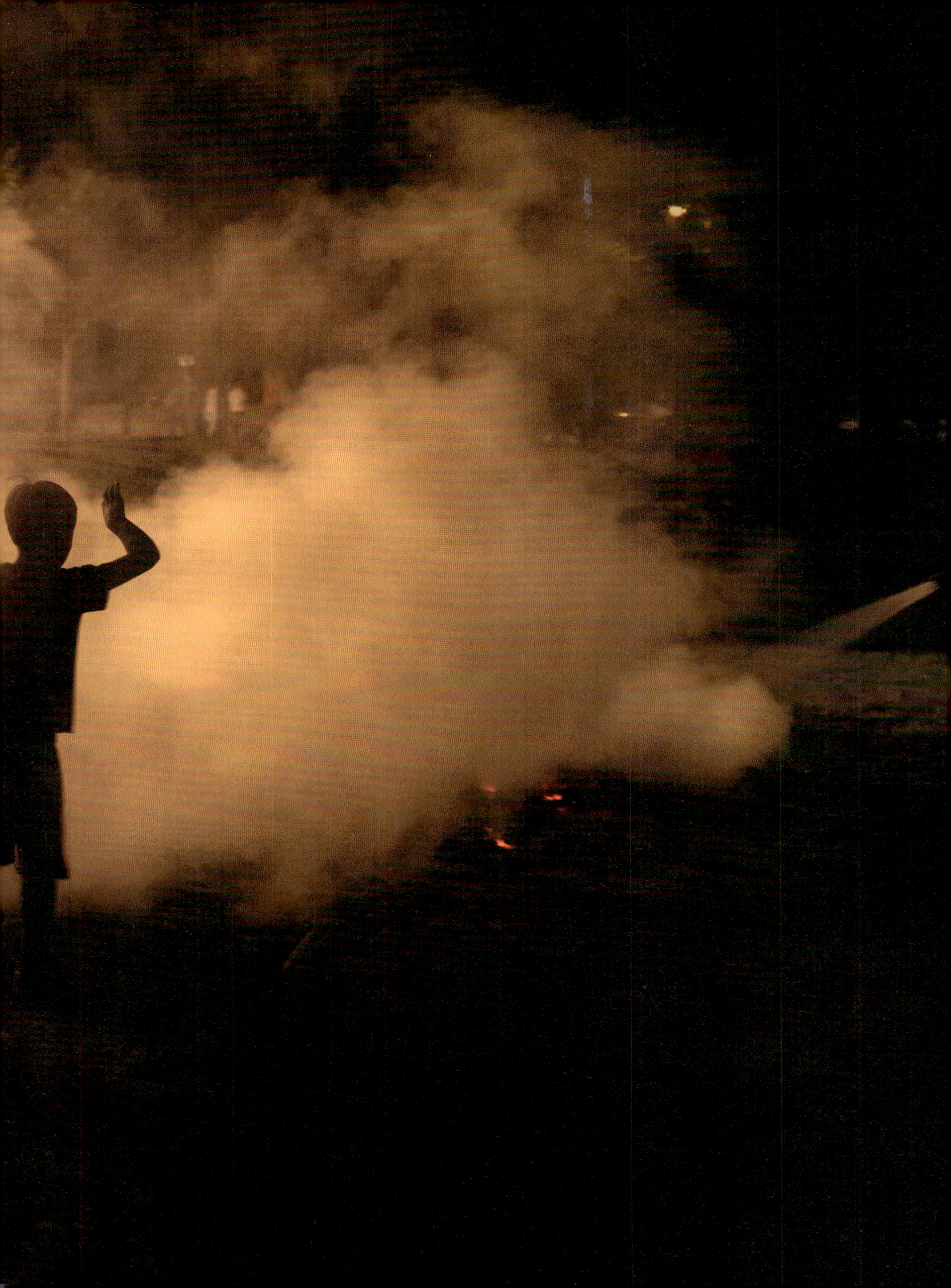

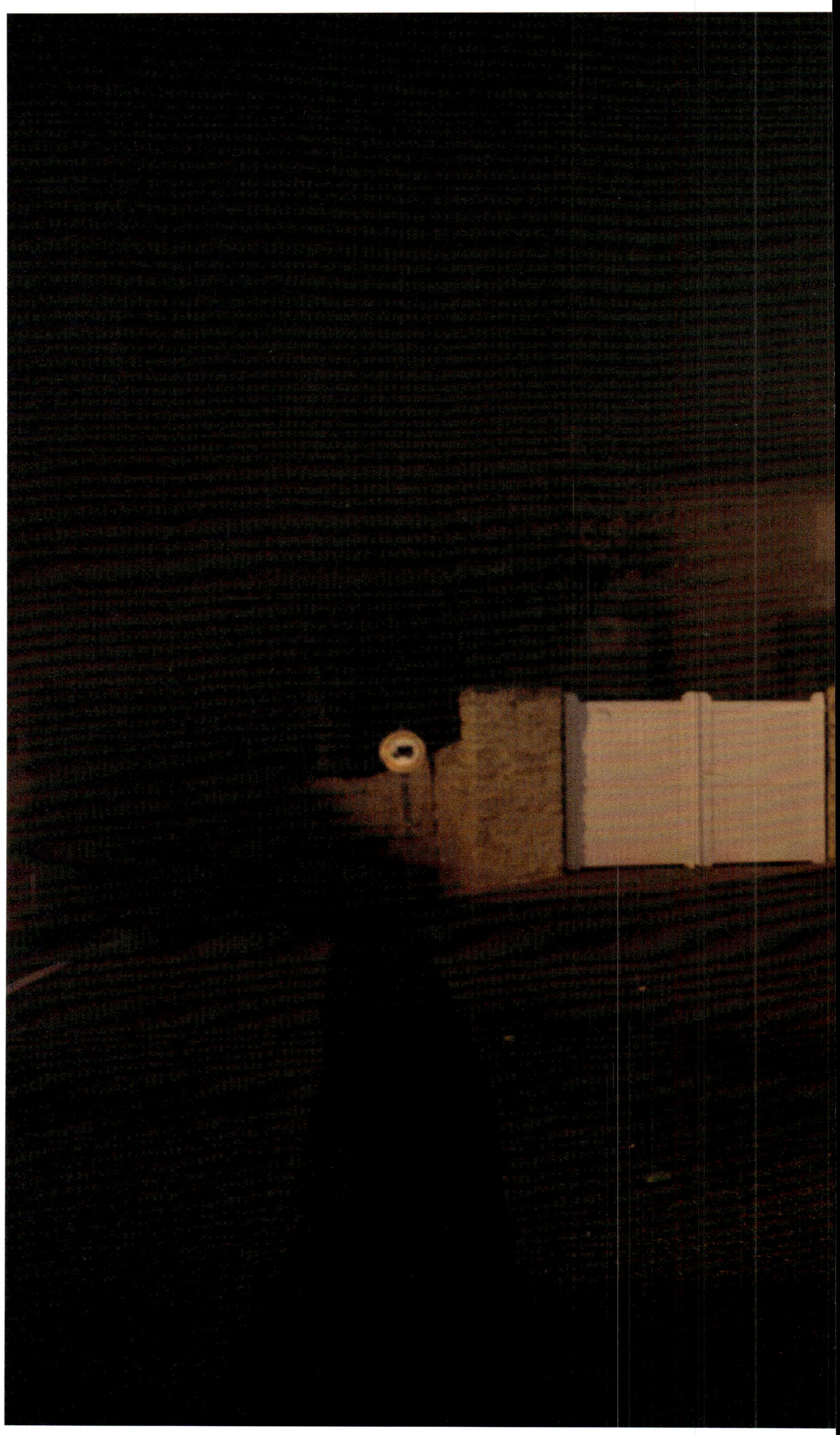

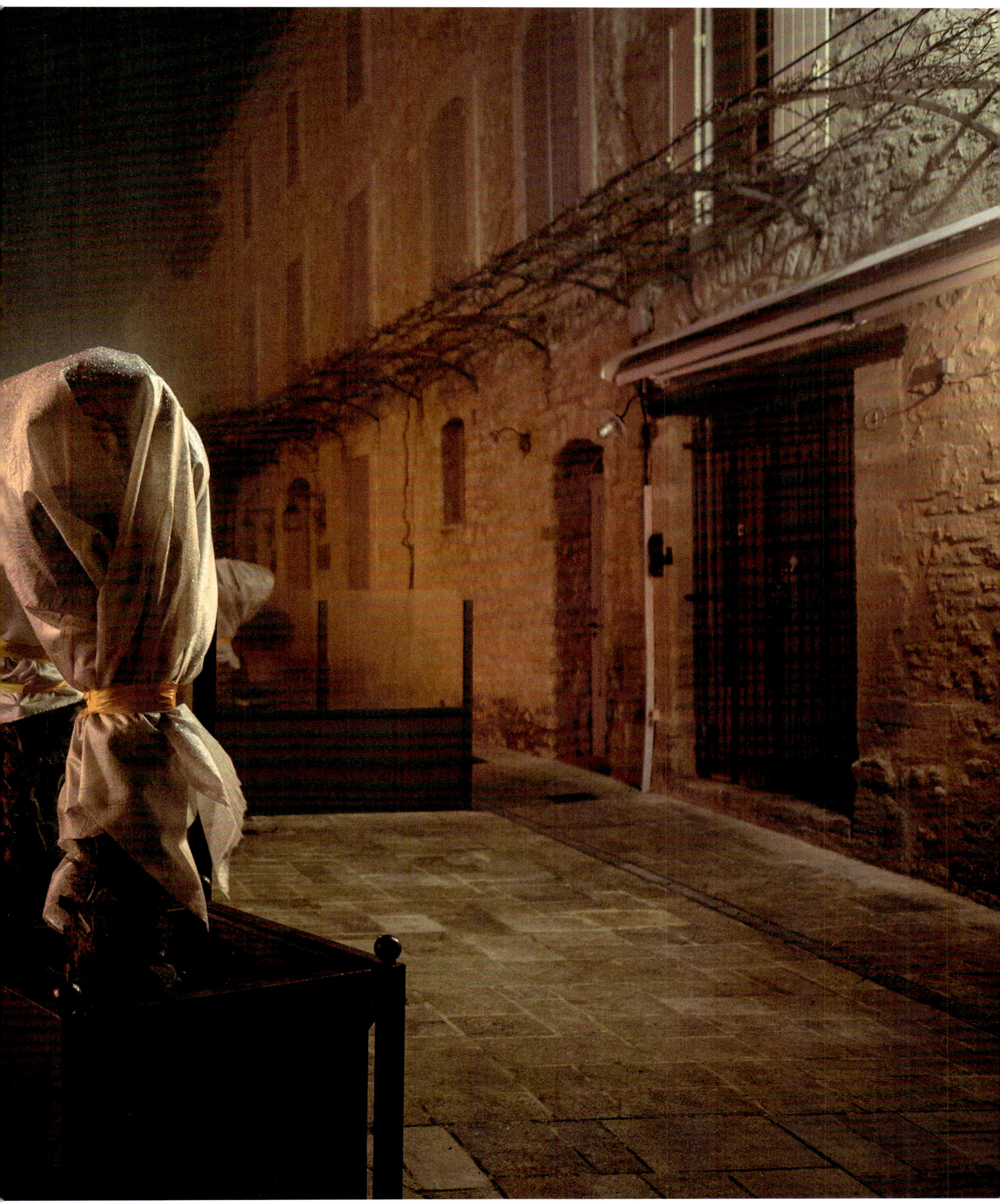

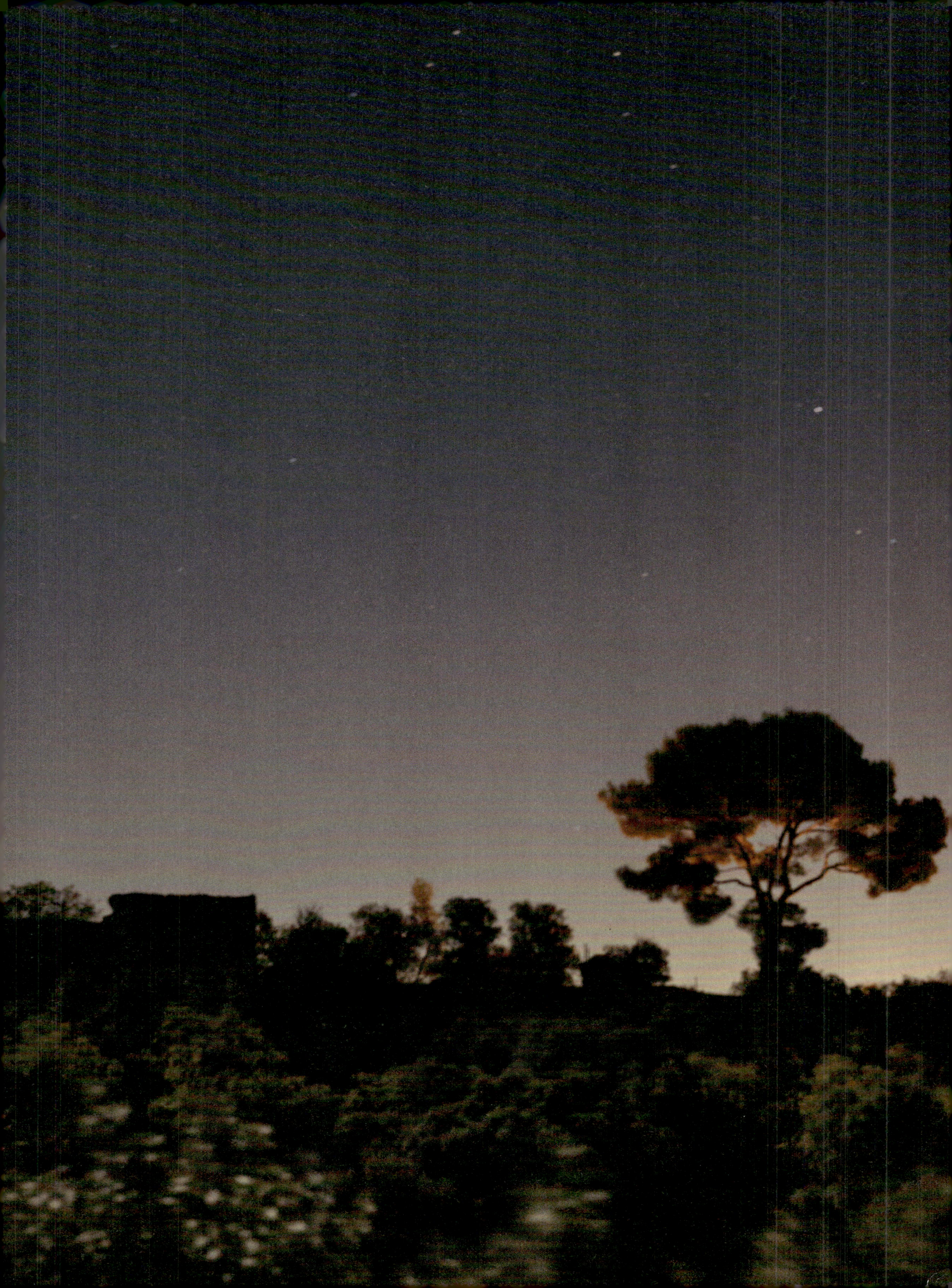

"I love you," the wind keeps saying to
everything it breathes into life.
"I love you and you live in me."

"Je t'aime," répète le vent à tout ce
qu'il fait vivre.
"Je t'aime et tu vis en moi."

—René Char,
So That Nothing There Will Change

MISTRAL

Rachel Cobb

In a small village in Provence, where I've been going regularly for the past forty years, the mistral is a frequent guest. It rushes in from north-facing windows and small air vents. Bedroom doors are propped open by two-kilo cast-iron butcher weights. Inevitably someone forgets to put one in place, and the report reverberates throughout the house. Any number of ceramic bowls and carelessly placed glasses go crashing to the terra-cotta tile floors. My young niece stands in the entrance. A gust of wind suddenly slams the heavy wooden door on her finger—a spray of red on the white plaster wall. Village kids, looking for amusement at night, take advantage of the mistral to muffle their monkey business. Loose shutters creak, chimneys howl, and nobody hears them.

The mistral is a gremlin wreaking havoc on our lives. It is everywhere. It is nowhere to be seen. People feel the wind without necessarily being aware of how it affects their lives. Anyone who has spent time in Provence is likely to have experienced the cold, dry wind that funnels down the Rhône Valley between the Alps and the Massif Central, gaining speed as it reaches the Mediterranean. Wind flows freely over borders. It cannot be harnessed like a river, depriving one country of a resource. Instead, it connects us. High pressure in the Bay of Biscay and low pressure in the Gulf of Genoa lead to a mistral that can extend all the way to the coast of Africa and high up into the troposphere.

As long as there have been inhabitants in Provence, they have endured the mistral. Archeologists have found evidence of prehistoric stone walls erected on the northwest side of fire pits that they believe were used as protection from the wind. Provençaux have many tales, myths, and sayings about the mistral. They maintain it lasts three, six, or nine days even though it regularly subsides after just one or two. They blame it for anything from migraines to crimes of passion.

By coincidence, Provence's most famous poet, Frédéric Mistral, shares his name with its most famous wind. Almost every town and village in the area has a sign for a Mistral street, avenue, or café. So not only do Provençaux experience the mistral's force as many as two hundred days a year, the word itself is inescapable.

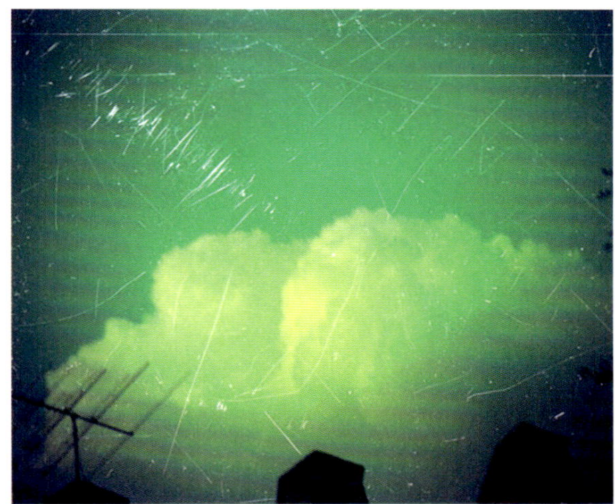

Nineteenth-century painters were drawn to Provence by the crystal-clear air that follows a mistral, but for Vincent van Gogh the wind was a torment. During the eighteen months he lived in Arles and Saint-Rémy, he complained about it in more than forty letters. On days when the wind blasted him, he tried laying his canvas on the ground and kneeling to paint; he tried weighing down his canvas with rocks; he even drove stakes into the ground and secured his easel to them and to nearby trees. All too often his effort to work en plein air was stymied by the "devil mistral."

If van Gogh and others could paint scenes of the mistral, I thought, why couldn't I try to capture it in images? It was not the first time I tried to photograph the unseen. I was eight years old and playing outside when I looked up and was sure I saw God in the clouds. I ran inside, grabbed my mother's camera, and clicked off all twelve frames, my first photographs. When my mother brought back the prints from the drugstore, she was not at all happy to find an entire roll of sky, and I was disappointed God had proved so elusive.

By the late 1990s, I was ready to try again. I set out to find evidence of the mistral and capture it in images. I went to a local library in Provence where a martinet of a librarian brought me books one at a time. I took notes from the dusty tomes, but I found very little to go on. I started talking to neighbors, to farmers at the market, and to workers who labored outdoors. They could all describe how the mistral menaced them, but not in a way I could use visually. I ran into a local friend, André, who knew an old shepherd. Perhaps he could be of some help?

André and I drove up to a hamlet on the south side of Mont Ventoux. In a stone and ochre-colored stucco house set against the hillside, his shepherd friend described to me—in his Provençal tongue—how his father's sheep were once lost on the mountain during a mistral, the sound of their bells carried away by the wind. The next morning, in a fierce mistral, I tried to photograph just such a scene. I drove up the mountain until the road ended, and I set out on foot looking for the shepherd's son, but all I found was limestone scree and some dead leaves bolting past. I could hear his sheep's bells clinking in the distance, but as I pursued the sound, it kept dancing away from me.

Chasing the wind became an obsession, often a frustrating one. When the mistral blew, I might drive an hour or two with a certain photograph in mind, only to arrive to sudden stillness. It felt like a game of you-can't-catch-me. It reminded me of when I was a child and I used to sail with my father. As our spinnaker suddenly went limp, he would declare, "The wind is a fickle woman."

Over time I began to notice signs of the mistral more and more. It was in the architecture. Provençal houses have traditionally been built with the wind in mind, not the sun. The northwest, windward side has few or no windows. The front door is always on the protected southern side of the house. You can tell when a house has been modernized—often by outsiders—because new north-facing windows have been punched through without regard to the mistral's force. In the Camargue, the marshy region at the mouth of the Rhône River, the traditional thatched cottages of the *gardiens* (herdsmen) are built with rounded lime-washed walls and slanting roofs facing at an angle to the prevailing mistral so that it flows around them. Iron belfries allow the wind to pass easily through them. Such iron-work campaniles are seen in almost every village and town of the region. If you plotted them on a map, it would show exactly where the mistral blows.

The Provençal landscape, too, reflects the effect of wind. It is a mosaic of vineyards, olive groves, wheat fields, and other plots separated by rows of cypress or poplars planted closely together as windbreaks. Mont Ventoux, also known as Mont Chauve (bald mountain), was once forested, but its trees were cut down for shipbuilding and charcoal production. The topsoil blew off, leaving a lunar landscape. Wind and rain eroded the chain of mountains known as the Dentelles de Montmirail so that they look like a lace border.

In agriculture and food production, the mistral can be useful. Winemakers are grateful when the mistral clears their vines of pests. It can help prevent rot. The combination of wind and sun aid in salt production in the Camargue. Even oyster cultivators benefit. In the Étang de Thau, high salinity leads to increased algae in the lagoon, so cultivators periodically pull their oysters onto racks to dry and kill the algae that robs them of oxygen. If there's a mistral, the algae dries three times as fast.

In between other work, I occasionally made my way back to Provence from New York to continue this project, but the pictures came too slowly. It was impossible to time my trips to catch the wind. It was clear I needed to spend a long period of time there. After years of photographing newspaper and magazine assignments where I would drop into a location rarely longer than a week or two, I was ready to sink into one place until I knew it deeply.

My husband and I moved to the village and enrolled our son in the local school. Day after day, camera at my side, I drove the same narrow roads and walked the same circuit around our village. I got to know the area so well I knew individual plants—watched them lose their foliage as the days turned cold and felt the excitement of seeing their buds emerge as the days lengthened. Here is a rose from my garden after two days of mistral. There is a quince that survived gusts of 100 kilometers per hour. This wind-bowed sapling is going to make it. The mistral slowly revealed itself.

I started this story using Kodachrome film and digging through a small-town library, and I finished it using digital cameras and the Internet. It's taken me a long time to put into words and images just this: The mistral—an unseen force—not only shapes the place where people live, but also who those people are.

To me, the French have a complicated relationship with the mistral. They have a reverence for tradition, rules, and order. Everything in its place. Then along comes the wind, the *sacré* mistral. They rail against it. They exclaim it's a menace. Yet secretly they respect it. It's *liberté*. Like a spirit, the mistral cannot be contained.

NOTES ON IMAGES

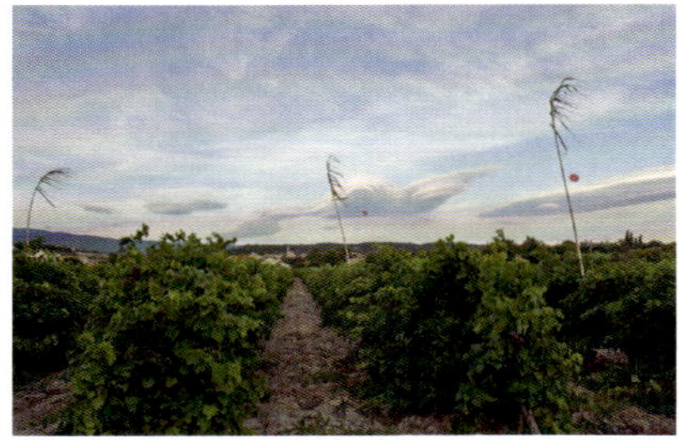

Outside the village of Modène, compact discs blowing in the wind reflect light frantically and scare away birds from the grapevines.

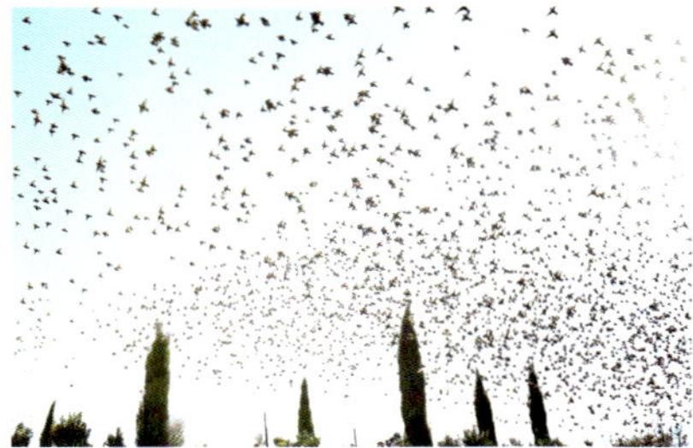

Devino-vent is a Provençal word that means a wind diviner. These forecasters were dead birds, usually martins, that had been dried and hung on strings in the kitchens of farmhouses.

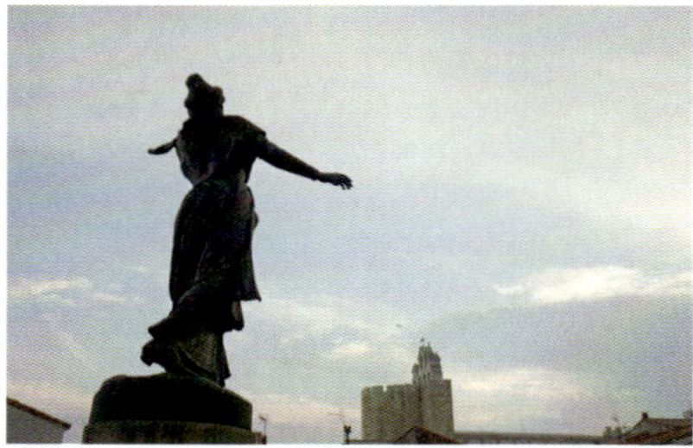

In the village of Saintes-Maries-de-la-Mer, at the edge of the Camargue, stands a statue of a windswept Mireille (Mirèio in Provençal), the heroine of Frédéric Mistral's epic poem of that name.

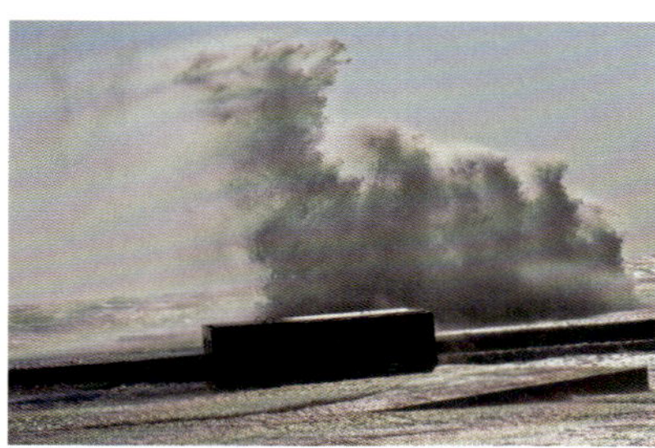

"Very poor atmospheric visibility also has been reported up to a height of 98 ft during cases of extremely strong mistrals because of a layer of spray that extends above the water surface."
—US Naval Research Laboratory, Marine Meteorology Division

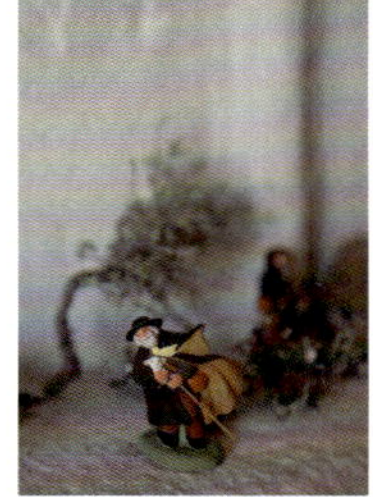

A windblown shepherd *santon*. *Santons* are clay figurines of saints represented by ordinary Provençal characters and used in crèche sets at Chistmastime. They were first made during the French Revolution when churches were closed and nativity scenes were forbidden. People took to creating their own crèche sets with local characters instead of known saints.

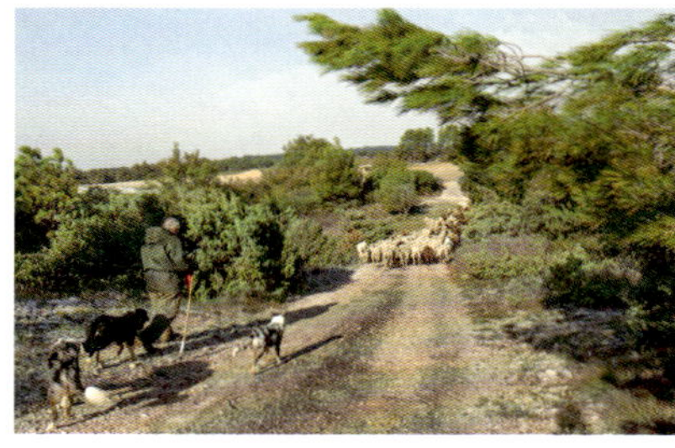

"The grass doesn't grow when there's a mistral, and it dries out the grass too," says shepherd Montagard. "I can lose my sheep on the mountain when they scatter and lose their way in the forest."

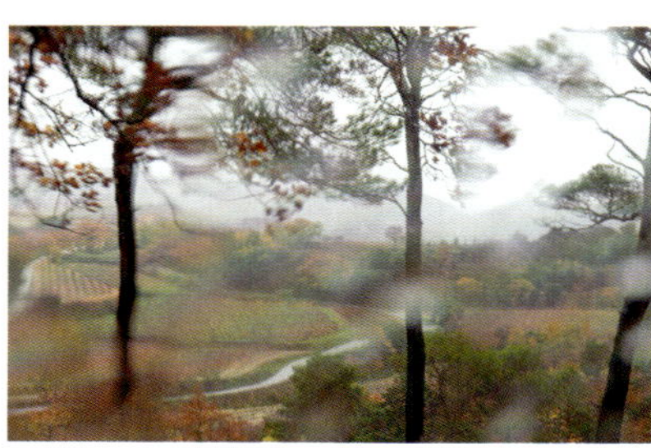

A regular mistral, with its cold, dry wind, clears the sky, but a mistral noir brings rain and clouds, usually cumulonimbus clouds.

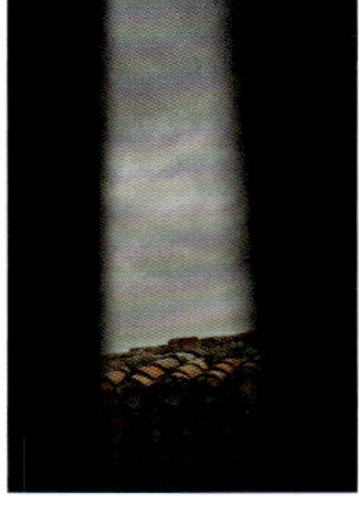

Throughout Provence, roof tiles are made from terra-cotta, laid in double or triple layers and set in mortar. Heavy stones are placed on top of the tiles to hold them in place during mistrals.

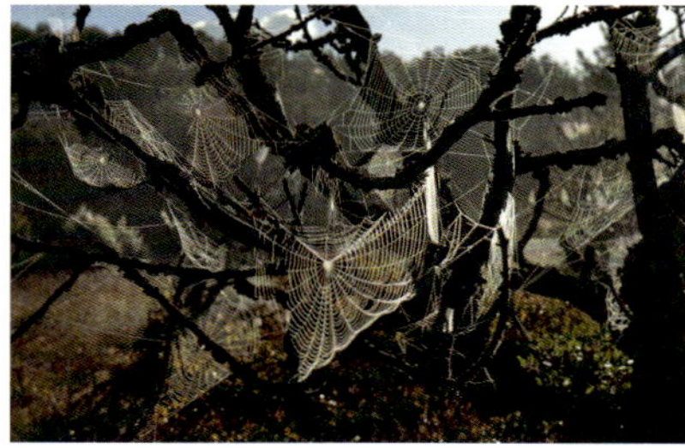

To cope with the winds, some spiders orient their webs to make them less exposed and others weave smaller webs.

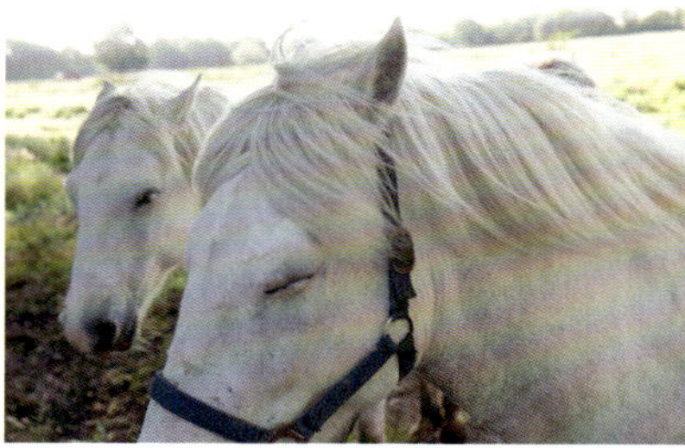

"The horses are ill at ease in the wind and react quickly to sudden movements."
—Laure Vadon, Mas Saint Germain, Camargue

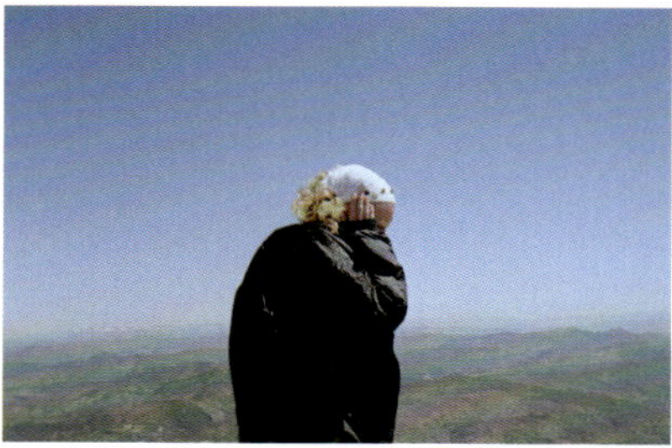

"Locals claim that a sudden feeling of dejection or even depression sweeps through them just before the mistral comes. Once the wind arrives, depression gives way to headaches and irritability."
—Oliver's Travels

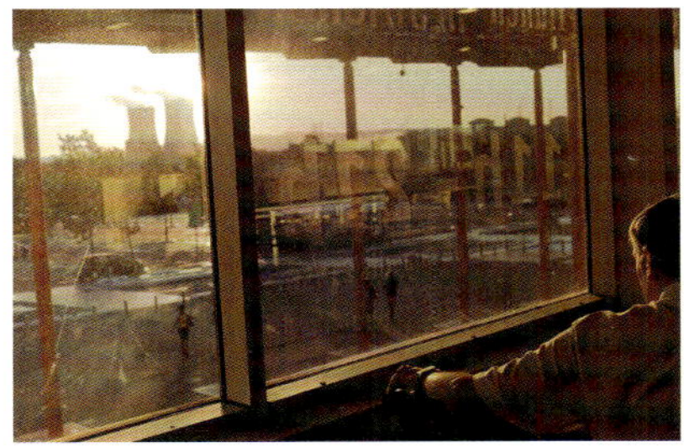

On February 28, 2013, at the Tricastin Nuclear Power Plant, there was a flash of blue followed by an explosion. The plant claims there was no cause for concern, but anti-nuke groups are unsure. Coordination Antinucléaire du Sud-Est points out: "The mistral was blowing 80-90 kph making it impossible to take accurate samples that would confirm or deny the presence of radioactivity."

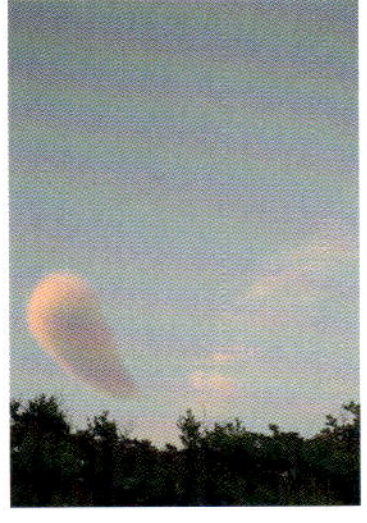

A mistral can produce this type of altocumulus standing lenticular cloud. When stable, fast-moving air meets a mountain, like Mont Ventoux, the air is forced up and over it. On the lee side, the air is forced down and up again in a series of oscillating waves that form into lens-shaped clouds. They appear stationary, but they are continually dissipating and reforming.

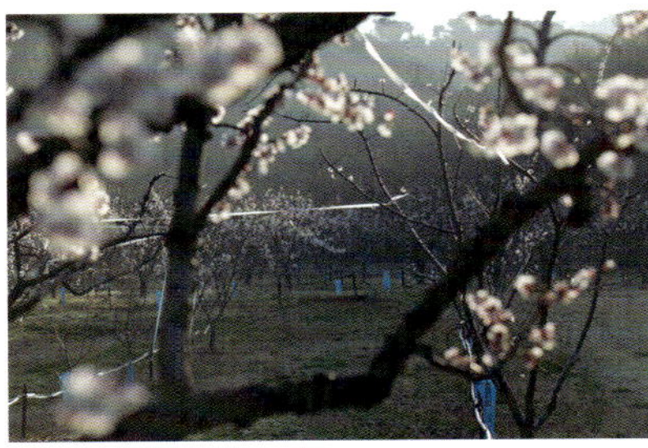

Farmers in Provence have found ways to make the wind work to their benefit. Strips of plastic flapping and humming in the wind act as an effective scarecrow to protect these cherries from birds.

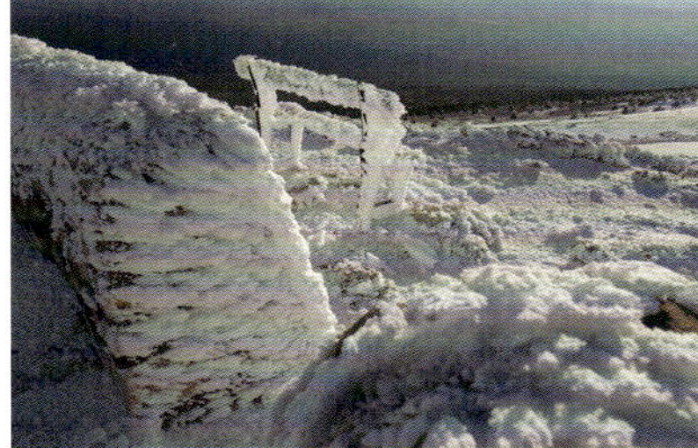

Although some dispute the origin of the name Mont Ventoux, Frédéric Mistral was never in doubt: "Geographers are incorrect in writing Ventoux instead of Ventour. The locals unanimously call it Ventour [windy mountain]." It is, in fact, one of the windiest places on earth.

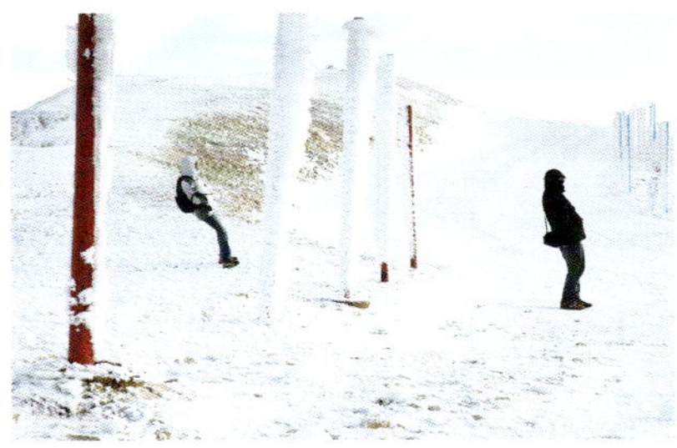

9 February 2013, 3:42 P.M., Col des Tempêtes, Mont Ventoux: gusts of 100 kilometers per hour, 11 on the Beaufort Scale. The mistral barrels down the Rhône Valley, slams into Mont Ventoux, and rushes through this opening, hence the name, Stormy Pass.

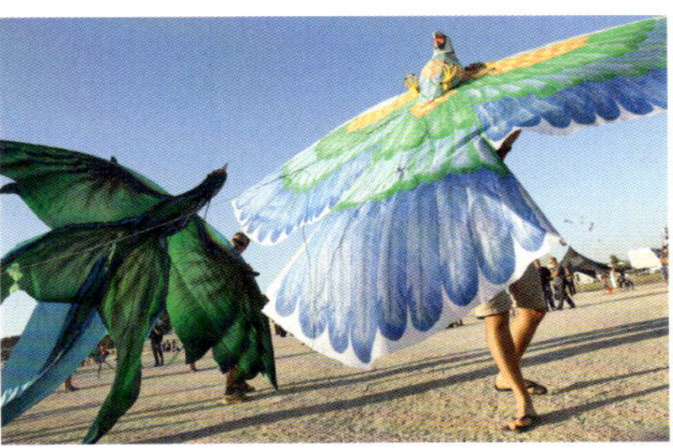

Wind itself is celebrated every September at the Fête du Vent on Prado Beach in Marseille.

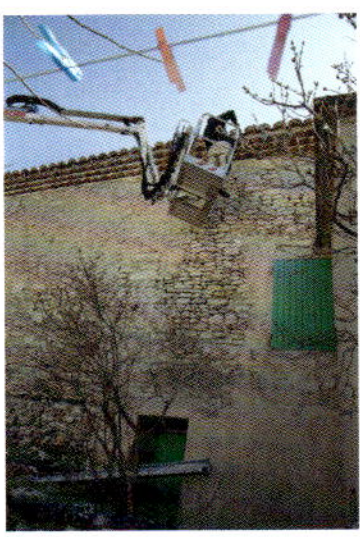

"We are on the front line of the mistral," says an agent of Allianz insurance company's Carpentras office. "People here know how to protect themselves." Allianz does not compensate insurers for damages caused by winds under 100 kph because, they reason, in Provence "that is just nature."

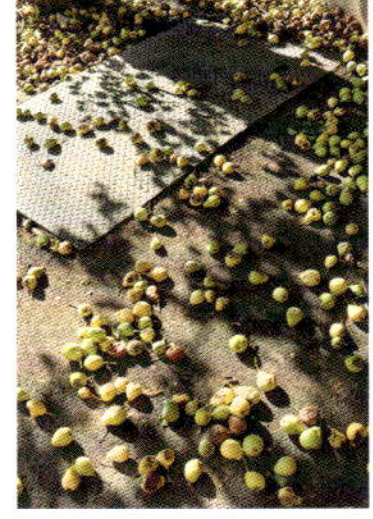

Windfall: an unearned, unexpected gain, a piece of good fortune. *Fruit tombé*: fallen fruit, windfall.

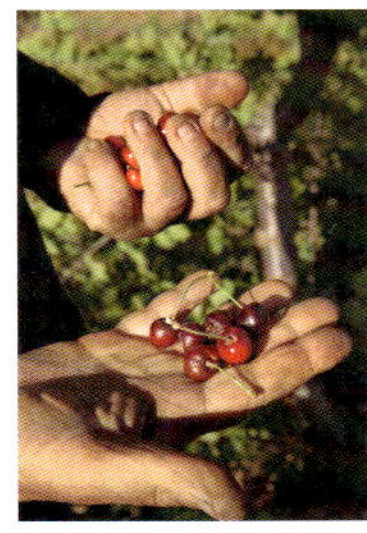

A strong mistral lasting several days damaged these cherries. Hanging on the tree, they appear bruised on one side.

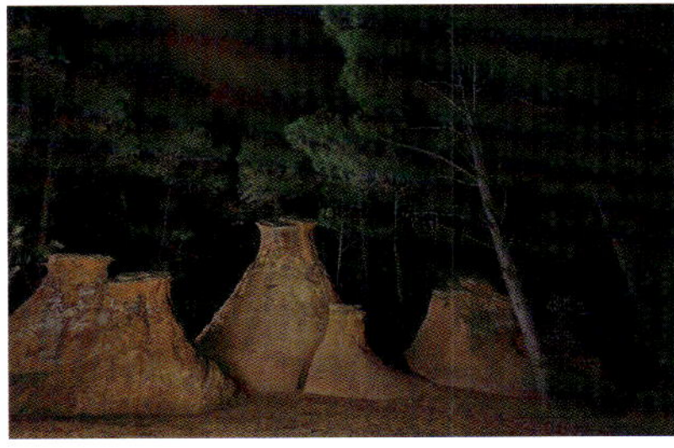

Outside the village of Bédoin, these rock formations called the Demoiselles Coiffées (coiffed young ladies) are made when layers of stone are eroded by wind and rain. They are also known as *cheminées de fées* (fairy chimneys).

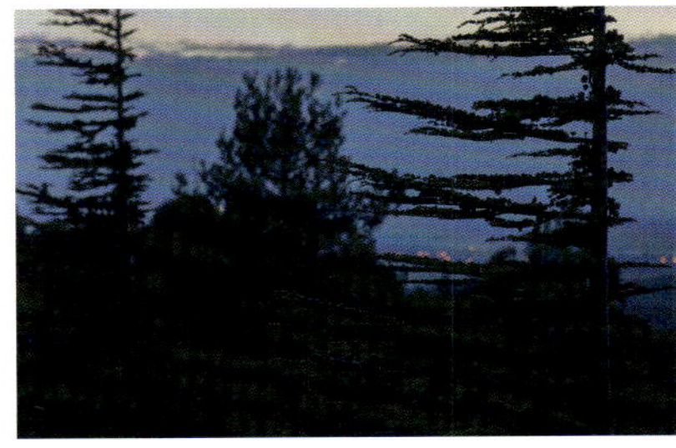

A *port en drapeau* is the form a tree takes when wind regularly blasts it from the same direction, causing its branches to grow on one side. *Port en drapeau* means a pole holding a flag, but it is also a term used for rag type.

Beaufort Scale of Wind Force for Land Areas

[illegible] mph [illegible] rises vertically

1: LIGHT AIR 1-3 mph Wind direction shown by smoke drift but not by weather vanes

2: LIGHT BREEZE 4-7 mph Leaves rustle, wind felt on face, weather vanes moved by wind

3: GENTLE BREEZE 8-12 mph Leaves and small twigs in constant motion, light flags extended

4: MODERATE BREEZE 13-18 mph Small branches moved, dust and loose paper raised, flags rippled

5: FRESH BREEZE 19-24 mph Small trees in leaf begin to sway, crested wavelets form on inland waters

6: STRONG BREEZE 25-31 mph Large branches in motion, whistling heard in telephone wires, umbrellas used with difficulty

7: STRONG WIND, NEAR GALE 32-38 mph Whole trees in motion, inconvenience felt when walking against the wind

8: GALE 39-46 mph Twigs break off trees, walking difficult, progress generally impeded

9: STRONG GALE 47-54 mph Slight structural damage, roof tiles blown off

10: STORM 55-63 mph Seldom experienced inland, trees uprooted, considerable structural damage

11: VIOLENT STORM 64-72 mph Very rarely experienced, accompanied by widespread damage

12: HURRICANE ≥73 mph Devastation

PAUL AUSTER, JULIAN BARNES, ALBERT CAMUS, RENÉ CHAR, NIKOLAY GAVRILOVICH CHERNYSHEVSKY, COLETTE, JOSEPH CONRAD, ALPHONSE DAUDET, JOAN DIDION, ALEXANDRE DUMAS, LAWRENCE DURRELL, FORD MADOX FORD, ANDRÉ GIDE, JEAN GIONO, W. SOMERSET MAUGHAM, FRÉDÉRIC MISTRAL, FRIEDRICH NIETZSCHE, PATRICK O'BRIAN, MARCEL PAGNOL, FRANCESCO PETRARCH, FRANÇOIS RABELAIS, JOSEPH ROTH, ROBERT SABATIER, GEORGE SAND, STENDHAL, ROBERT LOUIS STEVENSON, ÉMILE ZOLA

CORIOLIS EFFECT—the effect the earth's rotation has on the path

The Atlantic Ocean The Atlantic Ocean The Atlantic Ocean

A MISTRAL OCCURS WHEN THERE IS AN AREA OF HIGH PRESSURE IN THE BAY OF BISCAY AND AN

THE PRESSURE DIFFERENCE PUSHES THE AIR TO THE EAST, GENERATING A CURRENT, OR WIND, WHICH IS DEFLECTED AT A RIGHT

HIGH PRESSURE HIGH PRESSURE HIGH PRESSURE HIGH PRESSURE HIGH PRESSURE HIGH PRESSURE

bay of biscay

RIOLIS EFFECT—the effect the earth's rotation has on the pa

AS THE AIR IS PROPELLED FROM THE AREA OF HIGH PRESSURE TO LOW PRESSURE, IT VEERS TOWARD THE SOUTH, BRINGING IN COLD, DRY AIR FROM THE MASSIF CENTRAL AND ALPS.

THE COOL AIR ACCELERATES AS IT DESCENDS AND SPREADS OUT INTO THE MOUTH OF THE RHÔNE RIVER.

WITH FEW IMPEDIMENTS IN THE FLAT ALLUVIAL PLAIN, IT GAINS SPEED AS IT REACHES THE MEDITERRANEAN SEA.

SURE IN THE GULF OF GENOA.

FFECT.

RHÔNE RIVER RHÔNE RIVER RHÔNE RIVER RHÔNE RIVER

MAGISTER—Latin meaning "master" or "masterly" MAGISTRALIS—Late Latin

MAESTRAL—Languedocien Occitan MISTRAU—Provençal Occitan MISTRAL—French MESTRAL—Catalan

MAESTRALE—Italian and Corsican MAISTRÀLE—Sardinian MAJJISTRAL—Maltese

massif central massif central massif central massif central massif central massif central massif central massif central massif central massif central massif central massif central

alps alps alps alps alps alps alps alps alps alps alps alps alps alps alps alps alps alps alps alps alps alps alps alps alps alps alps alps alps alps

LOW PRESSURE LOW PRESSURE LOW PRESSURE LOW PRESSURE LOW PRESSURE LOW PRESSURE LOW

gulf of genoa

MY THANKS

To my husband, Morgan Entrekin, who has been like the mistral itself, a force of nature propelling me forward with his enthusiasm and his belief in me and my work.

And to our son, Allen, our great joy, who has accompanied me, since he was in a stroller, while I worked, and who has given up some fun along the way.

To my family, friends, and colleagues who have taken time to look at and to read my work and who have contributed to this book: Eduardo Angel, Elisabeth Biondi, Bonnie Cobb, Brodie Cobb, Olivier Cohen, Jim Colton, Jason Eskenazi, Edwin Gerber, Jessica Green, Ron Haviv, Patricia Herrero, Siri Hustvedt, Jeff Jacobson, Dean King, Mériam Korichi, Anders Lazaret, Santiago Lyon, Jonathan Olley, Terry McDonell, Renee Montagne, Ana Morris, Art Rangno, Eléonore Renié, Sarah Raper-Larenaudie, Dr. Jeff Reid, Elisabeth Ruge, Elissa Schappell, Maggie Steber, Robert Stevens, Chuck Sudetic, Mary Virginia Swanson, John Trotter, and Caroline Woods.
A special thanks to Jessica King for her translations and editorial insight, and to Paul Auster and Mary Ann Caws for their translations. And my deep gratitude to Bill Buford for writing a masterful introduction and for his friendship.

To everyone who generously allowed images of themselves to appear in this book: Daphne Beal, Michelle Bridelance, Thierry Bronne, Pascal Bulte, Kristina Deutsch, Allen Entrekin, Mayor Guy Girard, Christian Giraud, Didier Manzon, Daniel Michel, M. Montegarde, Pierre Vadon, and Sean Wilsey.

To Yolanda Cuomo, and her talented team, Bonnie Briant and Bobbie Richardson, for breathing life into this project and for helping me see it anew. To Chris Allan for making the color sing. To Andrea Albertini, and all of Damiani, for publishing this book.

I am profoundly grateful to you all.

MISTRAL

The Legendary Wind of Provence

RACHEL COBB

www.rachelcobb.com

BOOK DESIGN BY YOLANDA CUOMO DESIGN
Associate Designer: Bonnie Briant
Junior Designer: Bobbie Richardson

Color work and Kodachrome scanning by
Chris Allan of The Bridge, Williamsburg, NY.

Published by Damiani
info@damianieditore.com
www.damianieditore.com

Typeset in Fournier MT Std and printed on GardaMatt Ultra.
Printed in June 2018 by Grafiche Damiani—Faenza Group SpA, Italy.

ISBN 978-88-6208-618-9

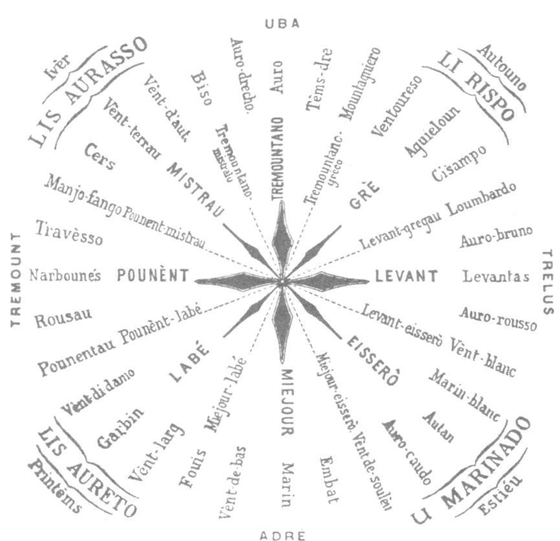
UBA
Ivèr
LIS AURASSO
Vènt-d'aut
Biso
Auro-drecho
Auro
Tèms-dre
Mountagniero
Ventoureso
LI RISPO
Autouno
Vènt-terrau
Tremountano-mistralo
TREMOUNTANO
Tremountano-greco
Aguieloun
Cers
MISTRAU
GRÈ
Cisampo
Manjo-fango
Pounent-mistrau
Levant-gregau
Loumbardo
Travèsso
Auro-bruno
TREMOUNT
Narbounés
POUNÈNT
LEVANT
Levantas
TRELUS
Rousau
Pounènt-labé
Levant-eisserò
Auro-rousso
Pounentau
Vènt-blanc
LABÉ
EISSERÒ
Vènt-di-damo
Miejour-labé
MIEJOUR
Miejour-eisserò
Marin-blanc
Garbin
Autan
Vènt-larg
Auro-caudo
LIS AURETO
Printèms
Fouis
Vènt-de-bas
Marin
Embat
Vènt-de-soulèu
U MARINADO
Estièu
ADRE